D0324373

SEP 1 2 1976

909.82   70 1624
BEALS C
GREAT GUERRILLA WARRIORS

Port Washington Public Library

Port Washington, New York

477 040169

MAR 2 9 1979
470 F

GREAT
GUERRILLA
WARRIORS

▼△▼△▼△▼

GREAT GUERRILLA WARRIORS

▲▽▲▽▲▽

by

Carleton Beals

Prentice-Hall, Inc., Englewood Cliffs, New Jersey

GREAT GUERRILLA WARRIORS
by Carleton Beals

© 1970 by Carleton Beals

All rights reserved. No part of this book may be
reproduced in any form or by any means, except for
the inclusion of brief quotations in a review, without
permission in writing from the publisher.

Library of Congress Catalog Card Number: 71-84997

Printed in the United States of America · *T*

13-368861-8

Prentice-Hall International, Inc., London
Prentice-Hall of Australia, Pty. Ltd., Sydney
Prentice-Hall of Canada, Ltd., Toronto
Prentice-Hall of India Private Ltd., New Delhi
Prentice-Hall of Japan, Inc., Tokyo

To Jorge Ricardo Masetti, killed in northern Argentina
fighting the Ongania dictatorship
To Luis F. de la Puente, killed in the Andes fighting
for the enslaved peasants of Peru
and
To Haydée Santamaría, courageous guerrilla in war and in
peace

CONTENTS

CONTENTS

1

BIG LITTLE WARS

The guerrilla hero of this decade is the Argentinean medico, Ernesto ("Che") Guevara whom I met in Havana a few years ago at a huge open-air dinner for thousands of Havana school teachers. They were celebrating "The Year of Education," the beginning of the spectacularly successful battle that wiped out the enormous illiteracy then plaguing Cuba.

Guevara arrived late, with a hint of a swagger, at the long platform of favored guests. He was clad in boots and an olive-green uniform, his hair tousled, his black eyes alert, a warm boyish smile on his mouth. A wispy beard scarcely covered his round cheeks and chin.

I arose from my seat, wanting to greet him. He was the miracle man of the Castro guerrilla war, a doctor suffering from debilitating attacks of asthma, a healer of wounded guerrillas, a builder of arms factories in the forest and mountain hospitals. He had led his starving little band across three provinces, through jungles and swamps to wage the crucial battle of Santa Clara that finally smashed the regime of President Fulgencio Batista.

There was a catch in his step. He swerved toward me, greeting me by name, though so far as I knew he had never seen me before. He gave me an *abrazo,* then held me by the forearms for a moment, speaking in a low, friendly voice.

Today his ashes lie in a jungle grave in inner Bolivia, near where he was murdered after his capture on October 8, 1967. He was leading a new guerrilla fight against the military dictatorship of puppet President René Barrientos. More than that, he hoped to arouse all the Andean peoples against their backward, feudal, land-holding regimes and their "imperialist allies," e.g. those who supported United States economic and political control. His Bolivian adventure is ended. The jungles are quiet again. The United States' secret agents, the United States' military advisers, the Green Berets have moved out of the area. United States helicopters no longer make their hawk-like flights.

Barrientos was apparently in the saddle firmer than ever. But before a year was out, his regime was bankrupt and shaken, the whole country in turmoil. Riots raged in four cities, the civilian cabinet was replaced by military rulers, congress was not allowed to meet. Martial law went into effect in August. Barriento's Minister of Interior, Antonio Arguëdas Mendieta had sent Guevara's *Bolivian Diary* to Raúl Castro in Cuba "to thwart U. S. imperialism" in Bolivia, and had fled abroad.

Briefly, the guerrilla *putsch* in South America appears to have subsided. The cynically opportunistic communists have broken with the various movements; in fact they had refused to aid Guevara unless they could have political control of the fight. But the lull is only an illusion. For despite some higher incomes resulting from the Vietnam war, most Latin American peoples are worse off than ever: there are more babies, less food, there is more unemployment, less hope. In many places there are fewer schools, fewer doctors, but more soldiers and more bureaucrats. The press is better controlled. Sullen nationalism and latent militancy, finding no immediate expression, worm deeply, unheard and unseen, like termites.

Che is dead, but his spirit lives. His name and his portrait appear on placards carried by demonstrators in scores of countries. The new youths of Mao's China hold his picture aloft. It looks out from Kremlin parades. The students of Bonn and Paris know him better than they do their own leaders. He has breathed life into Viet Cong battle charges. He has become a fetish, a cult in New York and San Francisco, in Algeria, Tanzania, Nigeria, and Guinea. His likeness looms skyscraper-high above the mass rallies in Havana, Cuba. He represented the militant spirit of our revolutionary age. He died for "freedom," fighting the black dragon of imperialism. He represented youth; he represented "the future."

Even before he left Cuba, Che had made an impact on friends and enemies. His treatise on guerrilla warfare has been a manual for the Green Berets—the counter-guerrillas being trained by the Pentagon in Panama, Guatemala, Puerto Rico and on the United States mainland. Since his death, books by him have appeared in English and many other languages. These books include his reminiscences of Castro's invasion of Cuba, and his *Bolivian Diary* which was suppressed by the Bolivian government and the C.I.A., except for a few garbled extracts, until its unabridged publication in Havana in June 1968. It is now translated and reproduced in nearly all countries. Evergreen Press in New York was bombed by anti-Castroites for publishing parts of it. Magazine articles about him have multiplied.

Guevara is not the first martyr of guerrilla warfare—which, after all is a hazardous occupation, be it in the urban jungles of the United States, or the wilds of Mozambique. A year before Che died, the priest Camilo Torres was killed fighting with the guerrillas in Colombia; Torres is now the hero of Catholic youth and students throughout all Latin America. These martyrs will not be the last.

Guerrillas are busy in at least ten Latin American countries. Despite the reestablishment of dictatorships—perhaps because of them—these struggles may well develop into a continental upheaval, a far-reaching crusade for liberation. This certainly was Che Guevara's intention.

Such violence has become almost a way of life all around the globe. What are the reasons, the methods, the goals? Is life everywhere so bad that it cannot be improved by gentler methods? Violence destroys certain abuses and institutions. It ends some slaveries, cracks up the cold pavement for new growths long smothered. Will this new freedom compensate for the new slaveries?

In the fifteenth stanza of his "Stanzas from the Grande Chartreuse" Matthew Arnold gave a description that suggests our century: "Wandering between two worlds, one dead, the other powerless to be born. With nowhere yet to rest my head, like those, on earth, I wait forlorn." Birth, like death, is a violent and immodest process, a presage of the new world. Both are harbingers of hope, as well as despair.

Guerrilla outbreaks have flared up on every continent except Australia. Guerrilla warfare—in the streets, in the hills—has become daily diet and threatens to break out in even more far-flung places. Riots in American cities and universities more and more assume organized guerrilla tactics.

Since the end of World War II, over seventy new countries have freed themselves from foreign rule. This has been done mostly by guerrilla warfare. Some of these new countries have since been semi-pacified by guerrilla victories and the establishment of independent or semi-independent governments. But as in Latin America, because of renewed oppression, feudal monopolies, and failure to develop economic resources—among other reasons—stability often has not been attained. This was to be expected. A number of European governments (as Belgium in the Congo) left the new regimes without a penny or trained men to carry on. In 1956 in Guinea, the French spitefully took out all aid officials and stopped their aid money. They even smashed all light bulbs and tore out pencil sharpeners. In this instance, an able leader (Sékou Touré) held things together. "Never mind," he said, "we prefer poverty in liberty to sickness in slavery." *

In Ruanda, Basuto, Bechuanaland, Nigeria, Aden, and elsewhere, the evacuating European Power installed reactionary elements to run the new governments. This precipitated fierce popular struggles to win the rewards of true independence. Meddling Belgian, British, French, German, Dutch, Egyptian, Chinese, Russian, and American agents and fortune-seekers have arrived for selfish reasons, not to aid the country or promote popular welfare. They have rarely contributed to stability. Nor have earlier patriot leaders always proven trustworthy.

* Quoted by Sidney Lens' *Africa: Awakening Giant.*

Sometimes reactionary leaders have seized power, as in Ghana and Indonesia. To paraphrase an African tribal proverb, "When the hyenas go away, the jackals are gleeful."

It is ironic that there are so many Little Wars in this era of atomic bombs, mighty jet bombers, new poison gases, and bacteriological and chemical warfare that have made a mishmash of the Geneva Conventions. Prior to World War II there were only fifteen Little Wars starting with that of Aguinaldo. Since then, a hundred and fifty coups or attempted coups have been wrought by guerrilla movements. Thirty-five major guerrilla struggles have occurred. Twenty or more are going on at this time.

The major cause of our century's desperate guerrilla revolts is patently imperialism in its various aspects. Conquest, foreign rule, financial and political penetration, periodic armed intervention. The reasons for imperialism and its irksome aftereffects must be known before we can begin to understand the unruly nature of one era. These have been clearly set forth by such writers as Lenin, Hobbes, Parker Moon, Mao Tse-tung, Scott Nearing, Nkruma. Latin American literature is rich with studies of the process.*

Absentee capital is foreign-owned and is bound to be hit hard by revolts. It is invested mostly in raw-product enterprises, usually in partnership with the powers-that-be; the landholders, the ecclesiastical establishment, the army. Inevitably this arouses antiforeignism. Alien ownership is identified with imperialism, which carved up and appropriated much of Africa and Asia in the previous century. Since then, the British and French empires have collapsed under the blows of guerrilla revolt and the militant new nationalism. A worldwide liberation movement is still fighting the remnants of such imperialism. The United States, with its maintenance of neo-colonialism status quo and its policy of armed intervention anywhere, has come to be considered the chief offender. The early Mexican agrarian guerrilla leader Emiliano Zapata saw his enemy not merely as the Carranza government but also as the United States embassy.

Behind this worldwide revolt are ugly facts. Eighty percent or more of the arable lands in colonial or underdeveloped countries were or are owned by a handful of whites or the elite. More than 50 percent of Paraguay's land is owned by twenty-five families who cannot survive without dictatorship. A large share of the remaining acreage is owned by foreign oil companies. In the starving countries of three continents, infant mortality customarily runs to around fifty percent or even higher. The death rate (except in Cuba where it is now lower than in Canada) is shockingly high. Doctors, hospitals, and medical knowledge are

* Isidro Fabela, Hall, Carnero Checa, Vicente Saenz, José, Juan Arévalo, Gregorio Selser, Mario Gil, Mariátegui, José Martí, Pablo Neruda, etc.

deficient everywhere. The entire country of Yeman, until recently, had
only five doctors. Most Vietnamese die without medical care. According to the Health Ministry of Venezuela (which has received more
foreign aid dollars than any other Latin American country), a million
and a half people—a fifth of the poverty-stricken population—are
afflicted with Chagas disease in which mosquito-borne parasites con-
sume the patient's flesh and his heart swells to twice its size.

In Iraq, the gulf between rich and poor was (and is) a standing
incitement to revolt. General H. G. Martin wrote in *Middle Eastern
Affairs* for March 1959, that 90 percent of Iraq's people are illiterate
and there has been little, if any, improvement. Their average life-span is
twenty-six years; their per-capita income is less than $90 a year. For
the masses in Asia, Africa, and most of Latin America, annual incomes
are even lower—around $50 in Salvador, Honduras, Ecuador, Bolivia,
Haiti, and Paraguay, among others. Nearly everywhere the population
is growing faster than the food supply or new means of production.
This is something for which neither the wealthy nations nor even any
successful guerrilla revolts are likely to find a quick or easy solution.
But the wealthy nations, themselves, are no longer able to operate outside their established power-forms, and dollars join the march of
decay. The guerrillas are able to make a more meaningful effort, for
a new frame and new substance are required everywhere.

Underdeveloped countries breed more than their share of under-
developed people. Dictatorships are merely an ugly reflection of wide-
spread suffering and sickness. The Guatemalan poet Rafael Arévalo
Martínez remarked, "The end product of endemic malaria among our
people is malarial government." Another writer has said: "A one-
product system breeds a one-product government—dictatorship."

Such conditions have existed for centuries. Many revolts have occurred but police states, often inspired from without, have ruled most
such subhumans for thousands of years and during much of the modern
era. Why are the poor now stirring out of their long-time lethargy?
Why, at long last, do they respond to guerrilla leaders?

Late last century, the rise of mass production made possible more
goods and comforts for populations in Europe and the United States.
Technological advances opened up incredible opportunities, churning
up hopes in the minds and hearts of the most remote backward peoples.
Unfortunately there is no way of quickly satisfying the universal
hunger, and few governments even try.

New industry injected into sweat-and-muscle countries lacking most
labor-saving devices tears the old society apart. It starts cracks and then
widens them. The gadgets of communication accentuate the contradictions: telegraph and cable; highways, railroads, and airplanes; newspapers, movies, radio, and television. The hopes created by new
productive power, even before our electronic age, vividly accentuated

the awareness and resentment of widening poverty and futility. Unrest spreads. Injustices accumulate. New interests, new classes are soon at each other's throats. The social breakup becomes inevitable. Guerrilla warfare strikes forth.

Now, before the industrial revolution has been mastered, the electronic revolution is bringing even greater maladjustment and more ubiquitous revolts. Norbert Wiener, scientist of the new Cybernetics, foresaw the wave of social consequences, the mass unemployment, the disorders and violence that would occur unless foresight were used. He predicted in his *Cybernetics* that within twenty years—which meant the 'seventies—the situation would become acute in the United States.

The irony is that the governments of the most technologically progressive countries (e.g., that of Napoleon III a century ago and the United States today) become the citadels of political backwardness. They ally themselves with the most nonprogressive feudal and militaristic elements in the various underdeveloped lands in the false hope of keeping order. However, neither system—industrial or electronic—can long tolerate the local straightjacket of feudal restrictions and illiterate populations.

The inefficient, self-sufficient feudal hacienda is unable to minister to the new cities properly. Yet the rise of large-scale absentee plantation agriculture and the growing of commercial export crops rather than foodstuffs, expands large-scale ownership and worsens the plight of the rural population. More peasants are flung from the morass of the back country into the ghettos of the new shining cities where slums grow faster than boulevards. Caracas, Rio, Buenos Aires, Lima, Madrid, Athens, Leopoldville, Saigon, Danang, Seoul, and Tokyo and other cities throughout Latin America, India and Asia are examples. Before long the urban guerrilla goes into action.

Unless the land can be distributed to the peasants or pass into the hands of the State, the old feudal military rule cannot be broken. Until it is, promises of progress and gradualism are fraudulent.

"The Communist conspiracy" is often a figment of the imagination. It is an excuse for maintaining the status quo. Actually such a conspiracy is usually merely one possible end product of unrest. Cypress guerrilla leader General Grivas said: "The British could never get it through their heads that one revolt was not a conspiracy but a movement of the people." The railroads broke down the isolation of Chinese peasants and broke up their centuries-old way of life. The liberators, the demagogues, the guerrillas, and the communists merely rode on the cow-catchers.

The new nationalism *is* one of the chief causes of guerrilla war. The communist leaders have been flexible enough to seek to promote, utilize, and direct nationalist forces everywhere; these leaders have been wise enough to ride with history—which means picking the winner. Most western leaders have preferred the short-range profit of playing the role of King Canute and setting their faces against history.

Essentially, nationalism is a conservative, even reactionary force that runs counter to a world supposedly being knit together by radio, television and aviation, by the newer forces of industrial growth, technology, and worldwide trade. In contrast, nationalism seeks to salvage the traditional culture and safeguard the sacred customs of the past. The Kenya Mau Mau fought desperately to preserve pagan dances, music, rites, and female circumcision. Thus the militant new nationalism brings together strange bedfellows from all classes of society. "No one knows what a nation is," California history Professor Henry Morse Stephens used to say. "All we know is, it is something for which men will fight." And Dr. Bemis of Yale has said that, in spite of the growth of international forces, "It is still the most powerful force operating in world affairs."

The new breed of guerrillas pushes nationalism into anti-imperialist war. They are knowledgeable about previous guerrilla struggles, their aims and methods. They have no truck with old style political parties, Right or Left. Elections, especially in illiterate countries, are controlled by the army and the elite and hence do not serve to promote reform but rather to confuse and manipulate the people.

Though their programs are rarely clarified, it becomes evident that the new fighters strive for truly national economies. They plan to utilize all resources, provide new enterprise, and prevent the disastrous and overall paralyses due to lopsided, haphazard foreign ownership that drains out as much or more than it puts in and pressures or controls native governments. They project programs—land, water, electric power, schools, medical care, better standards of living—to benefit "all" the people. Such programs are promoted also by powerful outside interests within existing political structures that often defraud or oppress the people.

The new guerrilla leaders, however nationalistic, look not to the past but rather to a new independent world. Therefore, as soon as the revolution has been a success, the reactionary and self-seeking nationalists—usually members of the more affluent groups—have to be purged, as they were in Cuba. Otherwise, those sloughed aside will soon discover that the foreigner was not so bad. They become new subversives, emigrees who plot (with foreign aid) to restore the lost form of government and their own special privileges.

How do guerrillas operate? Basically, as Che Guevara pointed out, guerrilla tactics and strategy are no different from those used in any war. The rules were first laid down by the Chinese author Sun Tzu in a famous treatise on military methods published six centuries before

Christ. Here and there in the Old Testament are instructions about
how to wage guerrilla-type war, though the chief admonition is to
have faith in the Hebrew God. Organized religion is always a hand-
maiden of power politics—but Tzu's keys to strategic victory provided
the basic hard-core Ten Commandments of guerrilla warfare.

> All warfare is based on deception.
> Ergo, when capable, pretend incapacity. When active,
> feign inactivity.
> When close at hand, make it appear you are far away;
> when far away, that you are near.
> Offer the enemy bait to lure him; feign disorder and strike
> him.
> While he concentrates prepare against him; whenever he is
> strong, avoid him.
> Anger his general and confuse him.
> Pretend inferiority and encourage his arrogance.
> Keep him under strain and wear him down.
> When he is united, divide him.
> Attack where he is unprepared; sally forth when he does
> not expect you.*

Modern treatises provide information on how to supplement rural
revolt with urban terrorism—as in Aguinaldo's documents and in
Guevara's book and in documents supplementing his *Bolivian Diary*.
All later writers have merely elaborated on Sun Tzu by applying his
formula to modern situations and political methods. The Filipino resistance manual, published in Madrid in 1900, was the first such document this century. (It is summarized in the next chapter.) It followed
similar lines, with detailed instructions on field tactics, particularly
mobility and surpise, though the authors probably had never heard of
Sun Tzu.

Lenin. had little to say about guerrilla warfare, though in 1906 he
published a short history of such outbursts from the end of the previous
century on. He called them bastard manifestations of the revolutionary
process. Lenin warned, however, that the true revolutionists, who
should use all methods for promoting the cause, should not under-
estimate or despise the guerrillas. He said that guerrillas are mostly
terrorists or anarchists, or social riffraff; it is best to be prepared to
take charge of them and give them meaningful purpose, especially
just prior to full-fledged insurrection and civil war. This thesis has
been vigorously disputed, even by Marxists. In late 1966 it caused a
serious split between the Venezuelan guerrilla movement and the Communist Party; pointed discussions have appeared in the Cuban
Cuadernos de la Casa de las Américas (No. 1 July–August 1965) and

---

* This is a prosaic summary. Actually his language is very poetic. A considerable
excerpt is given in Robert Payne's *Mao-Tse Tung*, p. 110.

in *Sucesos* and in *Política,* Mexico (Feb. 14, 1967). The Communists trying to obey this formula in Latin America have mostly fallen flat on their faces, since the guerrillas have resisted outside political manipulation.

In *Les Temps Modernes* (Paris, January 1965) Professor Regis Debray, now serving thirty years in prison in Bolivia, argued that a revolutionary guerrilla movement cannot be dependent upon any existing political organization, communist or otherwise. (Castro echoed this in 1967.) Inevitably, such organizations are imbedded in the sound milieu and corrupted by existing governments. The guerrillas must create their own political directives during the heat of campaign. In short, the Cuban revolution cannot repeat itself in Latin America. Guerrillas, as Castro himself insists, must and will work out their own methods, solutions, and aims according to local situations.

Interesting is the resultant schism between the New Guerrilla and the Old-line Communist. In Cuba, Castro who calls himself a nonrigid Marxist has thrown a considerable number of Marxists in jail for long terms. During his somewhat puerile onslaught on the Trotskyites in early 1967, he charged that they were in control of the Guatemala guerrillas then led by Yon Sosa. Yon Sosa quickly purged Trotskyites from his political organization but kept on fighting in a secondary role. A young pro-Communist then breezed into the hills but in 1967 was killed in an auto accident. A younger leader moved in, and early in 1968 the guerrilla movement disassociated itself entirely from the Guatemala Labor Party [Communist].

In Venezuela, the outstanding guerrilla leader Douglas Bravo refused to obey the Communists. They had made a suspicious deal with the government, apparently on Moscow's orders, and had ordered a halt to armed rebellion. He kept on fighting. Castro attacked the Venezuelan Communists severely—an ugly interchange that has not yet subsided. The other Communist Parties of Latin America have since boycotted his international reunions in Havana.

Castro insisted that a guerrilla force must be independent of outside political and tactical controls. This, he claimed, was why the Huks failed in the Philippines. The central board in Manila ordered guerrilla strikes everywhere on a given day, but they were unable to know the situation in each locale. This ran counter to all known laws of guerrilla mobility with reference to enemy concentration. Guerrillas everywhere must develop their own political authority. The matter came up again in Bolivia, where the local communists set up their price—political control of the movement—and refused to cooperate with Che. "Guevara's death lies not only at the doormat of the United States and dictator Barrientos but the communists," a guerrilla has charged.

These are merely strange and irritating quibbles for most Americans who are remote from leftist hair-splitting. But out of such quarrels, however petty, have come the forces that have shaken the world.

In addition to political insight, Che Guevara's treatise on guerrilla warfare provides practical information on how to manufacture explosives, grenades, and other essential light equipment; how to attack barracks, villages, towns; how to destroy communications, and how to ambush convoys. First, the attacker must be exactly informed about the enemy, his numbers, defenses, and arms. Never strike without superior numbers and only by surprise!

Either wittingly or unwittingly, Major Grivas and Giap adapted the precepts of Che and Mao Tse-tung to their own situations in Cypress and Vietnam.

Mao, in turn more or less reiterates Sun Tzu's findings in his own decalogue.*

1. Attack dispersed, isolated enemy forces first; concentrated strong enemy forces later.
2. Take small medium cities and extensive rural areas first; take big cities later.
3. Make wiping out enemy's effective strength our main object . . . not [the] . . . holding or seizing of a city.
4. In every battle concentrate an absolutely superior force, two, three, four, sometimes five or six times the enemy's strength, encircle the enemy forces, completely, strive to wipe them out thoroughly and do not let any escape from the net . . . avoid battles of attrition. [He provides technical details on how to attack.]
5. Fight no battle unprepared . . .
6. Give full play to our way of fighting: courage in battle, no fear of sacrifice, no fear of fatigue, continuous fighting, i.e. fighting successive battles in a short time without rest.
7. Wipe out the enemy when he is on the move, i.e. through mobile warfare . . .
8. . . . Resolutely seize all enemy fortified points and cities which are weakly defended . . . as for strongly defended forts or cities, wait till conditions are ripe . . .
9. Replenish our strength with all the arms and most of the personnel captured from the enemy. Our army's main sources of manpower and material are at the front.
10. Make good use of intervals between campaigns to rest, train and consolidate our troops . . . [Such] periods . . . should not be very long, and the enemy so far as possible should be permitted no breathing space. . . . Divide forces to arouse the masses; concentrate them to

* Condensed from Mao Tse Tung's *Collected Works*, Vol. X, International Publishers (1954) and *China Digest*.

> deal with the enemy. When the enemy advances, we
> retreat; we harrass the enemy camps, the enemy tires,
> we attack. The enemy retreats, we prepare . . . to ex-
> tend stable base areas . . . advance in waves; when
> pursued by a powerful enemy, employ the tactics of
> circling around . . . let the enemy pass, but close in
> again as soon as he passes.

How often and how successfully these tactics have been used by
the Viet Cong!

Mao advised, swift onslaught—preferably five minute attacks—
furious fighting, seizing arms, and rapid withdrawal. No matter if the
enemy calls such breaking off of an engagement a victory. What is
"victory" in imperialist language is known as "defeat" in guerrilla
language. President Johnson called the holding of Saigon during the
1968 Tet offensive a great victory for General Westmoreland. To the
N.L.F., the National Liberation Front of course, it represented a
humiliating defeat of the United States and the greatest Viet Cong
victory to date.

This is the N.L.F. tactic used time and again in Vietnam. Repeatedly,
as earlier in the Philippines, United States generals optimistically pre-
announce ambitious programs of encirclement only to find the trap
empty, the slippery foe not there. Too often, dead civilians have provided the bulk of the body count—a wry sort of victory.

"It is we, not the enemy who decides when and where there will
be engagements," and Dang Thanh Chen, President of the Viet Cong
Liberation Youth Federation (numbering 500,000, of which 100,000
had gone to the front). That was early in 1964. By 1967, with the
greater buildup on both sides and northern participation, United States
forces were painfully learning the realities of tropical warfare. They
sometimes trapped the foe—at least in publicity releases. But the
enemy, despite an allied force of more than a million men, largely
retained the initiative up through 1969.

As Castro told an interviewer in August 1966, the secret of guerrilla
success—especially at the outset—is mobility.

> The guerrillas must always be moving and avoid the error
> of fixed encampments, take great precautions against enemy
> infiltration, and always be aware that any messenger com-
> ing from the enemy zone runs the risk of being caught and
> forced to divulge precise information. When the guerrilla is
> still weak and inexperienced, failure to move about con-
> stantly is likely to be fatal.

Lawrence of Arabia stated the same ideas in his own peculiar way.
He cited Marshall de Saxe, "We [the Arab rebels] had nothing material
to lose, so our best line was to defend nothing and shoot at nothing.

Our cards were speed, and time, and hitting power . . . in Arabia, range was more important than force, space greater than the power of arms."

The guerrilla has certain advantages, some not easily overcome. He is able to thread trackless forests, which are well-known to him, rapidly with his lighter mobile weapons. The present day American G.I., it has been stated, carries seventy pounds on his back. He requires sixty pounds of food and supplies daily. He cannot go off the beaten track very far, very quickly, or for very long, even though the vulnerable helicopter now gets him to definite points quickly and brings in supplies and adds firepower.

Key outposts in rebel areas do not always have large enough garrisons to be safe from attack. Even if they do, they are vulnerable to rocket fire, which can destroy ammunition dumps, tanks, planes, buildings, and human life. American officers in the Philippines repeatedly complained that their forces were too small for safety—let alone to send out patrols which were usually ambushed.

Che Guevara noted that

> one of the weakest points of the enemy is transportation by road or/and railroad for it is virtually impossible to maintain a vigil yard by yard. At almost any point, a considerable amount of explosive charge can be planted that will make the road impassable and if it is exploded at the moment a vehicle passes, a considerable loss of lives and material to the enemy is caused, and at the same time, the road is put out of commission.

In Cuba in 1957–58, buses and trucks even close to Havana were blown up, and travel by road or train to Santiago became perilous. By 1968, in South Vietnam, only two trains were still running over a few short stretches of track, and in July one of these was destroyed.

Some of the most exciting episodes of Lawrence's *Seven Pillars of Wisdom* tell of dynamiting railroads and bridges. Dramatic tales are related of Villa and Zapata attacking trains and roadways. Villa developed bizarre methods to rip up miles of tracks rapidly. Mao Tse-tung's blows at transportation are an epic story.

Tunnel warfare is a deadly type of combat, one of the oldest forms. The Roman catacombs, for instance, long protected the Christian "underground." In the late forties, when the French reentered Hanoi in their effort to reconquer their lost colony, they found a half-deserted city. Then the enemy burst out of underground positions.

Viet Cong tunnels honeycomb whole districts. One labyrinth at Tuy Hoa, discovered in late 1965 by the 101st Airborne Division, was a mile long—large enough to sleep two divisions, or four thousand men. It took a week just to explore it. The most complex tunnel system lies about twenty miles northwest of Saigon in the Ho Bo woods, and is said to extend from Saigon to the Cambodian border. Built in three levels to a depth of forty feet, it contains kitchens, mess halls, dormitories, classrooms, hospitals, storerooms, and small "spider-traps." A small part of it was seized in January 1967 in a scorched-earth operation which wiped out every village in the area.

Tunnels do not always help the defender. In Nicaragua, Sandino knew exactly where American forces were concealed underground. He calmly occupied the town and blew off the head of every man who came up for air. On occasion, Viet Cong have been trapped before they could escape through the labyrinth; poison-gas blowers have been utilized to wipe out defenders.

Fidel Castro concluded his anniversary speech in Santa Clara, July 26, 1965: "The guerrilla struggle is a formidable arm against the imperialists, but it can never be an adequate or useful instrument for the counter-revolution." The chief reason: guerrilla war, more than bigger wars, is for political, not military or international power aims. Military victory that fails to obtain political backing is a useless victory, say all guerrilla writers. That is true for both sides. The outside invader rarely wins popular support; he merely gains limited acquiescence to his power, his money, or his terror.

With at least a few, money is sometimes more effective than political ideals. Vast expenditures dished out lavishly corrupt officeholders, generals, black marketeers, and others, creating an unholy dependence on the invading power. But the guerrillas have some advantages that can never be wholly offset by massive modern weaponry, cash, or propaganda. First of all, the guerrilla is not a foreigner. As Marshall de Saxe commented, "It is deep in the human heart that one must seek the source of victories."

Since the guerrilla is rarely a foreigner, he has a better intelligence service than do alien counter-guerrillas. In Vietnam, such guerrilla agents have been discovered in the highest United States offices and services. This has led to isolation of native special forces and workers and the use of Filipino, Chinese, and other mercenary and non-Vietnamese servants. (This tactic was also used in the war against Aguinaldo in the Philippines.)

Che Guevara has declared that no guerrilla movement can succeed unless all pacific possibilities—such as resort to the courts, propaganda, strikes, and mass demonstrations—have been exhausted. The people must have the feeling that because of excessive police power and the death, imprisonment, or exile of their leaders, they have no other recourse but to fight. The guerrillas then provide hope for liberation.

One Hundred and Fifty Questions to a Guerrilla, by the Argentine A. Gener, translated and published by the United States Senate Subcommittee of Internal Security, insists that a guerrilla movement must never move against a popular regime. The justifiable motives for revolt are: "Injustice suffered by the people, by a foreign invasion, the imposition of a dictatorship, the existence of a government of enemies of the people, a regime of oligarchies, etc."

Once the guerrilla program catches on among the masses, Yon Sosa has remarked, it moves "with the power and speed of a locomotive." It has proved a slow locomotive in Sosa's Guatemala, but is still running, and with a few more cars.

The 1958 joke in Cuba was: "What's that fellow Castro stirring up things for? According to the constitution, he's too young to be president."

"Don't worry, compadre," came the answer. "By the time he comes out of them thar hills, he'll be an old man with a beard." The beard, of course, was true prophecy.

Lawrence of Arabia remarked that the real secret for Arab success was their belief that the art of war was dialectics. In medicine, the knowledge of bodily weakness is all important; in the material world *knowing* becomes important. You have to know more than the enemy. You have to spread your message.

Today the "stained and ignoble" offspring is propaganda. Our ears are dinned to headache stage. But psychological warfare was doubly necessary for the Arabs and doubly effective because of the Germans' and Turks' dull, labored recourse to brute force. The guerrillas had to use something more subtle and effective than firepower or tactics. They had to arrange the Arab's mind "in order of battle . . . as carefully and formally as other officers . . . arrange their bodies." Secondly, "it was necessary always to arrange the minds of the enemy . . . then . . . [the] minds of the nations supporting us . . . since more than half the battle passes there in the back." Similarly, "the mind of the enemy nation and of the neutrals looking on, circle beyond circle." Lawrence added, "the printing press and each newly found method of communication favored the intellectual above the physical . . . [whereas] the regular officer with the tradition of forty generations of service behind him, stuck to the antique way of making war." But "for the Arabs, the dialectic was more than half the command, the secret of eventual victory."

Mao puts it more bluntly: "Arouse the greatest number of the masses in the shortest time by the best means possible . . . cast the net wide to win the masses, draw it in to deal with the enemy." But ideological and moral conversion take time, so "don't end the war prematurely, keep it going." A physical victory over the enemy is sterile without a prior victory over the minds of the guerrillas themselves and over the minds of the people.

Che Guevara is explicit: "Guerrilla warfare is a war of the masses, a war of the people . . . the guerrilla is a social reformer who takes up arms in response to the angry protest of the people against the oppressor and fights in order to change the social system that keeps his unarmed brothers in ignorance and misery."

In August 1966 Castro said in a somewhat contrary vein that "the best propaganda is success." He scoffed at the phrase "armed propaganda." How, he asked, can one conceive of guerrillas who, instead of attacking enemy vehicles and ambushing enemy patrols, dedicate themselves to going from village to village "making speeches?" He couldn't remember that he had made a single propaganda speech during the war itself.

"Bite and run" warfare, as Guevara called it, helps create instability and results in the repeated downfall of stopgap governments lacking popular support and confidence. The people become hopeless and apathetic or look to the guerrillas as the only way out. When such false governments of small cliques of self-seeking politicians and generals depend on outside invaders, the time comes, Mao concluded, "when a single spark will start a prairie fire."

Usually guerrilla warfare is started by daring leaders such as Abdel Krim, Mao, Sandino, Castro with a handful of daring men. Garibaldi set out to free Italy with seven men and a mule. Soon Sicily, southern Italy, and Naples were in his grasp. Castro began operations in the Sierra with only twelve men.

The leader's fame grows by means of mere survival, persistence, and steel nerve. The Robin Hood of the hills becomes a popular idol. Legends ascribe magical powers and invulnerability to the outlaw leader. Sandino, Villa, and Zapata were considered imperishable by their men. Zapata hoofbeats rode the sky like thunder long after his death. Aguinaldo was believed to be wholly immune to sickness or bullets. He was protected by the miraculous Antuing-Antuing charm, and his nickname was "The Invulnerable."

Aguinaldo was the first serious obstacle to the expansion of United States power in Asia, which began in 1853 when Commodore Matthew C. Perry "opened up" Japan. Since then resistance to the west in Asia has been Asiatic, not merely Communist—often not Communist at all. Ho Chi Minh has depended far more on nationalist than on communist doctrines. "Asia for the Asians," was a potent Japanese slogan, and it still moves more than two billion people.

Thus Aguinaldo was a portent of war to come: a warning that the deeper we go, the more costly the enterprise will become. There are no cheap Little Wars any more. The suppression of Aguinaldo and the conquest of the Philippines was more costly in blood and money than the entire Spanish-American War. As the first guerrilla figure of this century, Aguinaldo is even more important for our understanding today.

2

FROM AGUINALDO TO THE HUKS

> Damn, damn, damn the Filipino
> We'll civilize him with a Krag.

They were singing it over their lifted drinks in the officers' club in Manila. Their men had been fighting the Spaniards with their Krag-Jorgensen rifles—not much of a fight—but now they were fighting the Filipinos, and the brave Yankees were biting the dust.

The old Spanish walled-city of Manila had surrendered to the United States Army on August 13, 1898 following only token resistance. Since May 1—after Admiral George Dewey, following prewar plans, destroyed the Spanish fleet at the outset of the Spanish-American War—the city had been under his guns. It was soon surrounded by armed insurgents led by the young Independence leader, Emilio Aguinaldo y Famy, an exiled guerrilla chieftain who headed an Independence Junta in Hong Kong. Dewey had him brought from Hong Kong on the gunboat *McCullough*, May 19, to organize revolt.

Aguinaldo received a few weapons from Dewey and got in a big initial shipment which the United States Consul in Hong Kong provided with the exiled Junta's funds. Almost at once, 30,000 Filipinos rallied around the new flag of independence which Aguinaldo raised in formal ceremonies June 12, 1898, at Cavite Viejo, his birthplace, where he set up a new government for the moment acting as dictator.*

This was his second effort. In 1897, toward the end of his earlier guerrilla campaign, he had established a provisional government which had soon given up the ghost when he agreed with the Spaniards to go into temporary exile.

Admiral Dewey and the then-commanding United States General Thomas W. Anderson visited him in Cavite. Dewey congratulated him, "How beautiful your flag is! It has a triangle and resembles that of Cuba. Will you give me one as a memento when I return to America?" By then, Aguinaldo's forces were rapidly taking over the whole country.

---

* In 1966, June 12—rather than the July 4 set by the United States in 1946—was declared the legal Philippine Independence day.

16

He was in a position to seize Manila at any time. The city had been deprived of its water and nearly all food supplies. The place stank, and people were sick and dying. But the Filipino leader was persuaded to hold up his attack on the city until enough United States soldiers could arrive to participate.

United States volunteers came streaming off transport ships and elbowed Aguinaldo's men out of some of the deep trenches they had built to ring the city. Making secret arrangements with the Spaniards without informing Aguinaldo, Commanding General Wesley Merritt assaulted the city on August 13. It was a sham battle; only four American soldiers were killed. The Filipino forces, not knowing of the secret deal, leaped from their trenches and quickly took over the suburbs and part of the city.

The American soldiers immediately surrounded advanced Filipino units, and General Wesley Merritt ordered Aguinaldo's men to hand over their prisoners and retire. It was a critical moment; General Thomas M. Anderson, said subsequently: "The Philippinos were beside themselves with rage and disappointment."

The victory parade a few days later was wholly American—not a single Filipino patriot marched. From the outset, no Filipino soldiers were allowed within the city, though many had families there. Those who tried to come in were arrested. Soon Americans were detained when trying to cross through *Filipino* lines—though invariably, when furious protests were made by the United States high command, Aguinaldo ordered the release of such offenders—with apologies.

General E. S. Otis—sent with the largest reinforcements thus far and given full command—rode through the captured city in a carriage, observing the misery and sullenness of the people. He disliked Filipinos intensely, though he usually concealed this in his official communiques. His first remark to his companion, journalist Murat Halsted, was "Shall we have to give these people, as Charles Sumner would say, the ballot—ay, sir, the ballot?"

Halsted, who soon wrote an outright defamation of Aguinaldo and the Philippine Republic, replied, "A lot of them look as though you shall have to give them the bullet first."

Aguinaldo tried every ruse to gain recognition of his government from United States commanders and acquiesced to nearly all occupation demands, usually made with threats of force. Little by little, American military officers learned to use, if a bit awkwardly, his own expressions of goodwill, cooperation, and friendship. But it was only paper work. Frictions multiplied. Not once did American officers address him by his proper title of either general or President.

General Otis sent an ultimatum that the Filipinos evacuate all forces to beyond the city lines. The Filipinos wanted to fight then and there, but Aguinaldo restrained them. After prolonged dickering

—General Otis had no way of proving the validity of his arbitrary map of Greater Manila—the withdrawal was made, except for small sectors Aguinaldo considered vital for defense.

The mere presence of American troops in Manila created ill will. "The natives soon learned to dislike us." wrote John F. Bass, a long-time resident, in *Harper's Weekly*. "We plastered the town from end to end with beer and whiskey advertisements. Americans who have followed the Army have put their time and money into saloons. No other business attracts them."

American officers and others described the shooting of civilians; the swarms of adventurers; the soldiers' contemptuous epithets for the natives, whom they called *Yuyus;* and the looting of whole villages, such as Manaloyan and Santa Ana. Stolen goods were black-marketed to shady adventurers or to the Chinese. Even in the heart of Manila, soldiers went "curio hunting," breaking into private homes, wrecking the interiors, yanking jewelry off the women and sometimes stripping off their clothes. The murder of a woman and her child, "as a joke," in the Arrocero market, brought out an angry mob. A United States guard killed a child on Lacosta Street for stealing a banana from a Chinese.

As Bass wrote, we were "rough and tyrannical." They were considered "tricky and dishonest." The aims were too divergent for reconciliation: The Americans planned to seize and rule the islands; the Filipinos dreamed of independence and were ready to fight for it. Complete lack of knowledge ruled both sides; mutual hate was the answer.

Aguinaldo said sadly that if the Filipinos had to be ruled by an outside power, he would prefer Spain rather than a country alien in all its customs. "Why should we have to go back to our childhood and learn English?" Actually, for him, a Malay Tagalog with one-fourth Chinese blood, Spanish was also a foreign tongue, though he had studied it in the village school in Cavite Viejo and for three years in a Dominican preparatory school in Manila.*

After his father's death, Aguinaldo returned to Cavite Viejo to run the family farm; he taught the town school, then became mayor. As head of the powerful secret Masonic independence order, the Katipunan, he raised revolt. His guerrilla forces soon took over all Cavite province next door to Manila, and he set up a provisional government.

The Spaniards that year were being bled white in Cuba, where nearly two hundred thousand well-armed troops using scorched-earth terrorism and concentration bullpens had been unable to put down the guerrillas. Spain could not afford another full-fledged revolt in

---

* Tagalog has since been made an official Filipino language.

the Philippines. Fernando Primo de Rivera, uncle of the later dictator of Spain, was rushed to the islands. He negotiated for peace at Riac-Na-Bat (Split Rock) an Aguinaldo stronghold.

Aguinaldo demanded freedom of the press, the expulsion of all Spanish friars whose orders owned most of the land; equality for native Filipino priests; equal pay and preferment for Filipinos in government, in the army, and in the courts; and finally, island representation in the Spanish Cortes in Madrid.

Primo promised to effectuate the reforms if Aguinaldo and the other insurgent leaders would go into exile for three years. He offered 800,000 pesos ($400,000) for their arms. Half the money was paid over to him in Hong Kong, but the balance was never paid. The reforms were never made, and the Spaniards instituted a reign of firing-squad terror.

On his return to the islands on the *McCullough* in 1898, the Filipinos rallied to fight for the Republic, its flag, and its new independent government. Aguinaldo was a Tagalog. He spoke their language. He embodied their hopes. He was the incarnation of freedom and independence.

Even a churlish writer such as Edwin Wildman observed his great popularity.

> Aguinaldo's presence upon any occasion was marked with the utmost ceremony and parade. The people worshipped him and covered his path with flowers, the children dropped on their knees, and the natives doffed their hats in reverence. The love of feats, music and dancing was given full reign . . . his triumphal tours in the cities along the railroad line . . . [aroused] a fervor resembling religious frenzy. Triumphal arches were erected, mass-meetings of enormous proportions were held, and the prettiest girls . . . dressed in the colors of the Filipino flag blended with the Stars and Stripes, were hailed and cheered with delight . . . The spirit of liberty dominated the hearts of the people.

Murat Halsted visited his headquarters, across the bay from Manila.

> The day was August 27 and sultry. The power of the sun was trying. There was no air stirring. The hour was half past one in the afternoon. The village was Bacoor . . . where . . . the water was too shallow for launches . . . not deep enough a hundred yards from shore to float a canoe with a man in it . . . a spot . . . free from visitations of surprise . . .
>
> The church standing near the shore was large, stone built, and almost stately, but marked . . . by the shells of the Spanish fleet before the Americans came, because the insurgents had a way of appearing there and taking a peep

at misty Manila across the bay, nearly ten miles away . . . with a background of faint blue mountains, too distant to give the green tint. They reminded Admiral Dewey of his native state [Vermont] and the scenery about his native city Montpelier.

Aguinaldo's two-story house, set among heavy-leaved trees, had a conspicuous roof of reddish tile, like the roofs in villages of France . . . At a turn of the stairs to the second story stood two military guards. There were perhaps twenty-five armed men in sight. The arm was the famous Mauser. The swords seemed too large for the men, who . . . were not as large as the Japanese, but of the same small make-up and get-up and style with the [cocky] air that the Japanese military men refuse to part with . . . There was an atmosphere of enjoyment and importance and of great expectation . . .

The ladies of his family . . . were well-looking and dressed in highly colored and pleasing robes of silk, with bunches of lace and a flash of jewels . . . There was a tinkle of music in the house, not obtrusive, rather distant, a hint of the musical character of the people . . .

Don Emilio Aguinaldo y Famy . . . President of the Revolutionary Government of the Republic and General-in-Chief of its army . . . was . . . short and slender, as unmilitary in appearance as possible, dressing habitually in a single-breasted white coat and white trousers, showing thinness of limbs, often wearing a badge and carrying a little stick—articles of decoration of which he is said to be fond and vain. His eyes are cunning and his best feature. There is the light of the unusual . . . a glance that changes quickly from docility to a sharp glare and wild animal alertness. His feet are slender, his hands like birds, delicate with knotty joints and prominent nails, hair black, thick, coarse and perpendicular, with a fine gloss of vitality. His voice is low, with a softness so modulated that it is almost feminine, but that swiftly . . . changes [to] . . . a subtle tone . . . [seemingly] negating everything asked—the words blurred slightly from a habit of protruding the tongue . . . shading the low-spoken tones into indistinctness. The hands are moved as he speaks, not in a shaky, nervous style, but with a flutter. In his own apartments he moves in a gliding way, and is treated with deference. There is no question that he fully believes in himself, and that he has a tendency to exact ceremony . . . [He likes] to be . . . [addressed] "Your Excellency."

Aguinaldo, of course, had come back to the islands with the belief, derived from talks with United States Consuls in Singapore and Hong Kong and with Dewey's representatives, that the United States would assist him and the Independence Junta to establish a free Filipino government. He tried to get this in writing, but was repeatedly assured he could depend on the goodwill and generosity of the United States. In Manila, Dewey gave him further "hearty assurances." The United States had never sought colonies, had no need for them, and could be relied upon to act fairly.

Denied permission even to enter Manila, the Filipino President moved his government up in Malolos, twenty-five miles north. His cabinet included some of the best educated, wealthiest, and ablest men on the islands. At the very moment Otis ordered the Filipinos to get out of the fringes of the city—September 13—the first Filipino Congress in history assembled, one hundred delegates from all the islands.

Aguinaldo opened the session, dressed as usual in polished boots, and an immaculate white suit, with several emblems on his chest. He was given a standing ovation. His talk was brief and eloquent—a government of the people, for the people, the free government of a new nation. Cheers swept the gathering.

John Barret, former United States Minister to Siam, attended some sessions—one of the few Americans to visit the interior even that far. "The members," he said, with a certain condescension, "compared in behavior, manners, dress and education with the average men of the better classes of other Asiatic nations . . . [they] . . . conducted themselves with great decorum and showed a knowledge of debate and parliamentary laws . . . [equal to that] . . . of the Japanese Parliament."

In early September 1898, a United States Navy survey team (about the only Americans to go outside of Manila) reported that the interior, ruled by Aguinaldo, was well-organized, well-garrisoned, well-administered, and wholly at peace. The two officers, cordially received and banqueted, discovered to their surprise that the Filipinos were exceedingly literate, cultured, and refined, but the Americans were astonished by so much "ignorance" about the United States. The Filipinos criticized

> the attitude of our government toward the two races . . .
> under our jurisdiction . . . the Indians and the Negroes
> . . . [Their] deliberate oppression . . . [was] . . . a warn-
> ing of what they [the Filipinos] may expect . . . They have
> been told that we possess neither patriotism, honor, re-
> ligion . . . nor any other . . . refining influence . . . On
> one point they are united . . . Whatever our government
> may have done . . . [in driving out the Spaniards] it has
> not gained the right to annexation.

Most Americans displayed equal ignorance about the Filipinos. As Mr. Dooley wrote, "The American people on the whole don't know

whether the Philippines are islands or canned goods." President Mc-
Kinley himself admitted that before the war, he "could not have told
where those damned islands were within two thousand miles." It was
to be a bloody geography lesson.

The United States Paris Peace Commissioners and Congress ignored
the findings of the Navy team and tried to ascertain the potentials of
the Filipinos for self-government. They called in no Filipinos, no
Spaniards, no Asiatics, no representatives of Aguinaldo—only United
States Consuls and generals, plus several dubious European authorities. Few had ever been outside of Manila. Though scarcely con-
cealing their racial prejudices, most praised the Filipinos—but all
hedged on granting independence, which by then was an idea offi-
cially taboo.

Brigadier-General Anderson said:

> I submit with all deference that we have hitherto under-
> rated the natives. They are not ignorant and savage tribes,
> but have a civilization of their own, and though . . . in-
> significant in appearance, [they] are fierce fighters and for
> a tropical people, industrious. A small detail of natives will
> do more work in a given time than a regiment [of American
> volunteers].

The Senate hastened to delete the rest of his remarks. Before he
trimmed his sails to please Washington, Dewey himself stated, albeit
ungrammatically, "In my opinion, these people are far superior in
their intelligence and capable of self-government than the natives of
Cuba."

"There are sufficiently able and educated men among them to develop a large degree of autonomy or self-government," reported John
Barret in *Harper's Magazine.* But, of course, "they should be guided
and encouraged by patriotic and unselfish Americans, shouldering
the White Man's burden [sic]."

Hong Kong Consul-General Wildman [not the writer], did put in
a word of warning.

> The Philippine Islands cannot be dealt with as though they
> were North American Indians, willing to be removed from
> one reservation to another at the whim of their masters . . .
> its ten million people will demand independence, and the
> attempt of any foreign nation to obtain territory or coaling
> stations will be resisted with the same spirit with which they
> fought the Spaniards.

Aguinaldo said at one point, "We merit as generous treatment as
was given Cuba." He still harbored hope that he could win recognition. Perhaps, suggested Brigadier-General Anderson, the masses could
be weaned away from Aguinaldo "if we could win over some insurgent

officers and . . . conciliate the people." Unfortunately "we know how to fight, but we do not know how to conquer."

But McKinley had come under the thumb of Teddy Roosevelt, Henry Cabot Lodge, Senator Albert Beveridge, Alfred T. Mahan, *et al.* He told a Methodist Episcopal missionary committee at the White House:

> The truth is, I didn't want the Philippines, and when they came to us as a gift from the gods [sic] I did not know what to do with them . . . I thought first we would take only Manila, then Luzon, then the other islands perhaps also. I walked the floor night after night until midnight, and I am not ashamed to tell you, gentlemen, that I went down on my knees and prayed to Almighty God for light and guidance more than one night, and one night late it came to me this way . . . I don't know [how] . . . but it came to me (1) That we would not give them back to Spain—that would be cowardly and dishonorable, (2) That we could not turn them over to France or Germany—or commercial rivals in the Orient—that would be bad business and discreditable, (3) That we could not leave them to themselves —they were unable to exercise self-government—and they would soon have anarchy and misrule over there worse than Spain's was. There was only one thing for us to do; take them all and educate the Philippinos and uplift and civilize and Christianize them, and by God's grace to do the very best we could by them, as our fellowmen for whom Christ also died [sic], and then I went to bed and went to sleep and slept soundly.

[Most Filipinos were Catholics.]

The Filipino Congress sent Felip Algoncillo to the United States to try to win support for independence. He also asked that Filipino delegates attend the Paris peace conference with Spain, since after all, it was to decide the fate of the islands. Algoncillo was treated with contempt, but managed to talk briefly with President McKinley. Granted no satisfaction, he went on to Paris. The United States Peace Commission would not even receive him.

At the peace conference, the American commissioners agreed to recognize all Spanish private and corporate rights. This insured that the Dominican and other Spanish Orders would be paid for their vast land holdings and rice fields. It affirmed the Spanish ownership of railways, street cars, electric plants, and waterworks that were soon to become American owned. The United States delegates bought the Philippines from Spain for $20,000,000—something that could not have come about if Aguinaldo's government were recognized. As one senator, weak on arithmetic, remarked, "We have bought 10,000,000

Malays at one dollar a head, unpicked, and nobody knows what it will cost to pick them."

In the *North American Review,* Ex-President Harrison argued that the Paris commissioners had bought something Spain no longer possessed and could not deliver, something the United States did not possess and could obtain only by another war.

Aguinaldo promptly denounced the peace arrangements, but still pinned his hopes on prominent United States anti-imperialists who found the United States' entry into the colony-grabbing game of European powers a dangerous deviation from basic American principles. These anti-imperialists included former Presidents Cleveland and Harrison, Andrew Carnegie, Carl Schurz, William Jennings Bryan, William James, Mark Twain, Jane Addams, and a majority in the United States Senate—which refused to ratify the peace treaty.

McKinley toured the United States to drum up annexation sentiment. He took it for granted (as did nearly everybody else) that Filipinos were primitive savages, incapable of self-government. Despite the lack of treaty ratification, a landing force was sent to seize Iloilo on Panay Island, the second city of the islands. The Filipinos flatly refused to turn it over. They strengthened their defenses.

To attack could have meant war, but Otis received last-minute instructions to hold up the assault. On board four United States war vessels outside the harbor, men sweltered impatiently for weeks. Commanding General Marcus P. Miller fumed and sweated and kept urging immediate attack.

Ignoring the Senate, McKinley sent to Manila a proclamation asserting full United States sovereignty. The Americans do not "come among you as invaders and conquerors, but as friends to establish and maintain a government which will accord to the people what is the heritage of all free people [sic] the full measure of individual rights and liberty." The United States military government at Manila would "with all possible dispatch" extend its authority to the whole Philippine group. Those who took the oath of allegiance, McKinley promised, would receive "support and protection." All others would be brought under "the lawful rule we have assumed." The strong arm of authority must be "sedulously maintained" to bestow "the blessings of good and stable government under the flag of the United States."

The proclamation was angrily torn from the walls. Aguinaldo issued a bitter counter-proclamation disclaiming responsibility for the rupture of amicable relations. In a short time, he declared, his government had come to rule all Luzon, the Viscayan Islands, and part of Mindanao. This had cost no little blood and gold.

We entertained absolute confidence in the . . . traditions
of a people which fought for its independence—who posed

> as the champion liberator of oppressed peoples; we felt
> ourselves under the safeguard of a free people. . . .
>   I denounce those acts before the world in order that the
> conscience of mankind may pronounce its infallible verdict
> as to who are the true oppressors of nations and the tormen-
> tors of humankind; upon their heads will be all the blood
> that may be shed.

In Manila's *El Heraldo de la Revolución*, Aguinaldo attacked General Otis for declaring himself military governor of the whole country.
As chosen president of the nation, Aguinaldo was obliged " to defend
to the death its liberty and independence." Surely the United States
authorities had not brought him back to the islands "to fight the
Spaniards for the benefit of the United States."

Sullen fear now prevailed. It became impossible to hire natives to
perform the most trifling services. Anti-Americanism became so great
that a reign of terror resulted. "Even the women of Cavite province,
in a document numerously signed by them," reported Otis, "gave me
to understand that, after all the men were killed, they were prepared
to shed their patriotic blood for the liberty and independence of the
country."

The newspapers "violent and uncompromising . . . accused the
Americans of unjust treatment and the . . . indiscriminate use of
force against innocent Filipino residents . . . the shooting of stragglers who passed in the vicinity of American fortifications." The
breaking point was near.

Though deserted by wealthier and more timid members of his
cabinet, Aguinaldo remained at his post in Malolos, calm, determined,
unshrinking. He worked around the clock, always impeccably dressed
in his white suit and polished shoes.

The United States aim was to overthrow his government and impose American rule. Despite his previous aesthetic stance, Dewey
seized every Philippine flag he could find. Otis suppressed *La Inde-
pendencia*. Although its presses were carted off to Malolos, later to
other temporary capitals, it continued to be published until the beginning of guerrilla warfare.

Otis was horrified by secret plans printed in Tagalog, to take
Manila. This document revealed the tactics, used many times since,
of guerrilla fighters in urban resistance. Not even Che Guevara has
been so explicit. Dated January 9, 1899, it was addressed to "The
Brave Soldiers of Sandatahan of Manila," and sounds like later Black
Power programs in the United States. The secret Manila militants
were to keep watch on fellow countrymen. However, if loyal to "the
holy cause of the country," they were to keep on pretending to be
United States sympathizers so as to draw good pay and be able to
inform "the Committee of Chiefs and our Army officers" of any important matters.

The resisters should study American outposts and headquarters for places for surprise attack. Before any attack, four men should be sent in with a smiling demeanor, with a good present for the American Commander, while the others hid in adjacent houses. One, dressed as a woman, should kill the sentry quickly.

They were not to pause to seize the rifles of dead enemies, but were to keep on slashing right and left with bolos until the Americans surrendered. If bolos or daggers were not available, they should prepare sharp-pointed lances and arrows to drive into the bodies of the enemy.

On rooftops along streets where Americans customarily passed, four to six men should be stationed, ready with stones, timbers, red-hot irons, heavy furniture, boiling molasses, rags soaked in coal oil, and so on but no glass "as most of our soldiers are barefoot." Hot liquids should be thrown as bombs on Americans or syphoned out on them with bamboo tubes.

On the ground, the Sandatahan were to attack with determined ferocity and isolate Americans in small groups. Contingents outside the city would force the enemy line and join their brothers. The combat would be short. Such tactics would create so much confusion the enemy would not be able to use their firearms lest they shoot each other. "The victory will be certain, the triumph ours . . . Manila will be taken."

Property was to be respected and prisoners well treated . . . Consulates, banks, and commercial establishments were not to be plundered. The Chinese were to be respected. "Be on the lookout for those traitors who by robbery will seek to mar our victory." All were to remember the holiness of the cause for Liberty and Independence, their sacred oath, their immaculate banner, and the promises made to all civilized nations. "Filipinos are not savages, nor thieves, nor assassins, nor are we cruel." We are men "of culture and patriotism, honorable and very human."

Impatiently waiting off shore from Iloilo, General Miller wrote on January 5 that the Navy guns could wipe out the city "and should destroy it all, I believe it would be of advantage . . . as a newer city would be built up soon." Iloilo was finally shelled on February 11, with considerable loss of civilian lives. By then the war was already a week old.

Firing had broken out along the lines after a United States sentry killed a Filipino on the night of February 4. W. W. Grayson of the Nebraska regiment related what had happened.

> I yelled "Halt" . . . The man moved. I challenged him with another "Halt" . . . [He] shouted "Halt" to me. Well, I thought the best thing was to shoot him. He dropped. Then two Filipinos sprang out of the gateway about fifteen feet from us. I called "Halt" . . . and Miller fired and dropped

one. I saw that another was left. Well, I think I got my
second Filipino that time. We retreated to where our other
fellows were, and I said, "Line up, fellows, the Niggers
are in here all through these yards" . . .

The Americans retired behind the water main.

On Sunday morning, the Americans attacked in force, killing or
wounding some 3,000 Filipinos. Dewey's *Monadnock* sent in a rain
of shells that "put the fear of God into them"—or at least the fear of
steel and death. On Monday afternoon the Nebraskans stormed the
reservoir, and seventy-nine Filipinos lay dead on top. On Thursday
the Filipinos abandoned San Roque, across from Cavite, which was
set on fire. This was the washerwomen's town, and in the subsequent
United States victory parade along the Luneta, the officers did not
display their usual spic-and-span appearance.

Aguinaldo had tried to halt the fighting. "I sent a ranking member
of my staff under a flag of truce to General Otis to convey the message
that the firing on our side that night before had been against my
orders and that I wished to stop further hostilities . . ." General Otis
replied roughly: "The fight, having begun, has to go on until the grim
end."

Secretary of State Elihu Root, speaking at Canton, Ohio, soared to
unusual heights. "On the fourth of February an army of Tagalogs, a
tribe inhabiting the central part of Luzon, under the leadership of
Aguinaldo, a Chinese half-breed, attacked in vastly superior numbers
our little army in the possession of Manila, and after desperate and
bloody fight was repulsed in every direction."

Aguinaldo later wrote in his 1957 book, *A Second Look at America,*

> Had war been avoided—and it could have been pre-
> vented by a greater measure of good will on the part of
> the American military authorities approximating our own
> . . . American moral status today would be far more mas-
> sive . . . To us the war with America was . . . a great
> tragedy. From my first contact with the Americans in Hong
> Kong and Singapore, I had envisioned a motherland, long
> chained to starving by European imperialism, at last free
> and happy. To that dream we had dedicated every ounce
> to our efforts and energies. We had at last defeated the
> Spaniards on our own soil . . .

On February 6, the Senate hastened to ratify the peace treaty with
Spain. Anti-imperialist William Jennings Bryan put the deal across.
He hurried to Washington and made political hay out of national
tragedy. Gleefully he told his Democratic colleagues they should now
vote for ratification because the McKinley administration would not
survive an unjust war.

Aguinaldo told the world:

> What a spectacle . . . to see at the end of the century—
> called the century of enlightenment and civilization—a
> people jealous and proud of its own sovereignty employing
> all its great power . . . to wrest from another people, weak
> but worthy a better fate, the very rights which in its own
> case it believes to be inherent by natural and divine law
> . . . we shall fight to the last breath to revindicate our . . .
> independence . . .

General Otis launched a three-pronged attack into the interior to surround Aguinaldo. The Filipinos, in spite of inferior equipment, resisted bitterly. General Arthur MacArthur pushed fairly rapidly up the railroad line along the China Sea coast. Guerrillas were active. Soldiers dared not venture even a quarter of a mile from the roadbed. MacArthur's descriptions indicate some of the problems of guerrilla fighting. "The density of the jungle," he reported, "which prevented seeing any distance, made it impossible to keep the troops together . . . impeded and at times entirely interrupted their movement . . . to intercept the insurgent retreat was almost impossible . . ."

Generals Henry Lawton and Lloyd Wheaton, moving up the Pasig Valley, were slowed down even more by swamps, jungle, heavy rain, and raging rivers. They could not be supplied with adequate food or ammunition. Oxcarts sank to the axles in the deep mud. Oxen weakened and died. The native porters slipped off into the jungle, and the soldiers had to haul the heavily laden carts themselves. Sickness and exhaustion laid up more than half the men. The trap was never closed, but MacArthur stormed ahead into burning Malolos.

Aguinaldo had ordered his men to contest every inch of ground and had personally encouraged them at the river. When defense there was broken, he worked all night packing up, burning documents, and arranging for the shipment north of the printing presses that were more precious than the lives of his soldiers. He told the townspeople that Malolos had to be burned. They set fire to their own homes. He waited until the city was in flames, then boarded his train, already crowded with refugees. He set up headquarters in San Fernando, later in San Isidro.

Lacking men and materials, MacArthur was obliged to halt in San Fernando until the monsoons were over. Only 2,640 of his 4,800 men were fit for the firing line, the rest were so sick or exhausted they would not be fit "for duty as a regiment within any reasonable time." Otis had to call a halt everywhere.

Patriot war material was being brought in from the mainland. On August 27, the *Abby* out of Canton sailed into Bataán and delivered 500 rifles, 500,000 rounds of ammunition, 2 Maxim guns, 2,000 rounds of Maxim ammunition, and an American instructor.

"Arms," wrote Edwin Wildman, "even found their way into Manila

Bay on merchant ships . . . under false labels. Funeral processions became so numerous they aroused suspicion . . . caskets and hearses were found to be filled with Mausers." (Later the Viet Cong were to use the same cover-up.) General Otis admitted that he could not prevent supplies arriving in Manila from being smuggled to the interior. Aguinaldo had his own organization inside the city, a Junta headed by a Chinese *mestizo*. The Junta members were not arrested until the Spring of 1900, and even then no natives could be found to testify against them.

By the end of the rainy season, Otis had reinforcements and fresh supplies. In the South, Lawton, the most dashing of the United States officers and a giant, jovial man, pushed the patriots back from the edge of the city and from nearby lake shores. Shortly before being killed, he said:

> Taking into account the disadvantages they [the Filipinos] have to fight against in arms, equipment and military discipline—without arms, short of ammunition, powder inferior, shells reloaded until they are defective—they are the bravest men I have ever seen . . . What we want is to stop this accursed war . . . these men are indestructible.

Aguinaldo made his next stand at Tarlac near the coast, but his forces began breaking up. On November 12 he called a conference of military leaders at the hat manufacturing city of Bayambay (Pangasinan Province) to lay plans for guerrilla warfare. "Our troops," he declared, "henceforth will maneuver in flying columns and in guerrilla bands." He named commanders for the various provinces.

On moving into Bayambay, MacArthur reported to Manila, "The so-called Philippine Republic is destroyed . . . The Army itself as an organization has disappeared."

Aguinaldo's small force barely avoided encirclement by galloping up a deep mountain ravine. He forged on into the rugged northeast mountains. His rear was protected by twenty-three-year-old General Gregorio del Pilar, his most brilliant officer. Forty-four hundred feet up in the narrow Tila Pass, he constructed a stone barricade to command the zigzag trail below.

United States sharpshooters climbed an adjacent mountain hand-over-hand. Pilar was hit in the neck with a Krag-Jorgensen bullet. His body was "stripped of everything of value from the diamond ring to the boots." "Handsome lad," wrote MacArthur. "He believed in the right and not . . . personal greed or ambition."

Aguinaldo holed up in Palamón, a northeast jungle town high above the ocean. There, with the remnants of his government, his close aides and a small armed force, he directed guerrilla operations throughout the archipelago. Messengers slipped in and out daily. Adjacent villages sent food, all they could spare and more. So loyal were all Filipinos that for several years the United States forces had no inkling where he was.

Once American forces raided the town. Forewarned, Aguinaldo moved into the forest with his archives, his family, and entourage. The invaders had no idea he was nearby. His camp—the thick-thatched administration building, with its stripped sapling in front bearing the Philippino flag—could not be seen even from the trail. An outlook hut overlooked the sea and the palm trees below. Here work went on: writing letters, preparing wall posters to be secretly printed in Manila. Here were stored a great deal of rice, other supplies, and arms brought in from far places (even from beyond enemy lines) mostly on the backs of men. A "forty-coconut man" was considered pretty good. Even at night the labor went on by the light of palm-olive lamps.

To his secretary, nodding after a night of work, Aguinaldo said, "Those who love freedom need little rest or sleep, so wake up my good friend, and have your tea. A new work day is at hand."

Of those days of guerrilla warfare, Major Lee wrote, "Never in the history of similar warfare were greater difficulties presented. Often the rivers were so high that improvised ferries were swept away . . . the country was flooded, the roads quagmired and trails almost impassable."

Edwin Wildman wrote:

> Aguinaldo's renegade soldiers, leagued with the wild forest tribes and marauding bands in every part of the Archipelago . . . at our approach, would disappear like mosquitos in the daytime, upon our withdrawal they swarmed back . . . Even in the proximity of our army posts, where Americans attempted to engage in commercial operations, life was not safe. Given the least excuse, and a gun or a bolo, [the pacificos] would drop their work and offer a fight.

General MacArthur also described the problem, "The practice of discarding uniforms enables the insurgents to appear and disappear within the American lines in the attitude of peaceful natives, absorbed in that dense mass of sympathetic people, speaking a dialect of which few men and no Americans have any knowledge."

It became necessary to set up battle stations nearly everywhere. "Each little command had to provide its own . . . security and information by . . . patrols, explorations, escorts, outposts and regular guards." But the garrisons were too tiny to send out adequate scouting parties. The roads and the railroads also had to be guarded, and a large force had to be maintained in Manila where the people remained hostile. More plots to seize the city were uncovered.

Commenting on General MacArthur's pacification efforts, Wildman wrote, "Our outlying . . . posts were attacked constantly, and our engineers and civil functionaries engaged in repairing bridges and building roads, had to work with their guns within reach. Often these guerrillas . . . ambushed our supply trains and captured ammunition and canned goods." They fired upon trains and swooped down upon villages, terrorizing, carrying away loot. "It was like hunting needles in a haystack."

Filipino villagers received the Americans cordially but volunteered no information. "The general situation was . . . discouraging. The natives at large did not love us and contested our occupation with what little force they could muster—enough to make life unsafe and trade difficult, if not impossible . . . it was a slow process to catch, kill or disarm him."

Two hundred thousand Filipinos died in the process. Brutality won the upper hand; the horrible "water cure" was used by both sides. Regard for the lives of civilians and prisoners was discarded. General Jake Smith ordered Samar Island to be turned into a "howling wilderness." "I want no prisoners, I wish you to kill and burn, the more you burn and kill the better it will please me." This was an earlier version of Curtis Le May "We shall bomb Vietnam back into the Stone Age."

The role and methods of Filipino guerrilla warfare were set forth in a pamphlet put out on June 15, 1900 by the revolutionary Filipino Junta in Madrid. It began,

> The imperialists, want to reduce the Filipino people to slavery and confiscate our rich archipelago and, in order to hide their greed, allege that, without the interference, anarchy would be general, but the falsity of this has already been exposed . . .
>
> Our guerrilla will not have to give battle in the field, diseases will soon finish off the enemy . . . The guerrillas must seek out the sympathies of the people and defend them against bandits and thieves . . .
>
> They must make up for their small numbers by their ceaseless activity . . . by day, hide in woods and in distant areas, then, when least expected, fall upon the enemy and disappear at once to enjoy whatever spoils . . . taken from the Yankees, but they shall be careful not to rob their countrymen . . . the commander must never camp twice in the same place, always march at night, show himself only in places where he does not usually operate and fall suddenly on the enemy when least expected.

His spies shall keep him informed of the position and tactics of the foes. This "will be easy since all inhabitants are in our favor." Signals, passwords, and countersigns such as cuts on trees, heaps

of stones, strips of cloth, balloons, and fires were to be changed frequently, to prevent their meanings being discovered.

The proper use of artillery, infantry, and cavalry was set forth.
"When an attack is made on a pueblo occupied by the Yankees, our
forces shall divide into three platoons. First, the most active men for
the attack . . . The last two groups will lie in ambush in echelons, to
protect the first platoon when it takes off."

Five hundred Filipinos, divided into smaller groups which could
easily disappear, were enough for each province. "When the enemy
attacks, they shall retreat toward the base of operations . . . once
the enemy tires . . . they shall unite to fall upon them . . . with all
the advantage of position carefully studied beforehand. A surprise,
properly planned, always gives great results," and "a few guerrillas
are enough to win the most unexpected triumphs." But mainly it
should be made with superior forces by rapid marches, where the
enemy least expects it.

"Ambushes . . . can cause a big loss to the enemy with little . . .
to us. Men chosen for ambushes should be veterans, cool-headed,
able to reserve their energy until the right moment. Since the enemy
will imagine our numbers to be vastly superior . . . if the first volley
causes serious losses, the enemy will run for it."

"It is essential," the Filipino manual commanded, "always to have
a tactical plan, to thoroughly reconnoitre the ground to . . . take
every advantage of the conditions and to know the strength of the
enemy . . ."—one of the chief requirements also insisted upon by Che
Guevara a half century later. It accounted for much of the guerrillas'
success against the Batista army in Cuba.

On March 15, 1900, General MacArthur replaced detested General
Otis as military governor. Otis informed a United States Senate committee, "I did not like to believe that the whole people of Luzon was
opposed to us but . . . the Filipino masses are loyal to Aguinaldo and
the government he heads." Ergo, the one hope for peace for the
United States was to locate and capture or destroy Aguinaldo.

Not until March of 1902 were his whereabouts made known by a
Spanish renegade, L. Segovia, Major Frederick Funston at once laid
plans to capture Aguinaldo by trickery. Forged letters written on
captured stationery were dispatched to the President, saying that reinforcements he had asked for were being sent to Palamón. Funston
and four other Americans, disguised as engineers taken prisoner, went
along with an armed Macabebe force posing as Tagalogs.*

A long sea voyage from Manila to the northeast coast was followed
by a grueling ninety-mile march. Food gave out. The Macabebe com-

---

* The Macabebes were distrusted and hated by the Filipinos. Some have claimed
they were Mexicans, originally brought over by the Spaniards to perpetrate police
brutalities.

mander was so fat, whining, and sick that he had to be carried most of the way.

Aguinaldo, unsuspectingly arranged to receive the group with solemn ceremonies. The Macabebes suddenly wheeled and fired on the guards, killing numbers of them, then fired on the villagers. More shooting occurred inside before Aguinaldo could be taken. A wounded aide escaped out a window.

Aguinaldo was put under house arrest in Manila and finally took the oath of allegiance to avoid being exiled to Guam (where captured patriots were sent). He ordered an end to further bloodshed.

The Filipino president claimed that Funston exaggerated a false story for his own greater glory. "His method," said Aguinaldo, was "a cross between the Greek Trojan horse, the British Major Martin and the Russian tribunal-confession"—in other words, "brainwashing and torture." Still another version was told by the Spanish renegade L. Segovia.

Funston was hailed as the hero of the war and promoted to Brigadier General. Many Americans were outraged by the trickery used, but since when has deceit not been a major tool of war?

Even after Aguinaldo's capture, guerrilla war continued fiercely until well into 1903, more sporadically thereafter. Eventually, nearly all leaders were hung or shot. The coup de grace in 1906—though it was still not quite the end—was described by Mark Twain in his *Comments on the Killing of 600 Moros*. The "dark-skinned savages" had entrenched themselves with their women and children in an extinct crater near Jile. "Since they were bitter at us for having been trying for eight years to take their liberties away from them," they were a menace. The bowl was 2,200 feet above the sea, "very difficult of access for Christian troops and artillery." General Leonard Wood led his soldiers to the rim. "Kill or capture the six hundred," he ordered. The soldiery fired into the crater with artillery and rifles. After a day and a half it ended with a great victory. Five hundred ninety-nine Moros men, women, and children lay dead. Only one captive was taken and, with Wood looking on, was also killed. Mark Twain concluded, "The enemy numbered six hundred, including women and children—and we abolished them utterly, leaving not even a baby alive to cry for its dead mother. *This is incomparably the greatest victory . . . ever achieved by the Christian soldiers of the United States.*" President Theodore Roosevelt wired Wood congratulations for upholding the honor of the American flag: "I was never so enthusiastically proud of the flag till now." Such was the glorious battle of Mount Dago. The long guerrilla war groaned to a halt, and Americans governed the islands.

In time, feeble efforts at land reform were instituted. Vast estates of the Catholic orders were purchased (at great cost to the Filipinos) to be sold to tenants and other buyers, many of them foreigners. This of course did little for poorer farmers, and peasant revolts occurred in Tayug in 1931 and in Laguna in 1935. Sharecropping increased from 22 percent in 1930 to 40 percent in 1958. Today, large landholdings, made necessary by commercial export crops, are mostly in United States hands (i.e., the United Fruit Company and the Dole's Pineapple Corporation). Foreign ownership is more extensive than under Spanish rule. Peasant income is still infamously low.

Stanley Karomov summarized in the *Saturday Review*:

> Under U. S. colonial rule, Americans had a privileged market in the Philippines . . . American manufactured goods flooded the islands, thwarting local incentives to industrialize. At the same time, the U. S. stimulated production of sugar, copra, hemp and other export products . . . The Philippines therefore, typified the narrow "colonial" economy reliant on the U. S. for survival. To a significant extent it still does: Nearly half its export earnings depend upon special accords with the U. S. . . . Favored by the U. S., traditional landlords expanded their estates . . . by getting marginal lands, or dispossessed bankrupt farmers.

Philippine independence was granted on July 4, 1946. But vast Army and Navy bases were retained, along with many special privileges for Americans. Though subject to United States scrutiny and often overt interference, the Filipinos now largely run their own domestic affairs.

Manuel Roxas, the new president inaugurated under General Douglas MacArthur, was the most notorious Japanese collaborationist. The Japanese occupation had left the people hungry, ragged, their industry and commerce in ruins, the government without a penny. No nation ever began its career under less favorable conditions.

The United States distributed considerable food and clothing, and gave the new regime $35,000,000 to keep it alive—far less than it gave to most other Asian countries; far less in fact than went to enemy Japan. Some additional aid was provided thereafter.

Aguinaldo grows in stature. Communists now belittle him, but more and more he is recognized as the George Washington of the Philippines. Besides changing independence day to June 12 early in 1965, the government issued a special series of stamps to mark Aguinaldo's death. In due time, it is likely that an adequate biography of him will be written.

Guerrilla activity in the Philippines has continued to play an important part in the islands' history. The Japanese World War II invasion was fought by numerous Filipino guerrilla bands, chiefly by the Hukbalahap (The National Anti-Japanese Army), known in the United States as the Huks. These extreme Nationalists were not recognized by the (Douglas) MacArthur military regime that took over from the Japanese. They were denied the compensation paid to all other, less important, guerrilla bands, some of which were postwar paper outfits devised to grab funds. Even so, the Huks laid down their arms and prepared to participate in political life.

The Huk leader Mariano Balge told how their hopes were high after independence was granted. As the Democratic Alliance, they elected six deputies. But when the party opposed the "imperialistic" Bell Trade Act that favored American business interests and citizens over Filipinos, the Huks were thrown out of Congress. Their followers were persecuted, jailed, and killed. Survivors again took to the hills for many years of ugly warfare that still goes on. President Roxas boasted he would wipe them out in sixty days. It took ten years and massive United States help to curb them.

This heroic struggle is described by William J. Pomeroy in *The Forest*. An American, Pomeroy and his Filipino wife joined the Huks as schoolteachers and experienced the most formidable hardships and tragedies. They were sent to prison in Manila.*

The Huks were accused of being Communists, some likely were, but most were just hungry peasants, nationalists, and anti-imperialists. At one time they captured several large centers—Manila once seemed doomed—but they never secured a permanent foothold in the villages. Their leaders in Manila were finally rounded up and jailed or killed.

In a 1967 Havana speech, Fidel Castro attributed early Huk failure to the "political" committee in Manila. How absurd it was, he pointed out, to order simultaneous guerrilla attacks on a given date without proper knowledge of the situation of each unit.

The Huks have never completely abandoned the strugle. By 1962 they announced (under their new name Hunkbong Napagpalaya Ng Bayan—Tagalog for Army of National Liberation) that they had 130 armed fighters and 20,000 sympathizers. Since then, they have grown and expanded their operations. Leftist propaganda claimed in February 1968, that they controlled most of Luzon, an exaggeration though opposition to the Vietnam war has greatly increased their following.

One reason for guerrilla revival is the high rate of unemployment (now about 10 percent). The greater poverty of peasants and workers is partly due to a phenomenal 3.2 percent population growth, which throws nearly half a million new workers into the job-market every year. The Tweedle-dee and Tweedle-dum antics of the Republican and National parties, which alternate in the presidency, has added to popular frustration. *Prensa Latina* correspondent A. R. Karin remarked in 1967: "One is controlled by the U. S. Embassy; the other by C.I.A."

* After about ten years they were released. He now lives as a journalist in London.

The Huks seek to undermine Philippine support for the Vietnam war. Actually they get much of their arms and supplies from the area around Clark Air Base, where United States Army personnel spend about 50,000 dollars a month in the cafes, shops, and whorehouses.

A Congressional report declares that the American military effectiveness in Southeast Asia, depends primarily on the bases in the Philippines and the capacity of President Marcos to "provide the leadership the situation so desperately needs." Thus the growth of Huk force is a backdoor menace to the whole Vietnam enterprise.

Guerrillas often just fade away, but unlike generals, they usually return. Aguinaldo's revolt is not yet ended.

3

THE ROBIN HOODS OF MEXICO:
PANCHO VILLA

Pancho Villa, the Mexican bandit who turned guerrillera and social reformer, pushed his big sombrero back on his reddish hair, hitched his heavy crisscrossed cartridge belts and said wryly that if it weren't for the damned Texans he would plant the Mexican flag on the gringo White House. He made a try at it. His Columbus, New Mexico, raid on March 10, 1916, killed nearly a score of United States citizens and burned part of the city. General John Pershing was sent south across the border immediately with an invading expedition to get him "alive or dead."

It was the first widely publicized United States involvement with guerrillas since Emilo Aguinaldo. Guerrilla fighting had followed American occupation of Nicaragua, Haiti, and the Dominican Republic (1915–1916), but these disorders caused little fanfare except in Latin America. The Villa episode, however, made headlines around the globe.

Villa was a huge hairy fist defying the heavens. He lived with unbridled gusto and joviality. His quick savage temper, puckish humor, sudden whims, free-handed generosity, and brutal violence made dealing with him, said one associate, "like handling dynamite."

He began as a bandit outlaw, became a bonafide guerrilla of the Revolution, headed armies, imposed revolutionary laws in much of the north, printed money, seized Mexico City, and sat briefly in the carved high-backed presidential chair. He became a social reformer, believing in the rights of the poor, accepting the revolutionary slogan of "Land, Water and Schools."

A robbery during the final years of the Díaz dictatorship netted him 50,000 pesos; he said "I gave it all away to the needy except what I had to spend for my immediate requirements." When as a revolutionary he took a plaza, he often threw open the grocery stores and meat markets to the poor. He paid the owners on the spot, though sometimes with only I.O.U.'s. He bought food for hard-pressed villages. Once he remarked of Francisco Madero (to whom he was loyal even when Madero kept him in prison), "He is a rich man but is risking his life and his fortune to help the poor. If all rich men dedicated themselves to alleviating the lot of the unfortunate and worked for the benefit of the people and the country, all this bloodshed would be unnecessary." By a combination of terror and largess, he created farflung loyalties and obedience that more than once saved his life.

In one of his novels, Rafael Muñoz describes how in the desperate later years shortly before Pershing's 1916 invasion, Villa looked up Don Tiburcio, survivor of a reckless group known as "The Lions," who had fought with Villa. Villa asked him to rejoin. By then a simple farmer, Don Tiburcio protested that he now had a wife and child. Villa shot both, telling Tiburcio he no longer had a good excuse not to rejoin.

The story is probably apocryphal, but indicates the fear Villa's name evoked in a middle-class urban writer. Usually Villa had more valid reasons before he killed.

Villa's code was the product of simple philosophy. His devotion to his family, to his wife (to whom he was never faithful), to his two children, and especially to his mother, was boundless. Once a poor friend was in love with the daughter of a rich hacendado. Her father threw him out, but the father was being foreclosed by the bank for $25,000. Villa seized the bank president in his home and made him fork over $25,000 which the young suitor then gave to the girl's father. The marriage was soon celebrated in lavish style.

Whimsically, Villa sometimes also showered favor on bitter critics. He paid off the two thousand-peso mortgage of a vituperative small rancher and asked him if he still thought Villa was a monster. The man became well-to-do—and a fanatic Villa partisan.

Villa never forgot a favor or let an injury go unpunished. To a fellow bandit who robbed him of everything and later became a local judge, he gave the choice of death or giving up his position—and won another useful friend.

He hated gringos and killed many, but a few he liked tremendously. Numbers of Yankee adventurers helped train his men or fought with him. In the 1911 assault on Ciudad Juárez, he was aided by American cowboys led by Captain Oscar Creighton. (Among the adventurers was Tom Mix, who later used his talents to better advantage in Hollywood.) During Villa's efforts to help President Madero suppress the 1912 Pascual Orozco revolt in northern Mexico, Villa's American machine gunner, Thomas Fountain, was summarily shot by Orozco. The State Department heatedly told Madero that no American could be killed without due process. Since he was trying to suppress the killer Orozco, Madero thought this unreasonable criticism. If foreigners came to Mexico, they had to run their chances along with Mexicans.

Villa became a good friend of General Hugh Scott, who swore by him even after the Columbus raid. Villa was supplied—briefly but copiously—with arms by the United States Government, which never failed to stick its fingers into Mexico's affairs and thereby contributed to the bloodletting. Likely the subsequent shift of American support to Carranza provoked Villa to perpetrate the Santa Ysabel massacre and the raids into New Mexico in January and March of 1916.

But more than Americans, he hated Spaniards and Chinese. He killed many, sometimes having them pulled apart by horses. When he took Torreón in April 1914 (where 7,000 dead piled up), he expelled 6,000 Spaniards, telling them to go eat ham in Spain. This corresponded to popular prejudice: The Chinese monopolized the wholesale and retail food business of northern Mexico, and most other retail business was in Spanish hands.

Villa killed, but often felt compunction. He wined and dined one prominent prisoner, then embraced him, expressed regrets at having to shoot him, and wept copiously. Another time, obliged to have to gun down a beloved but traitorous subordinate, he gave out that the man had been killed by bandits. He brought the body to the man's wife, sat through an all-night wake, and was a pallbearer at the funeral. "I didn't want to hurt her feelings," he explained.

Though Villa took scores of women and married or pretended to marry many, he was otherwise devoted to his first (and only legal) wife, Luz Corral de Villa—a beautiful, serene, well-bodied, part Indian woman by whom he had two children. For them he bought much property in Chihuahua City and, when he ruled in the North, built for them a marble mausoleum at a cost of 200,000 pesos. (His own body was never to rest there.)

Villa's women were often from leading families. In spite of his stocky, gross appearance, their experience was not always without rewards. When necessary, he rigged up fake marriages, with an aide posing as priest or justice of the peace.

One hostile critic, Leone B. Moats, remarked: "His lust for blood and for women were equal. When he had satisfied the one, he would slake his thirst for the other." His chief weaknesses were women and cockfighting, and she quotes him as saying, "Women can be found everywhere, but good fighting cocks are damned scarce." But her anecdotes—how he stripped women naked, enjoyed them, then thrust them bareskinned out the door; how he forced a husband to watch him rape his wife—are apocryphal.

Though Villa had few of the Puritanical traits characteristic of most dedicated guerrilla leaders, his personal habits were mostly austere, if disorderly. He did not smoke or drink, but he ate whenever he was hungry and slept only when he had to. He rarely rested, never stopped working till he had finished a job, never spared himself any necessary hardship. He was aware that daring was often his best protection.

As Villa became a political force, a few young intellectuals rallied around him, such as José Vasconcelos, Martín Luis Guzmán, the Peruvian poet José Santos Chocano (soon sent packing). He got ideas from them, but pretty much followed his own instincts on all important matters.

Pancho Villa was born in Durango, probably in 1878. His father died when he was ten. At sixteen he was a sharecropper on the Gogojita Hacienda in Cantalán, where he lived with his mother, two brothers, and two younger sisters. Coming home from the fields on September 22, 1904, Villa killed hacendado Agustín López Negrete for violating his fifteen-year-old sister Marcella. He then fled into the nearby Sierra de la Silla in the Gamón range. Previously known as Doroteo Arango, he took his grandfather's name, Villa, calling himself Francisco (Pancho).

To understand Villa and his exploits, one must appreciate the life and psychology of the footloose men of the Mexican countryside. They have a sublime indifference to all civilized norms of conduct, morality, and sex. One must be able to appreciate their primitive responses, their frequent absurd generosities, their excessive bragadoccio, their hot touchiness, and their pride. The mestizos—men of mixed blood, the inevitable products of race conquest—belonged neither to Spanish nor to Indian culture. Outcasts from both worlds, their breed often had to lead lawless lives for generations, surviving by their wits and cunning.

More valuable to Villa than money was his far-flung knowledge of the country, of horses, and of men. He came to know every hidden trail, every pitfall. His memory was better than the most detailed map. Everywhere he managed to leave at least one faithful friend behind him.

In 1910 Abraham González (later a martyr to the revolutionary cause) had persuaded Villa to enlist in the fight to overthrow Dictator Porfirio Díaz. "For the benefit of the people," argued Abraham, "those persecuted and humiliated, those who have had their sisters and daughters violated, all their rights trampled upon."

Villa commented later:

> I came to understand, for nobody explained anything to the poor, what this thing they called the fatherland, the *patria*, really was. For me until then it had been only a bitter-sweet love for the open country, the deep ravines and mountains where I lived with boundless rancor toward everybody, for nearly everybody was on the side of the oppressors . . .
> For the first time, I heard the name of Francisco I. Madero, and I came to love and revere him, for he had unbreakable faith. He sent us his Plan of San Luís Potosí, where he had been held in prison until he escaped to the United States.

The Plan called for armed revolt, no reelections of president, vice-president, governors, and mayors; and for the return to the villages of communal lands stripped away during the thirty-year Díaz dictatorship. It named Madero provisional President.

In the Blue Mountains Villa began recruiting for the forthcoming Madero Revolution. He selected fifteen men, all perfectly armed and mounted. They wore embroidered gold shirts—The *Dorados*. From the very beginning, he realized that the major obligation of a leader was to see to it that his boys "never lacked anything ever." His true guerrilla role had begun.

He led them to within half a dozen miles of Chihuahua and slipped into the city to get instructions from Abraham González. This was October 3, 1910—the day before Congress declared Díaz president for another six years. Díaz had been dictator for thirty years—a glittering, cruel reign of "progress" in a land of maltreated serfs and slaves where the gringos were above the law and owned a large part of the country.

On November 17, Abraham dined at Villa's house in company with Cástulo Herrera. Herrera was to have command of all forces in the area.

Villa concealed his pique: "Abraham had had no chance to appreciate that I myself could have carried on the revolutionary campaign." But he told González: "You can be assured that my men will fight for the good of the people and the poor. I will always obey Cástulo's orders . . . We will fight to the last breath of life."

They set out for the Blue Mountains. Tears flooded into Villa's eyes as he left Chihuahua, a city he had come to love. "Never since I mourned that night for my mother, did I have so great a desire to weep."

He expanded his force to 375 well-armed volunteers. Cástulo ordered them to take the village of San Andrés. The federals and officials fled. The rebels began shooting exuberantly into the air. As Cástulo did nothing to restrain them, Villa ran into the plaza, shouting, "No one is to fire. Our ammunition is to defeat the enemy . . . Don't think it's going to be as easy as this morning. We haven't begun to fight." From then on, Cástulo was little more than a figurehead who tagged along but gave no orders.

As time went on, weapons and ammunition became less of a problem. There were illimitable supplies across the border and, as their power grew, there was plenty of money to buy them. Also more and more government equipment was captured or bought.

Years ago, when I was coming down from the Sierra Madre in Durango, I was stopped by a sentry on the outskirts of a small village. After the customary *"Quién Viva?"* I was taken to the Commandant.

"You were lucky," he told me. "The sentries have orders to shoot on sight. We are expecting a Villista attack."

The attack came at daybreak, and firing continued all day. Women went about their work as usual, carrying jars of water on their heads or washing clothes in the river. About nightfall a truce permitted the Villistas to occupy half the town until morning. That night both bands got drunk together and galloped up and down the streets, shooting at the stars—among other things—and shouting "¡Mueran los gringos! Kill the Yankees!" I was the only gringo within five hundred miles, but they embraced me affectionately, they called me "gringo" with great glee, offered me food and drink. At headquarters, the leaders of the two sides amicably drank mescal and dickered over the price of arms the federals would sell to the rebels. Thus, I learned that the government troops had a big stake in keeping the war going.

With only fifteen trusted men, Villa attacked a train. Federal Colonel Pablo M. Yépez was killed, but the train was carrying the entire federal Twelfth Battalion. Villa had to withdraw fast and was lucky not to be cut to ribbons. He took Santa Ysabel with little trouble and, 500 strong, set out for Chihuahua City.

It was too big a bite. His *Dorados* were quickly surrounded. They cut their way out, but Eleuterio Soto was left dead, and Villa was wounded. They retreated back to San Andrés.

General Pascual Ortiz, head of Madero's revolutionary forces, wired, "I have just captured this plaza [Ciudad Guerrero]. Come see me here about supplying you with ammunition."

It was a three-day ride. Villa and his men were joyously received. People offered to give up their homes, but he camped on the outskirts. "We demonstrated that the Revolution was an organized revolution, that the leaders gave guarantees and that their men loved order and respected the property and comfort of all." (More likely he did not trust Ortiz.)

The combined forces split into smaller bands and converged on Cerro Prieto, a strong point held by Federal General Juan J. Navarro. Villa's vanguard attacked at eight in the morning. It was his first formal combat and lasted more than three hours. Navarro's artillery proved very accurate; one of Villa's most trusted aides was killed. At that critical moment, Ortiz's cavalry arrived. Fighting ebbed and flowed all day, and the rebels were finally routed.

Villa led his forces back to San Andrés. The pre-Christmas holidays had begun, and he allowed most of his men to disperse to their homes. The Federals surprised the town. Villa resisted behind barricades at the railroad station till his men began showing up. They fled to Las Playas, where there was plenty of water and cattle.

The survivors were now poorly mounted, but raids brought in four hundred horses. The men contrived saddles of cowhide and halters of woven palm leaves or rawhide.

They surprised fifty Rurales and took their arms, horses, and saddles, then moved on through remote haciendas, villages, and mines. Everywhere they were royally treated. At one big hacienda, the owner opened the corn cribs, provided all the meat and grain required, even seated Villa and his officers at his own table. At the Naica mine, the workers were wild with joy, and the manager fed Villa's men and horses for three days and gave him 2,000 pesos in cash. He spent 1,500 of them for clothing for his ragged followers.

At Ciuda Camargo he captured seventy rifles and ammunition. Various towns and mines were occupied. On one occasion he sent word for the Federal force to come out of the town and fight him. "Whenever possible, it is the duty of those who fight to avoid that towns suffer the upsets of battle." He received an insulting reply and stormed the place.

He set out with two aides to spy out the situation in Parral, one of the major cities. They put up at the small stone house of a friend. Dressed in peon attire, they rode on stringy nags. Their rifles were to be brought into the city in sacks of charcoal.

"And so I came into Parral again—that city where I had become a man and where the justice of the rich or, better said, the justice against which we were fighting in the name of the revolution, had so often prevented men from making an honest living."

They nosed around, sizing up the four army barracks. As prearranged their friend brought their guns and good horses to the outskirts, but suspicious police took him to the Commandancia. He claimed that the horses were to take his sick daughter and her family to his country home. Villa and his two companions had to leave openly, in broad daylight.

An observer raced off to tell the Commandancia that he had just seen Villa's beautiful horse. A hundred and fifty dragoons surrounded Villa and one of his aides at the stone house. The two burst out the only door, guns blazing. Villa was slightly wounded over one eye; he hid among the rocks. A heavy snow fell all day. That night he went back to Parral where a friend provided him with a horse but no saddle.

He rode out for about thirty miles. Another friend gave him a magnificent horse and fifty pesos. But when he got back to the mountain where he had left his force, not a soul was to be seen. They believed he had been killed in the stone-house fight.

Nevertheless, in a few days he had gathered seven hundred and fifty well-armed men. "In war," he commented, "nothing is impossible. Some actions bring together a huge force, others defeat them. The one thing: never abandon the fulfillment of a military duty."

A message came through from Francisco Madero to bring all his forces to Bustillos. It was their first meeting. Villa spoke of the honesty in Madero's "loving eyes," of his strong faith, his charm and talent. "I see him little in body, but . . . very big in spirit."

Madero exclaimed. *"Hombre!* Pancho Villa! But what a boy you
are! I thought you already grown up. I wanted to know you, to em-
brace you for all I have heard about you . . . How many men have
you got?"

They rode out in a buggy to review them. The leader spoke from the
plaza kiosk in front of the municipal palace. That speech drove away
all of Villa's lingering doubts about the little *caudillo*. "Listening to
him I understood why that man could govern and guide us, why all
revolutionary men were obliged to triumph or die with him."

Orozco showed up. Should they attack Chihuahua, the capital.
"What do you say, Don Pancho?"

"Don't do it," was his quick answer. "Even if we could take it, we
don't have enough men or arms to hold it. We should continue our
guerrilla system, mostly near the frontier where arms and ammunition
can be readily obtained."

Villa worked north, reaching the Rio Grande on April 29, 1911. The
revolutionary forces then converged on Ciudad Juárez, across from
El Paso.

There, some time later, Martín Luis Guzmán crossed from the
United States to join Villa. "Ciudad Juárez is a sad sight . . . compared with the bright orderliness of the opposite river bank . . . Yet
. . . our hearts danced as we felt the roots of our being sink into something we had known, possessed, and loved for centuries, in all its
loutishness . . . all the filth of body and soul that pervades its streets
. . . We were Mexicans."

Guzmán described his first meeting with Villa.

> He had on his hat, his pistol and cartridge belts. The rays
> of the lamp shone straight into his face and brought out the
> gleam of copper around the brightness of the whites of his
> eyes and the enamel of his teeth. His curly hair lay in a
> tangled mass between his hat and his broad curved fore-
> head. As he talked, the short ends of his reddish moustache
> made moving shadows across his mouth. His attitude, his
> gestures, the movement of his eyes, gave him a resemblance
> to a wild animal in its lair; but an animal that defends
> itself rather than one that attacks. He was a big powerful
> man—"an oak, a lion, a rock."

Each soldier—

> seemed to have across the breast ten or twenty cartridge
> belts with hundreds and hundreds of shells. The brims of
> their enormous hats seemed to weigh them down, making
> them still more squat. Every question and every answer
> made it plain that there were two different, two irrecon-
> cilable worlds whose only point of contact was the chance
> fact that they had joined forces in the same struggle. We,

> poor visionaries . . . had come armed only with the feeble
> experience of books and our early ideals, and into what had
> we walked? . . . into the tragedy of good and evil, which
> knows no compromise . . . no middle ground . . . Pancho
> Villa . . . had more of a jaguar about him than a man . . .
> a jaguar whose back we stroked with trembling hands,
> fearful that at any moment a paw might strike out at us.

Outside of Ciudad Juárez was also camped the famous Giuseppe Garibaldi with one hundred fifty Italian and American soldiers of fortune. One of Villa's men was disarmed on passing through his camp. Villa sent a note asking Garibaldi to restore the man's equipment. Garibaldi wrote back, "If you think yourself man enough, come get it." At once, Villa led thirty picked men to Garibaldi's camp. He met Garibaldi, took away his revolver, then disarmed his entire force.

"Señor Garibaldi, let this be a lesson to you that we Mexicans do not allow any foreigner to abuse us . . . You should be grateful that I don't shoot you."

Madero, who adored Garibaldi, came to see Villa. "I want you and Garibaldi to be friends." Villa and the Italian gave each other the customary *abrazo*, and Villa returned the arms.

Fearing international complications from firing across the United States border, Madero did not want to attack Ciudad Juárez where the federals were now bottled up. Orozco and Villa felt the attack could not be delayed. Time, food and morale were running out, and Díaz was rushing reinforcements north. Villa and Orozco agreed to send a small patrol to fire on the Federal outposts. This would bring in more men, and the engagement would become general.

It worked. Madero had to commit all his forces to the attack. This was at 3 P.M. May 10, 1911.

Villa's men were caught in cross fire from a corral, a school, and an alley. But Villa drove on through, taking the railway station where he threw up breastworks of railroad ties. By nightfall, he had driven the Federals back toward the main headquarters. From there they trained artillery down the streets, so Villa took to the houses, breaking through walls, block after block. It was slow work and took all night. They finally reached the marketplace.

Navarro hit them hard with machine guns and his artillery blasted walls down. But Villa's men attacked on all sides from the honeycombed houses. Navarro surrendered at 3 P.M., May 11th.

Villa's first effort was to get food. By 4 P.M. bakers were delivering hot bread—to the prisoners first, then to his own men.

Orozco wished to shoot Navarro. Madero, as provisional president, refused to permit it. Orozco in turn told Villa he was displeased with Madero's cabinet appointments, particularly Venustiano Carranza, Díaz' ex-Governor of Coahuila. "Show up at Headquarter Barracks with fifty armed men. If Madero refuses my requests, disarm the Presidential Guard."

Orozco went to see Madero. In a few minutes he shouted out, "Disarm the guard." Villa did so.

Madero rushed out, "You, Pancho, are in this, too!"

General Aguilar of Madero's staff claimed that Orozco and Madero quarreled violently, that Orozco pointed his revolver at Madero and his cabinet ministers. But Madero reasoned calmly with him, and they finally emerged arm in arm, seemingly good friends. Of course, Orozco had wanted to seize power and had hoped to cause a melée in which Madero would have been killed—for which Villa would have been blamed. Realizing he had been tricked, Villa rearmed the guard and left for his quarters. Raúl Madero took him to talk with his brother. Villa resigned and offered to turn over his troops.

"Very well. Shall we put Raúl in Command?"

"Whatever you order, Señor Presidente. But for them to respect and obey Raúl, you must tell them it is only a temporary arrangement, that you have sent me off on an important commission."

"Why not? I'll give you 25,000 pesos so you can set yourself up in private business." Madero finally persuaded him to accept 10,000 pesos.

Villa took only five men and went south by rail to San Andrés. The people there were starving, so he bought 500 hectoliters of corn from the Blue-Eyes Hacienda and distributed it.

The Díaz regime was collapsing. Agrarian rebel Emiliano Zapata was sweeping through the south. Rebels sprang up everywhere like mushrooms. City after city fell. At 10:30 on the night of May 21, 1911, in front of the Juárez customs house by the light of auto headlights and candles, Díaz was to turn the presidency over to his Foreign Minister, Francisco de la Barra, until elections could be held, and his governors were to resign.

When the news reached Mexico City, a great crowd surrounded the Chamber of Deputies and streamed through the city shouting "Viva Madero!" Presidential Guards held off the rock-throwing mob at Díaz's residence on Cadena Street.

The old warrior lay inside, suffering from an abscessed tooth, but he refused to resign. "I came in with bullets. I will go out with bullets." His wife Carmen, the Archbishop, and his Finance Minister José Yves Limantour, came to his bedside to plead with him. At two-thirty in the afternoon, he reached for his pen. Shortly after midnight, General Victoriano Huerta escorted him to the Vera Cruz train, and embarked on the *Ypirango,* bound for Europe. De la Barra was sworn in the following morning. All over the country governors either resigned or were driven out by guerrillas. Thirty years of tyranny and "progress" came to an end.

On June 7, Madero made his triumphal entry into the city on the heels of a terrible earthquake. Elections were held October 1, and Madero was sworn in as President on November 6.

Villa was living quietly in Chihuahua at his house at 500 Tenth Street and running a butcher shop. Toward the end of the year, Madero called him to Mexico City for consultation. The President feared that Orozco planned an armed coup.

"All I know," Villa told him, "is that he spends a great deal of time with Juan Creel [an ex-Díaz governor] and Alberto Terrazas." These were the two biggest landholders in the state and bitter enemies of the revolution.

"Keep an eye out," said Madero and sent Villa back to Chihuahua.

At Madero's request, Villa made a second visit to Mexico City in February and dined at Chapullepec Castle with Madero and his family. By then the situation was darker.

As Madero was essentially a decent man, a strange dreamer who believed in vegetarianism and spiritualism, he consulted soothsayers, Ouija boards, and crystal-ball gazers. As often happens during revolution epochs, he was caught and crushed between contending forces he never understood. The military were plotting; the old regime was plotting; foreign interests were plotting; the United States Embassy was doing everything possible to undermine him. Guerrillas were still fighting everywhere. Treachery stepped on the heels of more treachery.

If and when Orozco revolted, Madero told Villa, he was to take up arms at once and promised him whatever aid might be needed.

In Chihuahua City, under officer Antonio Rojas seized and held the Chihuahua penitentiary. Another Madero officer showed up at Villa's house with sixty men and asked him to lead them to retake the place. Villa went at once to the palace. There stood Orozco beside the new revolutionary governor—Villa's friend, Abraham González.

Villa looked Orozco in the eye. "If you are planning to betray the government, be frank with me. But you'd better have your pants well buttoned up."

Orozco turned pale. "My pants are well-buttoned. Will you help us put down the Rojas revolt?"

"Certainly, Señor. Let me have one hundred well-armed men and well-mounted men."

"But Rojas has two hundred."

"No matter. That's all I need." He asked Abraham for written authorization for him to recruit and arm whatever men he needed and to requisition necessary supplies.

Villa armed his eleven butcher-shop employees (all *Dorado* veterans) and took them to the railroad station where the one hundred promised regulars were expected. Orozco sent word to take Rojas out of town on a trip—"and don't waste a single cartridge."

Villa realized that Orozco had faked Rojas' seizure of the penitentiary to start trouble. He galloped out of town fast with his eleven men. To Orozco, he dashed off a note: "I am going out to the wilds to prove to you that I am an honorable man."

Right away he had 150 well-armed men. In a few days he had a force of 500. His name was magic. He led them back to a town near Chihuahua.

Orozco's father came out by auto to see him. "I have matters to discuss with you."

"Let us have lunch first."

The older Orozco said, "I have come to ask you not to support Madero. I am authorized to give you 300,000 pesos if you'll go to the United States and keep out of the affairs."

Villa refused bluntly. It was snowing, and he gave the old man the serape off his shoulders. "The cold doesn't matter to me," he thought, as Orozco's auto rolled off. "Worse is to have the sad fate of being the father of a traitor."

He took Santa Rosalia. The weather turned warm, and he watched a big dust cloud approaching. A dust cloud was a perfect signal. The approaching force was approximately 500 men. He retreated from the town, luring the enemy after him, then attacked. Even Porfirio Díaz, who had previously fought against the French, would have applauded his tactics. Villa captured much ammunition. But Orozco had moved fast. By March 25, the Madero forces were badly routed. Madero's General González Salas blew out his brains on the military train. The Indian General Victoriano Huerta, now over sixty, was put in charge.

Thus Madero put himself into the hands of the Díaz army. Men who were bound to betray him, and were doing so even then. "A praetorian guard smell was creeping into his regime," said Mrs. O'Shaugnessy, wife of a United States Embassy official.

Huerta was a gross, fat Indian. He was an advanced alcoholic but also an implacable old Díaz soldier—"a bull-dog in a yard of military mongrels," ruthless and bloodthirsty. "Kill your enemies," he said, "and let God hold the inquest." He took over a defeated army with little morale, immobilized by typhus and black smallpox, and hammered it into a fighting instrument.

Villa, ordered to place himself under Huerta's command, led the advance guard and went out to take towns on the flanks. Villa had much more experience in cross-country fighting and made Huerta choleric when he modified orders and plans. Summoned by Huerta, he sent word he was ill in bed and postponed the meeting until the morning. Again, Huerta was furious.

Villa's aide and close friend Tomás Urbina was arrested. Villa sent Huerta an ultimatum that unless Urbina was released within twenty-four hours, he would free him by force.

Urbina was released, but soon Villa was called to headquarters, where he was disarmed and ordered shot. The President's brother Raúl and other officers intervened, but Villa was actually facing the firing squad when shouts were heard outside the corral. Thanks to Raúl, a telegram from Madero arrived, sparing Villa's life.

"I never have feared death," mused Villa. "But for the first time I knew the secret of losing and dying. Afterwards I felt more confident than ever that my life would not be extinguished without due reward." Biting his nails angrily, Huerta sent Villa under guard to Mexico City. He was thrust into the penitentiary and held for months, mostly in solitary. Fellow prisoner Emilio Montaño, taught him to read and write. He managed to get books; Dumas' *The Three Musketeers* delighted him.

The chief charges brought against him were that he had been insubordinate and had misappropriated 150,000 pesos illegally levied on the merchants of Parral (which he had captured before Huerta was sent north). In response Villa produced his authorization from the governor to make requisitions and proved he had used the money to pay his soldiers and to buy food and clothing. He indignantly turned down a well-known visitor's proposal that he secure his release by joining in a plot to overthrow the government.

His personal messages to Madero brought no replies, and he decided to escape. He bribed a young court employee, Calixto Jaureguí, with a hundred peso bill, promising some day to give him the lottery houses in Ciudad Juárez.* The lad visioned himself as no longer a shabby clerk but as a free fighter in the hills. "The words of the guerrilla whirled about my mind, grotesquely mixed with the figures of the eagle with its wide outspread wings that I had seen on the hundred peso bill when I looked at it in the street light."

Jaureguí sawed through the bars of the prisoner's window facing the court, and Villa walked boldly out the front entrance of the prison, garbed as a court lawyer. He held his handkerchief to his face and pretended to be coughing. A few blocks away, he and Jaureguí entered an auto his brother Hipólito Villa had in readiness and were driven to Toluca. Still disguised, Villa reached the Pacific Coast and after some close squeaks, made his way north to the United States.

By the end of 1912, the Madero government estimated that more than two hundred guerrilla bands were operating. Madero was no more able to satisfy their revolutionary demands than he was powerful enough to suppress the violent threats and intrigues of the old guard, who were backed by the United States Embassy, then headed by Henry Lane Wilson. Madero was caught in the middle.

* Later he did, though the best gambling places he gave to his brother Hipólito Villa.

Late in 1912, General Félix Díaz, nephew of the fallen dictator, raised a revolt in Vera Cruz. He was captured and court-martialed, but Madero brought him to Mexico City and freed him.

Félix Díaz promptly gained control of troops and attacked the national palace. Driven off, he seized the Ciudadela—the national arms factory on Balderas Street. An unnecessary artillery duel with Madero's General Huerta resulted in the terror of "The Tragic Ten Days." Fantastic bonfires burned the dead in the streets.

Henry Lane Wilson persuaded President Taft to send troops to the frontier (which further augmented disorder) and arranged with Huerta that he take over the government. Wilson handpicked the future cabinet.

The betrayal was staged on February 18, 1913. Gustavo Madero was seized in a public cafe and murdered. President Madero and Vice-president Pino Suárez were taken after a deadly fracas in the Palace and were assassinated in a dark street behind the palace four days later. Mexico was horrified and roused to revolt against the usurper.

The hour to strike had come again. Villa bought horses and re-entered Mexico to begin the long fight against the new dictator. He swam across the Rio Grande at midnight on March 26, 1913 with 9 men, 8 Winchesters, 9 pistols, 36 pesos, a silver watch, and nothing to eat.

Everywhere people rallied to his support; once more he became a guerrilla in the hills. "He slept in one place and woke in another, he fired on the rearguard of passing columns and fled like lightning; at night he harrassed battalions in the camps and was gone before they could fire, and every day his force and his supplies increased."

Huerta's General Antonio Rabajo wired the Secretary of War in answer to a query as to Villa's whereabouts, "I have the honor to inform you that according to all information which is true and verified, Villa at this moment is in all parts and none in particular."

Resistance had already been initiated by Venustiano Carranza, Governor of Coahuila, who issued the Plan de Guadalupe as "The First Chief of the Constitutionalist Revolt." In Sonora, Alvaro Obregón, Elías Calles, Adolfo Huerta, and Benjamín G. Hill revolted. "Tamborino" Francisco R. Serrano, who banged a tamborine in the circus, joined up. He was to become a general until one day Obregón ridiculed him as a "hungry coyote" and had him shot. General Manuel M. Diéguez took up arms in Nayarit and Jalisco; Pablo González in Tamaulipas, Jacinto B. Treviño in Coahuila, and "Socialist" Salvador Alvarado in Yucatán. Mexico was on fire everywhere. In the South, agrarian leader Emiliano Zapata who had never laid down his arms was fighting against Huerta's brutal General Robles.

Villa rallied behind the new constitutionalist leader. On May 23

Carranza named him general, with command over all forces in Chihuahua and Durango. Villages, towns, then cities fell before Villa's onrush; the best generals of the army were beaten. On June 19, he stormed Casa Grande, freed Madero prisoners, and shot 95 *Orozquistas* —since Orozco had joined Huerta.

Carranza was thrown back from Torreón. Villa marched down and took it, then wheeled back to Chihuahua City held by ten thousand men. Bloodily defeated, he galloped on to Ciudad Juárez. With a handful of men he got in concealed in a coal car, took over, and set up a government. That was when Martín Luis Guzmán and Vasconcedos joined him. Villa swirled back to Chihuahua and five thousand Federals died; the rest fled.

John Lind, President Woodrow Wilson's personal emissary, threatened armed intervention. Huerta flouted him and on October 9, closed the Chamber of Deputies and marched eighty-four of its members off to the penitentiary. In the north, Villa was confiscating haciendas right and left, while United States Consuls protested on behalf of Englishmen and Spaniards. Villa's officer, Robert Fierro (some writers say Villa) murdered the Englishman, W. H. Benton when the latter angrily protested the loss of his Santa Gertrudes estate. It caused an international incident.

Ambassador Henry Lane Wilson moved heaven and earth to get Huerta recognized. He believed that Mexico needed a strongman and misjudged the strength and popular fury behind the revolutionary program. Mexico could no longer be ruled by die-hards. American business was now considered a principal enemy, and the land was engulfed in a tidal wave of antiforeignism.

On February 14, 1914, President Wilson brusquely recalled Ambassador Wilson and lifted the embargo on arms to the revolutionary forces. On April 21, United States Marines swarmed ashore in Vera Cruz on a flimsy pretext. Huerta's troops pulled back without a fight, but the townspeople, students, women, and children fought savagely from window to window, door to door. More Mexicans died than Americans were killed in Villa's later raid on Columbus.

Universal hatred for the gringos almost insured Huerta's perpetuation in power—the very thing Woodrow Wilson wanted to prevent. Mexico flamed with patriotic fury against the Yankees. Though they were receiving American help, both Carranza and Pancho Villa denounced the occupation. Even the guerrilla of south Mexico, Emiliano Zapata, offered to aid the detested Huerta against the United States and moved a big force to within a few miles of occupied Vera Cruz.

The revolting Constitutionalists kept closing in on Huerta. Between April and June, Villa occupied a dozen principal plazas. His *Dorados* struck terror wherever they rode. His forces swelled to ten thousand, twenty thousand, fifty thousand. He had become a leader of an army. On June 18, he avalanched into Zacatecas (against Carranza's explicit orders). A popular *corrido* told of Villa's success:

> Hah! You drunkard Victoriano
> Your evil heart will skip a beat
> When you hear of Zacatecas
> Where your troops have met defeat.
>
> On the twenty-third of June,
> I address those who are here,
> Pancho Villa stormed the city,
> Taking it by front and rear.
>
> All the streets of Zacatecas
> Were piled high with Federal dead,
> And those who were not slaughtered,
> Early in the day had fled.
>
> Some Federals were so scared,
> They hid in women's skirts,
> Pulling them over their trousers,
> And mantillas over their shirts.

On July 15, 1914 Huerta turned his government over to provisional president Francisco S. Carvajal and fled the country on the *Dresden*. He escaped from painter Dr. Atl, who wanted to exhibit him in a cage in Europe as a chimpanzee and make himself a millionaire. Villa and Carranza signed an agreement that they would keep on fighting until the regular army was wholly destroyed.

But all too soon, an ugly squabble occurred between them in Saltillo. Villa flatly refused to turn over his command to the bearded *hijo de la chingada* * and kept on fighting as he chose.

General Obregón, the most able general the prolonged revolution produced, took Guadalajara just ahead of Villa's forces, and entered Mexico City on August 15, again just ahead of Villa, from whom Carranza had withheld coal for his trainloads of troops.

Obregón led the army of the northwest into Mexico City, with his tall ferocious Yaquis beating primitive drums. Speaking from the Palace balcony, he upbraided the press for its defamation of the Constitutionalists and handed his pistol over to María Arias, a teacher, who had defied the Huertistas—"the only valiant fighter in the Mexican revolution."

He quartered his troops in the cathedral, where they cut down the magnificent Zócalo plaza trees for firewood. Prominent citizens were put to work cleaning the streets. During this and later occupations he made a heavy levy on city merchants and the Church.

* Son of a whore.

Rebel soldiers smashed into the abandoned palaces of all the wealthy families so favored by Díaz, palaces costing from several hundred thousand to half a million dollars—the Escandóns, Lascurains, Limantours, and Casasuses—and destroyed or carried off furnishings and art objects.

Carranza quickly took charge. He was stolid, implacable, and enigmatic behind his dark glasses and enormous gray beard. (I served on his staff a few years later.) No leader of his type had emerged since the days of iron-faced Benito Juárez. Able General Felipe Angeles, in charge of Villa's artillery, said Carranza was a reactionary stuffed shirt. He often acted like one, but the stuffing was of stern stuff.

Carranza sent Obregón north to put down disobedient army remnants. Villa tried to arrest and execute him. But they met in Nogales in the state of Sonora, on August 29 and signed a neutrality pact to settle their differences. "If you hadn't gotten here when you did," said Villa, "the *Dorados* of the North would be swarming over all Sonora." An amplified agreement, signed in Chihuahua September 3, recognized Carranza as provisional president.

But within three weeks, Villa openly broke with Carranza.

Villa remained in control of nearly all the North. He was giving out land to the peasants and money to work it and buy seed, opening schools and hospitals. When money gave out, he printed more! Railroad rates were reduced and free passes given to poor seeking work. He raised wages, stopped the smuggling of liquor and drugs into the United States, instituted price controls on food, and staged Sunday night band concerts in all towns.

On September 5, Carranza called for a meeting of revolutionary leaders and generals to name a provisional president (himself of course). A counter-Villista convention opened in Aguas Calientes on October 10, a place the caudillo controlled.

Villa had a dare-devil quality the Constitutionalist leader lacked. But it was impossible, said one of Villa's ablest intellectual associates, to think of him as "the standard-bearer of a devoted, reconstruction movement. He was too unpredictable, uncontrolled and blind." He sought power at any price and tolerated no opposition to his will, his orders, or his caprices. But except for a Carranzista contingent, all the Aguas Calientes delegates rallied behind Villa's banner. Villa's French-trained military adviser, General Felipe Angeles, was made chairman. The anti-Carranza delegates were soon reinforced by a Zapatista delegation of fifty armed men who had refused to attend Carranza's Mexico City convention.

It was one of the strangest gatherings in history. Each of the two hundred delegates had pistols close to his hands and a cartridge belt full of shells. There was an occasional enthusiastic pistol shot at the ceiling. Delegates applauded by banging their rifle butts on the floor. Women sat on the laps of some. Between speeches they sang *Cucaracha*, the Villa marching song.

> *La Cucaracha, La cucaracha,*
> *Ya no puede caminar*
> *Porque no tiene, porque le falta*
> *Marihuana que fumar.*

> The little cockroach, the little cockroach
> Cannot travel any more
> Because she has no, because she's lacking
> Marijuana for a smoke.

While the delegates were listening to the oratory of Zapatista lawyer Antonio Díaz Soto y Gama (who had drawn up much of the southern guerrilla's radical land program), Martín Luis Guzmán went to see Villa. The general was standing near his telegraph operator. The expression in his feral eyes filled Guzmán with giddy fear. Some men, Guzmán commented later, are separated by "limitless space," without any common denominator.

"There are more hats around here than we need," growled the caudillo. One of his closest friends and officers, General Monclovia Herrera, had defected to Carranza in Chihuahua. "How does the treacherous ungrateful cur dare turn on me like that!"

Guzmán was puzzled. "Too many hats?" he asked.

Villa strode up to him and shouted, "My boys are killing each other. Now do you understand?" He paced furiously. Every three steps, he said between clenched teeth, "The damn son-of-a-bitch!"

Word came that one hundred seventy of Herrera's men had surrendered. Villa whirled to the operator and sent orders that every last one be shot. He pushed back his sun helmet and shoved his hand through the reddish hair, then scratched his head as if his brain were itching.

"What do you think of all this, my friend?" he demanded softly.

Shaking in his boots, Guzmán told him it was wrong to shoot prisoners who had surrendered. "There are going to be a *lot* of extra hats around, General."

Villa remained calm, though his eyeballs rolled from side to side. "Why is it wrong?"

"The person who surrenders," Guzmán said, "spares the life of others. The one who accepts the surrender has no right to order the death sentence."

Villa's eyeballs stopped rolling. He yelled at the operator to send word to stay the executions. Nearly an hour went by. Villa fidgeted. "Will my counter order get through in time?" he kept asking anxiously.

When word finally came that it had, Villa mopped the sweat off his forehead with an air of great relief.

Not a word more was said about the incident. But after dinner that night as Guzmán left, Villa said out of a blue sky, "Thanks, *amigo*, for that thing this morning—that business of the prisoners." Over the years, however, Villa had Herrera, his family, and all near relatives murdered.

The convention declared both Carranza and Villa ineligible for the Presidency and named Eulalio Gutiérrez, the Zapatista choice to that office. A fisherman, stevedore, small shopkeeper, and petty lawyer from Tamaulipas, Gutiérrez was occasionally courageous—a rather honest, florid little man.

For his part, Carranza outlawed the convention and the two guerrillas, Villa and Zapata. They moved their armies on Mexico City. The Villistas now had new words for *Cucaracha*.

> *Con las barbas de Carranza*
> *Voy a hacer una toquilla*
> *Para verlo en el sombrero*
> *Del General Pancho Villa.*

> With the whiskers of Carranza
> I'm going to make a nice cockade
> So as to see it on the sombrero
> Of the General Pancho Villa.

The confusion in Washington was greater than in Mexico. Villa held a friendly get-together with General Hugh Scott in El Paso. Rifles, ammunition, machine guns, and light artillery flowed across the border to Villa's army—to bring peace and order to Mexico!

Carranza began evacuating Mexico City on November 18 and fled east to Puebla. For him, the future was now as black as a wolf's gullet. He was hemmed in by the two armies, and the United States Marines still occupied Vera Cruz. But they evacuated the port on November 23, and Carranza set up his government there.

On the 24th, Obregon led his troops out of the capital—west via Toluca. General Pablo González, who had just tried to assassinate Villa but who had also thrown off allegiance to Carranza, held the nearby silver town of Pachuca with 10,000 troops. Zapata's southern agrarians entered the capital November 27. Villa entered soon after.

At this time, it is wise to examine Villa's southern counterpart, since their lives were to flow largely together from this point on.

4

THE ROBIN HOODS OF MEXICO: ZAPATA

Emiliano Zapata was born in 1879, in San Miguel Anencuilco—part of Villa Ayala in the mountains beyond Cuernavaca. His parents were small farmers. Emiliano had seen his father weep when the local hacendado, backed by the soldiery, stripped away his little farm and reduced them to sharecropping.

As a young man Emiliano became a *mediero* (a fifty-fifty sharecropper) growing melons on the Textepango hacienda. He dressed as a *charro* (or rancher) in an embroidered jacket, skin-tight, buckle-under trousers, and an enormous sombrero. He was an expert horseman; accordingly, the hacendado sent him to Mexico City on an errand. There Emiliano looked over the owner's horses and was astonished at the fine stables and the marble pool for bathing the animals. In contrast, the people of Morelos lived in dirt-floor huts, their nakedness barely covered with rags.

In 1908 the local soldiery stole the village communal lands of Ayala, turning them over to Ignacio Torre Mier, a Díaz favorite. Emiliano assembled the peasants. He was then a lean, hungry-looking youth of twenty-nine. "We must send a commission to El Presidente."

Clad in their cleanest white "pajamas," wearing sandals, and holding big sombreros, the peasant delegation haunted Mexico City's marble corridors for weeks until their supply of tortillas was exhausted. Then, never having been heard, they trudged home again over the mountains.

This time, Zapata led them into the fields. "It is our land. We will take it back."

The army rode in fast. Zapata hid in the mountains, but was arrested and sent to the army. He became a sergeant in the Ninth Cavalry Regiment, and in some mysterious manner, got hold of a few thousand pesos and bought his release from service.

He escaped to Chietla in Puebla, where he sharecropped for a year. Returning to Morelos, he began campaigning for Patricio Leyva for governor against Pablo Escandón. Escandón was a Díaz Científico —as the elite were called—who owned most of the land of Morelos, thanks to Díaz. With the aid of the army rather than any actual election, he was deftly seated in the governor's palace in Morelia. Emiliano called the people together again. "The only way we can vote is with guns in hand."

Zapata had learned about Madero's program of "Effective Suffrage and No Re-election" from his friend and mentor, Professor Otilio Montaño. His little Junta sent Palbo Torres Burgos north to consult with Madero. He returned, saying he had been named chief of the revolt in the south, with Zapata second in command. But Burgos was soon betrayed with the rest of the group by their erstwhile friend Patricio Leyva and was shot on March 23, 1911.

Zapata miraculously escaped and rode toward Los Hornos ("The Kilns") with a handful of armed men. Six more joined him in San Rafael Zaragoza; thirty more in Huachumanta ("Abundant Cane"). But only eight were mounted and well-armed. More recruits kept joining, and in Los Bueyes ("Oxen") he divided his followers into small bands and rode through more villages. His forces kept growing. In Axochiapan ("River of Flowers") the priest gave him a fine horse and saddle, and he set out for Teotlalco ("Holy Ground"), a place large enough to seize funds.

Zapata later said proudly, "We did not ask the foreigner for a single cartridge, nor a single gun, nor one peso. We have taken everything from the enemy." He quickly raised three thousand men. They went into the fray swinging only machetes, but they soon captured carbines, ammunition, even artillery. In short time, they had ample war equipment taken from the Porfirio Díaz government forces.

At Tlayacapán ("Multitude") the strong garrison of two hundred Rurales fled, and Zapata pursued them relentlessly for six hours. That was April 4, 1911. With several thousand Indians behind him, Zapata took Jantelelco ("Edge of the Stone") a village of pomegranates and the birthplace of the brave independence priest, Mariano Matamoros. Zapata set up headquarters under Matamoros' monument in the plaza. He was surrounded by men with Winchesters at the ready; all the streets were full of revolutionaries armed to the teeth. Those who wished to see him were searched and brought in blindfolded.

With him were his brother, one-eyed Eufemio; several commanders and colonels; and Professor Montaño. "We need you intellectuals," Zapata told him. "Once the battle starts, no god can stop it."

On May 3 ninety soldiers and twenty-five Rurales gave his force a bad beating at Jonacatépec ("Onion Hill"), a town of 10,000 inhabitants. Zapata gathered his dispersed men together. He told them how to fight. "Hide in the barrancas and creep up close, on foot, silently on all side. Thirty of us"—his most faithful followers—"will make the direct attack. When we fall back toward the big rocks, strike from behind. Go in shooting, go in with knives. Spare no one. We have to kill all those flea-bitten *canallas*."

Zapata moved quickly on Matamoros Izucar and took it after a few rounds. By then guerrillas were fighting all through the states of Morelos, Oaxaca, and Guerrero. Already Zapata had an excellent espionage service, wrote Taracena, with "blind persons, beggars and messengers."

With forty-eight hundred well-armed men, Emiliano moved on toward the important hot-springs spa of Cuautla ("Place of Trees") the main city of the area.

> This is how I remember the city. You José Morelos, will climb over the rocks with men and work down over the big pool where the sulphur springs gush forth. Frighten the swimmers out naked and they will run with cut feet toward the barracks. Make a lot of noise, yell your goddamned heads off. We will occupy the city. Most of the soldiers will run to the barracks. Once they are trapped, they'll try to get away.

But the garrison held out for nearly a week, expecting help from from Mexico City. The Díaz army heads were more concerned about the Madero revolt in the north and were not yet overly alarmed by that in the south. The garrison got no aid. When their ammunition dwindled, they were wiped out almost to a man.

The Zapatistas entered the city May 14, "committing crimes," said Taracena. Zapata did exact heavy contributions from all the merchants, but he put a stop to looting. He insisted that property and lives be respected, and he released two high-level Científicos taken prisoner.

In the north, Villa and Orozco were storming into Ciudad Juárez. Torreón, one of the large cities was hurriedly evacuated by the Díaz' Federals, and the rebels killed Chinese and looted the Chinese bank. Pachuca, the silver city near Mexico City, was captured.

On May 21, 1911 Cuernavaca rose in arms and, when the citizens of the town took it over, Zapata hastened there to make it his headquarters.

Madero entered Mexico City, but despite the revolutionary victory, seemed to prefer the reactionary Científicos to his own followers. He even assisted De la Barra to disarm the revolutionary forces and restore the regular Díaz army to control. Clashes occurred everywhere.

Zapata refused to lay down his arms but went instead to Mexico City to talk peace. He put up at the little Hotel Coliseo. He agreed to disband his men and retire to private life provided his people were given arms and no troops were sent against him.

But when armed revolutionaries attacked the penitentiary to liberate Zapatista leader Abraham Martínez, a frightful slaughter occurred in the bullring. Zapata threatened to march on Puebla. Madero wired him that the matter would be straightened out at once.

Instead, Victoriano Huerta was sent to Morelos to get rid of

Zapata. The southern guerrilla was well intrenched, but Huerta moved on relentlessly, seized Yautépec ("Hill of Black Corn"), a place of thirty thousand, and kept on advancing, burning villages, killing, and looting. Zapata protested against the cruelties and the violation of the Madero agreement. He advanced on Cuernavaca with three thousand men.

Hoping still to settle matters peacefully, Madero met Zapata, in Cuautla on August 18, 1912. They walked toward each other with a few aides and embraced in the wide central street. They talked things over at the city palace. Zapata complained bitterly of the violation of their earlier agreement and of Huerta's brutality. Madero was full of praise for Zapata's support, but secretly, he was a bit contemptuous of this tall young Indian with grayish eyes.

Already there were stories that the southern bands were looting, holding drinking orgies, raping, and engaging in senseless violence. Certainly the Zapatistas had perpetrated their share. But every such crime in the south was attributed to Zapata personally. Certainly he was no mild mannered gentleman.

Madero had managed to sidetrack that wildman Villa. It would be even easier, he believed, to persuade this man of the south, who had never moved in urban or civilized circles, to give up fighting. In spite of Zapata's power and incredible exploits, he had the air of the *humildes*, of the long abused southern peons, singularly polite men used to submission and obedience. Madero completely misread the guerrilla's gentle manners. For all his apparent deference, Zapata was a fierce soul who would never submit to any man. His ideals were never to be broken in war or parley.

True, Zapata was impressed by this eager, näive leader of the rich family of the north, so trim, so well educated, so polite, every inch a gentleman. But this was the sort he had learned long ago to distrust. Bit by bit his respect faded.

"Now that the victory is ours, we must have peace," Madero began, touching his small black beard.

"Everybody wants peace."

Sure that the humble Zapata would be overwhelmed with largess, he offered him several magnificent haciendas or, if he preferred 100,-000 pesos to go abroad.

Zapata had already taken or burned a hundred such haciendas and seized many times that amount from banks and rich owners. "I cannot abandon my men."

"We can take care of them also."

Zapata shook his head. "No, Señor Madero, we are fighting for lands for everybody."

"But that must be done gradually. First, the main thing is to have a free government."

"The main thing is for every man to have a piece of land, schools, and a gun—always a gun. Our boys don't understand the fine elegant *políticos* of Mexico City. We do not trust them."

"You intend to keep on fighting?"

"That depends upon that fine-feather, De la Barra, and his Científico gang. He has sent soldiers against my people." Zapata finally agreed not to fight if Federal forces advanced no further and committed no more abuses.

But Zapata was no simpleton. Two days after his talk with Madero, a great crowd of twenty thousand persons in Mexico City shouted "Viva Zapata! Death to Huerta!" He had his urban guerrillas ready to move.

The reactionary head of the cabinet, Carlos García Granados, could not read the signs. He refused to recognize the new Madero-Huerta pact. "The authorities will not treat with an outlaw." And so the war went on in Morelos and elsewhere. On August 22, Huerta disarmed the people of Yautépec. He instituted a reign of terror everywhere. Whenever outnumbered, the Zapatistas withdrew to the nearby hills, waited till the Federals moved on, then came down to eat and dance with the people. Huerta's soldiers controlled only the soil their boots briefly trod.

Zapata led his forces to the gates of Mexico City. In Milpe Alta he burned the town palace and other buildings. After defeating the government forces in Otumba, he told his men, "Boys, we shall soon be having dinner with De la Barra in the Federal District. You must show him we are good sharpshooters."

"He [Zapata] is our foremost 'brigand,'" remarked Mrs. Edith O'Shaughnessey, wife of the United States Charge d'Affairs. "His slogan is 'Mexico for the Indians.' He wants to wipe out everything between us and Montezuma." It sounded clever on paper.

Madero was elected President on October 25. That same day, García Granados told the Chamber of Deputies that due to secret elements in the government orders against Zapata were not being carried out. The Under-Secretary of War said the real reason was that the number of Zapatista supporters was growing in every village. The pro-Madero deputies demanded that García Granados resign. The next day, another great crowd in the streets demanded he get out. He resigned the following day, and Zapata withdrew his forces to the slopes of high Ajusco, overlooking the city, which for more than a hundred years had been a guerrilla stronghold.*

Madero was inaugurated on November 6. The notorious wealthy reactionary Pedro Lascurain was made Secretary of Foreign Affairs and head of the cabinet. Other Científicos were appointed.

Zapata had already sized up Madero as a well-intentioned but un-

---

* Marshal Bazaine, during the French occupation, had burned it to the ground.

informed man beclouded by his wealthy background. That same day, November 6, the southlander harangued his followers a few miles from the capital in pine-clad Jiguero canyon. He told them to stand firm until they received lands. "Even though society speaks ill about us, history will justify us when the new generations begin to enjoy well-being, which we are planting with bits of our flesh and the tears of our wives; this same society that today curses us for the 'crimes' which we commit to obtain the resources to carry on our fight, will bless us." It was a forerunner of Castro's "History Will Absolve Me" speech.

He retired to the lonely Ayoxutla mountains in Morelos, and there he and Otilio Montaño drew up the Agrarian Plan de Ayala. On November 28, Montaño stood on a table in a thatched *jacal* and read it. Zapata said a few words. "This is our program. 'Land and Liberty' is our slogan." Musicians from Misquetzingo played the National Anthem. Zapata slouched in a chair, his eyes remote and hazy, then stepped forth tall, slim, and stern to review the men. They paraded down the village street, with "black silk flags, embroidered with skull and crossbones. The church bells were rung; fireworks were shot off." Zapata shared a glass of tequila with his aids, then vanished into his headquarters.

Madero—so Montaño read that day to the little gathering—had betrayed the revolution and was not recognized as President. The Supreme Power was to be put into the hands of Pascual Orozco (a strange myopia) or, should he decline, Emiliano Zapata. The manifesto called for the distribution of a third of all large haciendas to the peasants, the *campesinos*. The original *ejidos* of communal village lands, woods and waters usurped under Díaz by the hacendados, were to be taken back by the villages.

"Should we publish this?" asked the editor of Medero's paper, the famous *Diario del Hogar*. "By all means," replied Madero, "so everybody will know what a crazy man Zapata is."

Madero himself was being called "crazy, crazy, crazy," with fist blows on the table, by United States Ambassador Henry Lane Wilson. Even the President's own brother, Gustavo Madero, was getting a laugh at diplomatic gatherings with his *mot*, that the Maderos were "a family of clever men, the only fool among them was chosen for President."

But the Plan de Ayala was not the work of a lunatic. From the day it was issued, land distribution—an issue largely evaded by Madero— became the pivot of the whole revolution. The Plan de Ayala was unanimously endorsed two years later by Villa's 1914 Aguas Calientes convention. To offset Zapata's plan and its popularity, Carranza later issued his famous land law of January 6, 1915 for the restoration of *ejidos*—even to villages "not able to produce old titles." In short, land distribution, not political reform, became the chief goal. It was embodied in the 1917 Querétaro constitution as Article 27.

Madero, in his famous prerevolution book of 1910: *La Succesión Presidencal* set forth the claims for electoral reform, and mentioned land reform only vaguely. But Andrés Molina Enríques, in his earth-shaking *Los Grandes Problemas de México,* called land monopoly the major cause of the unrest which overthrew Porfirio Díaz. In his *La Revolucíon Agraria de México,* he traced the landholding abuses back to the Spanish conquest, when the native Mexicans had been driven off their holdings and forced to cultivate infertile or wild mountain tracts.

After Independence, Spanish-style encroachments on the *ejidos* or communal lands were continued. Land hunger lay at the root of the fight—more than half a century before the 1910 revolution—against the Church, which at that time owned more than half the land of the country. Then under Díaz dictatorship, millions of acres were handed over to favored Científicos and Americans for a few cents a hectare. The Indians and many mestizos were treated worse than animals. For the peons—"caught for life— toiling, sweating, diseased, half starved, swarming in rubbish huts, that would shame a pig— their only solace" lay in drink, fornication, and the promise of a better existence in the next world.

At a dinner given by Henry Lane Wilson, Mrs. O'Shaughnessy said, "We screamed with laughter at Mr. Potter's cutting from one of the big New York dailies, which quite solemnly states that Zapata is a natural product of the Díaz rule and is merely avenging the innocent and oppressed ones . . . What twaddle people read." But Zapata's later biographer, Baltazar Drumondo wrote, "Zapata was the first philosopher of the true revolution and before him, none had faced up to the agrarian problem of the country."

After the Plan de Ayala, Zapatisto gathered new strength in all of southern Mexico. In January, Madero called in General Juan Andrew Alamazán, who had been fighting in Guerrero under the Zapata banner. Madero offered him 100,000 pesos and forces with which to pretend to join Zapata and, according to one version, kill him. Almazán would enjoy a permanent pension to live in Europe.

Almazán refused point-blank and was put in prison. On his release in July, he went directly to the southern revolutionary front. Zapata was suspicious of him, so with a small force he went off on his own to Guerrero again to fight quite successfully against Madero.

On April 25, Zapata entered Cuernavaca with between four and five thousand men. The city, full of refugees who had suffered elsewhere, was anxious to surrender. By then, all Guerrero, south Morelos, and part of Puebla were firmly in guerrilla hands.

On July 20, General Genoveva de la O, one of Zapata's most trusted officers, assaulted the Mexico-Cuernavaca train and reportedly killed all soldiers and passengers.* On August 11, another train was assaulted on the Cuautla-Jojutla run, and two newspaper men, suspected of planning to assassinate Zapata, were shot.

Zapata was accused of many crimes and murders. But as we are discovering from our Black Power guerrillas, the revenge of a people abused for four centuries, is not likely to conform to middle-class standards. One of Zapata's worst detractors states that during his many years of struggle, the guerrilla leader executed only one hundred forty-eight people all told—a small number compared to those killed by Porfirio Díaz during his rule; by Villa; by the Maderos or, later on, by Carranza, Obregón, and Calles—all of whom sat in the seats of power. Of all the caudillos, Zapata was probably the least bloodthirsty. But he was the most pivotal person in the struggle against the feudal classes, so he naturally bore the brunt of more calumnies.

As we saw before, a week after Zapata took the capital in 1914, Villa finally entered. Trainload after trainload of Villista troops were brought in. On December 4, he and Zapata met by previous arrangement and embraced in Xochimilco. Together on Sunday, December 6 they made their joint triumphal military entry into Mexico City. For the joint victory parade, at least fifty thousand fighting men rode or marched along the Paseo to the Zócalo, to the National Palace.

The two chieftains rode side by side. Villa, on his famous horse, *Siete Leguas,* ("Seven Leagues") was clad in hip-length leather boots, a dark uniform with small officer's patches on the shoulders and a single line of metal buttons; and a plain military cap with a shiny black visor and a Mexican eagle plaque.

Zapata, riding his beautiful white horse, wore a light tan gold-embroidered charro jacket, a neck-stock, and dark tight ranchero trousers with embroidered stripes, that buckled under his instep. His Morelos sombrero, with horsebraid bands at the base of the tall peaked crown, was smaller than usual—only about four feet across.

Behind them came the *Dorados,* veterans of half a thousand battles, and the Zapatistas, who had captured all the South. They were sandal-shod, white "pajama" peasants who had galloped across the seven states, fighting, burning, killing, looting, seizing the big estates, and turning them over to the *Indios.*

Down the splendid paseo that Emperor Maximilian had laid out, past the Independence Monument (shattered by a terrible earthquake) and the garden glorietas with statues of Hidalgo, Morelos, Aztec Emperor Cuautemoc, the latest conquerors led their troops.

---

* I once asked Genoveva if the story was true. He grinned broadly, neither affirming or denying. He seemed to take pride in being considered a monster.

Rival bands played northern music then southern music alternately.

The chieftains and their staffs entered the National Palace at 3 P.M., stood in the balconies, and acknowledged cheers. Inside, they eyed the high-backed, red-plush, gilded Presidential chair—actually a replica, since Carranza had carted the original off to Vera Cruz. "We should try it," said Villa, "You go ahead, it's not my style." But he took it.

Five days later Zapata left to attack Puebla, which he entered on December 15. It was retaken by Carranza's General Benjamín Hill on January 2. However, the Villa-Zapata Conventionists took over Monterrey (the chief city in the north), captured Guadalajara, (the chief city in the west), and drove Pablo Gonzáles out of Pachuca. He reached Tampico with only three thousand men.

The two guerrillas and their puppet president Eulalio Gutiérrez ran the government for several months. The soldiers, particularly the Zapatistas, were surprisingly orderly. Little looting occurred. Villa's first public act was to round up the orphan children begging on the streets and sleeping in doorways, and take them to Chihauhua to be educated.

But Carranza's Constitutionalist forces were regaining strength. They were aided by the "Red Labor Battalions" of Vera Cruz, the millions provided by General Salvador Alvarado from the State-owned henekuén monopoly of Yucatán, and the organizing genius of Alvaro Obregón. Before long, thirty thousand well-organized troops were at the gates of Mexico City. On January 13, 1915 President Gutiérrez fled from the capital with a few soldiers and, allegedly, three million pesos, and surrendered to Carranza. General Roque González Garza took over the palace as acting President. On January 28, he, too, fled —to Cuernavaca.

Obregón again took over the city despite a stinging shower of Zapatista bullets. On February 18 he assembled 180 priests in the National Palace and demanded a contribution of 500,000 pesos. They refused and were put in jail, except for two who were obliged to seek the money from the well-to-do. The soldiery cleared a Catholic protest manifestation out of the central plaza. All foreign businesses and many Mexican stores were closed for refusing to pay levies. "When the food riots begin," Obregón said, "I won't stop them." Washington, which had provided his weapons, was shocked and protested sharply.

Obregón left to fight Villa in the north, carrying off 127 priests as prisoners in a cattle car. "We can't all get in there," complained one. General Benjamín J. Hill retorted, "Captain, shove them in. If any are left over, shoot them." They all got in without being shoved.

The Zapatista forces reoccupied the Mexico City plaza on March 13, and Roque Gonzáles was reinstalled in the Palace. But now Mexico City suffered real famine; people were dying. Food prices soared to incredible heights. Counterfeit money appeared. Huge crowds gathered before the Gobernación building for maize, and the Red Cross, acting for an International Welfare Committee, distributed food at the old Palace of Mines.

With eleven thousand men Obregón seized Celaya, a place famous for its candy makers on March 31. Villa's *Dorados* outnumbered his forces five to one. Not waiting for Urbina to bring more artillery from Juárez he attacked at once.*

At Celaya, Villa faced a great strategist and tactician. Obregón was patient and methodical, cool and cat-like, daring and imaginative. His discipline was perfect; things were neat as a brand-new pin. He saw to it that his men were always well armed, well clad, and well fed.

At Celaya he threw up barbed wire in front of trenches manned with machine guns and concealed six hundred dragoons to one side on high ground, ready to move when the first *putsch* had been thrown back. Villa's galloping forces moved forward in three columns. They hurled themselves in vain against the barbed wire and were mowed down in an artillery cross-fire. Villa's guns mistakenly plowed into his own cavalry.

Villa led his *Dorados* in repeated mad charges and overran Obregón's front positions. Some defenders tried to flee; Obregón ordered them shot on the spot. A column of 1,500 fresh Carrancista reinforcements saved him.

Without a cartridge remaining and 1,800 of his men dead, Villa fled, with only twenty *Dorados* left at his side, across a field strewn with bodies and discarded rifles. "I was so humiliated, I wondered why I ever believed I was a general. I would rather have been beaten by a Chinaman than by Obregón."

Villa reassembled his forces in a line from Silao to León. He still had more than 30,000 men, and reinforcements were pouring in. He returned to attack furiously, and lost 1,400 more. On June 2, 1915, during the seesaw engagements that followed, Obregón was hard pressed. He was knocked off his horse by an artillery shell which left his right arm dangling by a piece of skin. An aide prevented him from shooting himself.

General Benjamín Hill took over, concentrated all the forces, hit Villa hard and broke him.

Obregón had lost an arm, but Villa lost two major battles and the war. He lost even more. He lost his magic and his claim to national

---

* Actually Urbina had gone off to bury a million pesos' loot in gold and jewels. It was rank betrayal, and later Villa risked his life to hunt him down. But at the last minute, too moved by memories to shoot him, Villa handed him over to dread Roberto Fierro. Shortly after the execution, Fierro was drowned trying to cross a swollen river with his part of the loot. Rumor has it that his men killed him to steal it.

leadership. His forces were pushed relentlessly north by Obregón, who was on the march long before his wound healed. Aguas Calientes fell on July 10, and 4,000,000 Villla cartridges were lost. San Luís Potosí fell on July 16.

Villa's rearguard under the ferocious Fierro cut behind Obregón, retook Léon, Celaya, Querétaro, and San Juan del Rio. But these were mere guerrilla raids, without firm support. Driven back to Chihuahua, Villa was reduced once more to small guerrilla tactics. For a long time he was hell-on-wheels and continued his whirlwind forays, even into major cities, but his hour had passed. Mexico wanted peace, and he could not provide it.

On July 17, Zapatistas captured nearby Pachuca, the silver city, and were able to take back Mexico City—their third entry—the following day. The church bells rang out, but the people were hungrier than ever. Even so, bull-fighter Juan Silveti killed bulls in the ring, and three theaters put on a play, a comedy, and vaudeville, seats were only fifty centavos, the cheapest commodity in town.

Fighting continued in and around the city and, by August 2, the Carrancistas took it back once again. But the Zapatistas retained control of nearby Xochimilco and the slopes of Ajusco, and, off and on, the suburb of San Angel. The valley was still full of Zapatistas attacking whoever ventured forth.

On October 15, 1915, nine Latin American governments recognized Carranza. The United States followed suit in December, though Carranza firmly rejected all attempts to impose conditions. No executive in Mexico's history has ever been more touchy about Mexico's sovereignty. Even so, all-out arms aid now went to Carranza, which hastened the disintegration of Villa's forces. He led 6,000 men with heavy artillery to take Sonora, and was achieving success. General Plutarco Elías Calles was in bad straits. In the face of General Scott's protests, the United States allowed Carranza's forces to cross United States territory to help Calles. As a result, 2,000 *Dorados* lay dead at Agua Prieta in Sonora. Of the 6,000 Villistas, only 600 returned with Villa through the harsh Sierra Madrea snows to Chihuahua.

Infuriated and bitter, Villa considered himself grossly betrayed by the United States. On January 10 an outlaw officer of his, Pablo López, murdered eighteen Americans in Santa Isabel on their way to reopen the American-owned mines in Cusi. Villa persistently denied that López had acted on his orders.

Then on March 9, 1916, López raided Columbus, New Mexico, killing nearly a score of citizens and burning part of the town. Whether Villa participated in or even ordered the fray—he claimed he did not —is a moot question. General Scott believed his denials. But feeling in Texas and other border states was so bitter that more "Greasers" were gunned down by citizens, police, and rangers than Americans were killed in Mexico during the entire twenty years of the revolution.

The Pershing expedition rolled into Mexico on March 17 with 12,000 troops; 18,000 more were strung along the border. But his advance came to a quick halt: Carranza forbade him to move east, west, or south, or to use the railroad. This order was backed up by actual bullets, deaths, and casualties. To avoid war, Washington ordered Pershing to respect Carranza's orders. Thereafter, he chewed his nails in the hot sands for nearly a year.

Villa continued to attack well-known towns. On May 3, Villistas again crossed the boundary, killed three United States soldiers at Glenn Springs and destroyed buildings. Badly wounded in an attack in Chihuahua, Villa hid out in a cave and was near death from a bad leg wound. He recovered, gathered five thousand men, boldly took Parral, Jiménez and, after a few days' battle, Chihuahua City, capital of the State.

He had grown more savage. Stores were looted; forced loans were imposed. Whole blocks were burned down; many Chinese were massacred.

Fresh government forces finally drove him out. With incredible rapidity he moved on to distant Torreón and stormed in. The Carranza commander committed suicide. By December 1, Villa's forces numbered ten thousand men, compared to the handful when Pershing came to take him "alive or dead."

To the South, all through the early part of 1916, seesaw battles were fought with Zapatistas in all the towns ringing the capital. In February, Zapata, personally in charge, lost Amecameca but drove back strong forces under Gonzáles, from Tres Marías, Cuautla, and Huitzilán ("Place of Thorns"). Several Zapatista officers defected, but Zapata caught and executed them. One was his earliest companion-in-arms, one-eyed Morelos.

The Constitutionalist government issued additional agrarian regulations, but Zapata put out several strong manifestos and held a Sovereign Revolutionary Convention in Joquilla, Morelos. It accused *Carranzismo* of being leagued with the *terratenientes* (the large landholders) and President Wilson. In October he sent a message to the diplomatic corps that the Carranza government was spurious; that Carranza had reinstated the big landholders, closed the labor union offices of the *Casa del Obrero Mundial,* stripped workers of all rights, and killed leaders of the teachers' and electricians' strikes. Carranza had declared martial law and was cheating the people with false paper money. Zapata attacked the frenzied anticlericalism of the authorities, the thievery of politicians and generals, and his failure to pay his soldiers.

It was May before Gonzáles pushed past Tres Marías and on to

Cuernavaca. His troops also occupied Cuautla and Yautépec. Even
so, Zapata's guerrilla activities grew more energetic. Amecameca,
Otumba, Villa Ayala, Contreras were attacked. Zapata's troops entered
Tlanepantla, the "little pyramid town," just outside Mexico City.
González accused his fellow Constitutionalist and Minister of War
Obregón of selling the Zapatistas arms through the painter, Dr. Atl,
who went and came between both bands with immunity.

Though the state of Morelos was now occupied by four strong
Federal units, the Zapatistas still attacked and briefly held numbers
of important towns. The Federal soldiers, who were from the south,
were hit by malaria, dysentery, and other diseases. On November 7,
a troop train carrying four hundred Carranza soldiers was dynamited
and every man killed. The usual antiguerrilla brutalities were resorted
to. People were forced to evacuate their homes; villages were de-
populated and burned. When the people of Tlaltizapan could not pay
him the money he demanded, Federal Colonel Jesús María Guajardo
killed 180 unarmed citizens, alleging they were Zapatists. Carranza
sent him a message of praise.

But by February 14, 1917 González had to evacuate Cuernavaca.
It was first stripped bare by his soldiers. In a short time, all of Morelos
was back in the hands of the Zapatistas. Tres Marías was retaken, and
Gonzáles had to retreat to Tacubaya (part of the capital itself) with
7,000 ragged soldiers reduced to malarial skeletons. A large part of the
states of México, Puebla and Tlaxcala were held by the guerrillas, but
their leader—one of Zapata's most trusted men, General Domingo
Areña—went over to the Carrancistas. It was a bad blow, but Zapata
still had 70,000 men under arms and largely controlled twelve states
as far north as Durango. He maintained a propaganda agent, General
Jenaro Amuezca, in Cuba.

Meanwhile Pershing was still biting his nails. Soon after, in February
1917, he went home, his mission having failed. Villa again took Chihuahua "to celebrate Independence day" and as a Bronx cheer for
Pershing. Villa fell on other cities and boldly reattacked Ciudad
Juárez.

He streamed in through cut barbed-wire defences in two bloody
assaults and occupied everything but the high fort, which was ready
to surrender. Artillery shells began falling on the city from Fort Bliss,
and United States Negro troops crossed the river. Villa had to flee.

The townspeople fired on the Americans, causing fifteen casualties.
The American Colonel demanded that the Carranza Commandant in
the fort protect American soldiers from snipers. In a clipped reply the
general gave United States troops fifteen minutes to get the hell out
of town. They did: on their heels came Mexican soldiers and a platoon
of animated Mexican drummers, wildly cheered by the people.

Villa and Zapata continued their guerrilla operations throughout the

Carranza administration. During those touchy years, I was once caught in a village attacked by the Villistas. Afterward I left the capital of that state in the caboose of a freight train, the first in a long time to make the attempt. We entered a broad valley. Our train made a wide circle along the foothills. The Villistas were burning a hacienda far across the plain, and they took to their horses to try to cut us off. After a time, they shot from the hip—at which they were expert— or galloped bridles free shooting from the shoulder.

One conductor, a lively little fellow from Aguas Calientes, stood in the middle of the big open side door of the caboose, firing back with his rifle. When it was empty, he shoved it into my hands for me to re- load. Then he jumped up and down (a perfect target) shaking his fists at the Villistas, shouting: *"¡Hijos de la puta! ¡Cabrones! ¡Soy su padre!"* *—and other picturesque oaths. The engineer piled on the steam; the empties of the long train and our caboose bounced and swayed and rattled as we gathered speed over the long untended roadbed. Finally our train ducked into a canyon, beyond further pur- suit.

But by then Zapata was the real menace for Carranza. His watch- fires could be seen from Mexico City; there were skirmishes in the out- skirts. The father of Orozco, while on another mission of bribery, was seized and shot. Just outside the city, dead bodies dangled from tele- phone poles, and swayed in the wind gruesomely. Trying to get to the Zapata camp, I was turned back by Federal soldiers, but cut across the fields and made my way to Cuernavaca; Zapata was not there.

On January 21, 1919, he issued another long manifesto, citing the wrongs Carranza had done to the peasants, the labor unions, and the country. Infuriated, Carranza told González that he had to get rid of Zapata at whatever cost. González then called in Colonel Jesús María Guajardo, guilty of various massacres, to plot Zapata's assassina- tion. Guajardo proceeded to write Zapata that he had had serious per- sonal difficulties with González and wished to join the revolters. He firmly believed, he wrote, that the revolutionary forces would triumph.

Zapata sent back a formal invitation, saying that Guajardo would be received with deserved consideration. Carranza was informed that Zapata seemed to be rising to the bait.

Guajardo reaffirmed his faith in the revolutionary cause. He claimed to have men, horses, and arms and suggested that still another regiment would follow his lead into the Zapata camp.

On April 1, Zapata wrote back that he had received favorable re- ports about Guajardo's abilities and honesty. He and his officers and men would be received with open arms; he would have everything he wished on the revolutionary side. Zapata instructed him to move the

---

* Sons of the whore! Big goats! I'm your father!

following Thursday against General Victoriano Barcenas, a turncoat
Zapatista, in Cuautla—"a very bad element."

> That is where you must begin: by disarming Barcenas and
> his men. Prepare the blow carefully. You will leave his dis-
> armed forces in Chinameca, but send Barcenas and his
> officers to me at the Tepehuajo ranch. After that we shall
> decide what else you shall undertake. I warn you, you will
> have to act with great celerity and energy. Various federal
> officers and their units in and about Cuautla, are merely
> waiting for the word as to when and where they should join
> up.

He outlined a general plan, in coordination with Pancho Villa and
General Felipe Angeles, for a swift domination of all Mexico.

To gain time, Guajardo wrote back that same day that Barcenas was
not in Cuautla at the moment. He himself was waiting for twenty
thousand cartridges to be sent him not later than the tenth. They
would be necessary for future operations. He asked what plazas he
should attack after Cuautla and named three possible towns.

Zapata suggested that he attack Jonacatépec at once. He would
send aid, and a Federal turncoat officer would join him with a hundred
men. He suggested that a hundred trusted men try to intercept
Barcenas, who undoubtedly would hurry back to Cuautla.

On April 8, Guajardo made a simulated attack on the Federal forces
in Jonacatépec. There was much firing and many daring charges. There
were many dead, reported the colonel; the bodies had been buried
immediately.

In Manconadero, he shot 159 Federal soldiers whom, he said, the
peasants had accused of abuses. Zapata could not believe Guajardo
would cold-bloodedly shoot his own men and instructed him to come
to Tepaltzingo with an escort of thirty men. Guajardo showed up
with six hundred and a machine-gun. Zapata embraced him and
greeted him as a "General." He ordered promotions for all those who
had assisted in taking Jonacatépec. They rode together amicably.
Guajardo left for nearby hacienda Chinameca, where he had invited
Zapata to a banquet the following evening.

The next morning Zapata rode on down toward Chinameca with
150 men. False reports came in that an enemy force was approaching.
Zapata sent all but a few of his followers to take care of any trouble.
Guajardo sent him a horse to come to the hacienda. With some hesita-
tion—for he had only ten men available to accompany him—Zapata
rode out on the fine gift horse.

At the hacienda he was paid full honors by guards and a bugler.
But as he rode on in, the guards turned their guns on him and his
men, mowing them down. Others fired from the doors and roof of the
house.

Zapata's riddled body was taken to Cuautla. Thousands of peasants came to the funeral. He was buried "very deep" in the municipal graveyard, and a white angel was put over his grave. It bore a stone parchment reading: Plan de Ayala. Noviember de 1911. At its feet were the words: FREE LAND FOR ALL IS THE IDEAL OF THE REVOLUTION. The marble slab read:

> TO THE MAN WHO REPRESENTED
> THE POPULAR REVOLUTION
> THE APOSTLE OF AGRARISMO . . .
> WHO NEVER LOST FAITH . . .
> DEDICATED AS A HOMAGE
> BY HIS COMPANIONS IN THE STRUGGLE
> ANENECUILCO 1879. CHINAMECA 1919.

Some years later, as an honor delegate to an agrarian convention, I visited the tomb with Soto y Gama, president of the National Peasant League. The little white angel seemed inappropriate for the gaunt rider of the hills who was now supposed to gallop in the clouds. It did not seem as impressive as the thousands of Morelos sombreros which made a river of golden straw and black felt flowing in a human torrent toward the shrine.*

Even those who feared Zapata were filled with revulsion by the ugly betrayal. Though González held on to his military command for a year longer, he was ignominiously booted out of the country when Obregón took over the government. Guajardo was captured in the north, tried, and shot. Even before that, Carranza's popularity was reduced to almost nothing. Only the most corrupt army elements continued to support him.

Even so, in 1920, Carranza tried to impose "Meester" Ignacio Bonillas, so favored by Washington officials. Soon revolutionists were moving in on the Carranza government from all sides, and he had to flee to Vera Cruz.

I was then an instructor to Carranza's personal staff. Even as big posters were being daubed on the city walls announcing that Carranza would never give up the capital, I watched the looting of the Palace. Everything moveable—even old broken drums and bugles, as well as 70,000,000 pesos in gold—was carted down to the trains in Buena Vista station. Twenty-three trains were jam-packed with soldiers, officials, cavalry horses, war material, mistresses, parrots, archives, and gold.

Several of the chests of gold along the runway had lost their lids, and twenty-peso gold "Aztecas" spilled out under the running feet of

---

* Since then an impressive and noble monument has been erected.

train-men and weeping relatives. Everybody was too frantic to pay any attention to the money.

Hard-riding rebel cavalry galloped into the city even before the last train pulled out, riding past school children who had taken over the traffic guidance of a city without police. Guerrilla rebels soon blocked or wrecked the fleeing trains. Carranza had to take to the hills on horseback. A guerrilla leader murdered him in his sleep in Vera Cruz state. So died a stubborn, implacable patriot. He did much to restore administrative order, but little to carry out the mandates of the Revolution.

Adolfo de la Huerta from Sonora was made provisional president until a bayonet-made election could install Obregón, the real boss. The country, weary now of war, was soon pacified.

Nevertheless, Villa was still fighting on and on—but to no purpose. He was sinking back into the bandit status, the outlawry with which he began his career.

Indirect overtures came from De la Huerta that Villa lay down his arms. Villa distrusted the emissaries. He took Parral again, then in July 1920, "to show that Pancho Villa didn't make his tortillas out of goat's meat," he crossed the terrible Mapimi desert and took Sabinas, a town in a rich corn and sugar-cane valley flanked by ore-bearing mountains. There he tore up fifty miles of railroad track. Then he wired De la Huerta, offering to negotiate peace.

To show his goodwill, the president rushed three trains north in charge of General Eugenio Martínez (a soldier Villa trusted) carrying food, clothing, supplies, and gold with which to pay Villa and his men. After parleys and a personal telephone talk between the President and the guerrilla, a formal agreement was signed on July 28, 1920.

Villa was rewarded with the big Canutillo hacienda outside Parral, a vast cattle-ranch of 160,000 acres. It had a fine Casa Grande, a big colonial church, and houses for the peons. Villa, the one-time sandal-shod peon, had become a great feudal lord, but not in the old style. Part of the estate he gave to some fifty favorite *Dorados* who rode away with him from Sabinas after the surrender.

Thus began the great guerrilla's final years. He was still young (only forty-two). He had defied the police and the Díaz Rurales. He had learned all the tricks and tactics of good guerrilla fighting and had become a fantastic myth, a hero revered for his constant championship of the poor. His name terrorized the powers-that-be and was used to frighten children. Time and again he had put Washington into a sweat. He had come to head great armies and be the near-monarch of all he surveyed. Now he settled down to the life of the land-owning class he had so long harassed.

He worked hard, made Canutillo over into the most productive ranch in the land, and shared his prosperity with those who worked with and for him.

July 20, 1923 was going to be a clear, hot day. At eight in the morning, after a customary business trip to Parral, Villa started back to the ranch in his gray Dodge touring car. Five bodyguards rode with him. From a house in Plaza Juárez, a fusillade of bullets mowed them down. Meltón Losoya, a small rancher, and six of his friends and relatives had been waiting in that house for 102 days for the right opportunity.

A shot pierced the windshield, hitting Pancho in the chest. More followed. The careening car bounced over the sidewalk, as all seven men began pumping lead into it. Pancho—some claim—managed to draw his Colt and shoot one of the assassins, Ramón Guerrero, through the heart. But Villa gasped and died, twelve bullets in his body, four in his head.

The actual chief of the assassins, Jesús Suárez, a Durango legislator, claimed it was personal revenge and a patriotic act, because of the blood and bitterness Villa had brought to Mexico. Suárez was jailed briefly, but was pardoned by the President. He was said to have suddenly become wealthy. Had Obregón authorized the murder? Most people whispered that the new candidate, Plutarco Elías Calles, was responsible; he had feared Villa was planning to reenter politics and perhaps revolt. Current at the time was the macabre pun: "Who killed Villa?" Answer: *"Callese"* (be quiet.)

The afternoon following his death Villa was quickly buried with full honors but a minimum of fanfare in the Parral cemetary—not in the great mausoleum he had built in Chihuahua. A plain gray slab marked his grave. But even after death the great guerrilla did not rest in peace. Some years later, his grave was ransacked and the skull stolen, though one account states that "he was beheaded before being interred." Various fictitious news reports said that it had been bought by Ringling Brothers; by the University of Chicago for scientific purposes; that it was in the hands of the United States government, which had earlier put a $50,000 price on his head; that it was in an anthropological exhibit in California. More likely, somebody with necrophiliac talents made a pulque mug out of it.

In 1966, Villa's name was engraved in gold in the marble of the Chambers of Deputies, which thereby raised him to the honor of a national hero.

His death was the end of more than a decade of violence and bloodshed. In good part, the long struggles of Zapata and Villa ushered in a new and more just era of peace. In due time, the hoped-for great land reform was carried out by President Lázaro Cárdenas. But with the death of Villa, the day of the Mexican guerrillas was over.

5

YANKEE GO HOME: SANDINO

Until the recent capture and assassination of Che Guevara, this century's most popular hero throughout the Latin-American world has been Augusto César Sandino. For nearly seven years (1927–33) he fought for the independence of Nicaragua against invasion by the most powerful military nation in history—the United States.

Sandino's David and Goliath exploits became the theme of song and ballad, articles and novels. "Flea versus the elephant," Argentine writer Gregorio Selser called his struggle, in his two-volume biography of the hero and in *The Mad Little Army*. Sandino's ghost haunted every inter-American reunion and aroused angry crowds against good-will emissaries such as Hoover, Nixon, Eisenhower, and Stevenson. "Our model and inspiration," said the now-dead Guatemalan guerrilla leader, Luis Augusto Turcios Lima in 1966, "is not Lenin or Mao or Castro but Sandino."

His fame reached far beyond Latin America. Humble folk from Capetown to Jakarta came to know of his exploits, though few recalled the names of the American aviators who made Chinandega and Ocotal bywords of infamy all over the world.

Most people in the United States knew nothing about what was going on in Nicaragua, but twenty years later the hosts of Mao entered Peking bearing banner-sized portraits of the Nicaraguan hero. His three-story high picture loomed over the half-million people at the July 26 rally of 1966 in Havana. The Brazilian diplomat, Carlos da Silveira Martines Ramos, wrote:

NICARAGUA

Traveler, if you should arrive at its ports
    Full of hopes and illusions,
You would kiss the soil that Sandino
    Fertilized with the blood of lions.

Oh, noble Nicaragua! Your destiny—
    A blend of bitter tears and chants—
Bears the cruel brand of divinity,
    Which makes of one heart a thousand hearts.

74

That is why your banner flies in the sky—
    An everlasting piece of your soil,
Shining with glory and tragedy,
    Of love and defiance and desire,
Woven by the songs of Darío *
And by Sandino's sword of fire.

In Nicaragua, the so-called bayonet-and-dollar diplomacy was facing up to its first serious challenge since Aguinaldo. How could events in a despicable little banana republic affect our national destinies. Accepting the State Department's propaganda, the press branded Sandino an "outlaw bandit," and made no attempt to get his side of the story.

One Cuban guerrilla leader told his men, "We are not merely thirty men, we are six million people"—a thought that has buoyed up other guerrillas elsewhere. Support by the people is indispensable. The people, as Mao Tse-tung put it, is the sea in which the guerrilla swims.

At the outset of his famous treatise *Guerra de Guerrillas (War of Guerrillas)* Che Guevara, makes the distinction between bandit and guerrilla clear.

> Gangs of bandits . . . have all the characteristics of the guerrilla army: homogeneity, respect for the leader, courage, knowledge of the terrain, and often a good understanding of the proper tactics. The one thing the bandits lack is the support of the people, so inevitably these gangs are captured or exterminated by government forces.

Bandits flourish in times of catastrophe, as during the terrible Brazilian droughts of Pernambuco and Cerará when despair created a delirium of destructive hatred, a frantic attempt to escape universal misery. Only occasionally did such last-century men become leaders of more meaningful revolt: men such as Antonio Conselheira in Canudos or Manuel dos Anjos Ferreira—"Little Basket," *O Baloio*— in Maranhão from 1838–1840. The bandit pops up like eczema on an unhealthy body during evil periods: an ugly, blind, antisocial backlash against tyranny and injustice. The present bands operating in the Argentine Pampa and the hills, attacking ranches, have resulted from semicollapse of the country, the breakdown of public services, and top-heavy urbanization. Such bandits seek self-enrichment, adventure, or mere survival. Of late, since Guevara, bonafide guerrillas have appeared, guerrillas who wish to abolish injustices and overthrow the state.

The distinction was blurred in the United States Civil War, when lawless bands ravaged both North and South. Before that, Nathaniel

* Rubén Darío was Nicaragua's great poet, hailed as the writer of the first "modernist" poetry in the Spanish language.

Bacon of Virginia and Daniel Shays of Massachusetts, the Minutemen of 1776, and most Indian braves such as Chief Joseph of the Nez Percé, were guerrillas, and able ones. That "damned swamp fox" Francis Marion fought the British and Hessians, "with a ferocity which only Civil War can breed," using much the same tactics as guerrillas use today in the jungles and paddies of Southeast Asia.

Because he must retain the sympathy of the people, the guerrilla has to limit his terrorism largely to his known enemies—easy to distinguish foreigners, abusive native collaborationists, and officials. Help the people and share everything with the people, were injunctions repeated often by guerrillas Sandino, Tito, Mao, Castro, Ho Chi Minh, and Nguyen Huu Tho.

The guerrilla, like the bandit, does not abide by existing statutes or genteel rules of war. He recognizes no authority except his own. The guerrilla, "the Jesuit of warfare," wrote Che, *must* act "different from the romantic and sporting conceptions with which we are taught to believe war is always fought." In Algeria and Vietnam, as elsewhere, deeds that guerrillas consider legitimate are considered atrocities by his foes, whatever their own terroristic methods—as those of the British against the Mau Mau of Kenya. In parts of South Vietnam, "anything that moves is a Viet Cong," be it a water buffao, a baby, a peasant in the rice fields. Naturally, the body-count is always high. But anything that promotes the guerrillas' cause against the enemy and his ruling society, of course, is "justifiable": robbery, kidnapping, arson, even assassination. The guerrilla seeks to establish his own law, i.e. what he considers justice and freedom for the people. When a United States officer on the scene labeled Sandino an "outlaw" and ordered him to lay down his arms, he retorted that the only outlaws in Nicaragua were the Marines.

The highest United States officials repeatedly denounced Augusto César Sandino as a "bandit" and "Communist," which he never was. Through such publications as *Ariel in Honduras* and *El Repertorio Americano* in Costa Rica, he repeatedly set forth his program, available in all Spanish-speaking lands but not in the United States.

The credibility gap was pointed out bluntly by the *Review of Reviews*, April, 1928:

> The American public had no information about the Nicaraguan chief [Sandino] except what came from government sources. The State Department and Marine officials call him a bandit and outlaw, and many newspapers have accepted those terms . . . What sort of a man is he? What actually is he trying to do? The first effort to answer this question has been made by the *Nation* [which] . . . commissioned Carleton Beals to interview him.

On January 5, 1928, eight months after Sandino began his long heroic struggle, I entered the cable office on San Juan de Letran Street in Mexico City at 4:40 P.M. I was handed a wire from Oswald Garrison Villard, editor of *The Nation*:

CAN YOU PROCEED IMMEDIATELY NICARAGUA FOR NATION SENDING EXCLUSIVE STORIES AMERICAN POLICY MARINE RULE POPULAR FEELING ETCETERA, REACHING SANDINO IF POSSIBLE . . .WIRE COLLECT.

It was high time. Either Sandino's accusations should be disproved, or American policy should be rectified.

Would the marines let me land? Could I get my information out? The dangers of travel in difficult country in a war zone where American planes were bombing indiscriminately did not particularly preoccupy me; the one big question was, would Sandino receive me? He had little reason to love Americans. If half the stories about him were true, he would shoot me.

By five o'clock, my reply to Villard was winging north:

LEAVING HERE SATURDAY VIA GUATEMALA. GATES TO SANDINO OPEN BUT UNADVISABLE ANNOUNCE THIS . . . BEFOREHAND FOR IT WOULD INCREASE RISK SPOIL CHANCES.

Charges of disloyalty would be leveled against me. (Later a few brickbats did come, mostly from the Mississippi mud-bottoms and from white Texas women's clubs.) But my firm belief was that disloyal people were those who suppressed the facts and damaged their country's honor by using their powerful positions to promote improper deals, collect unsavory loans, and stage undeclared wars. The real enemies of the United States were those destroying our friendship with the whole of Latin America. It was not a crime those days— as it is today—for a newspaper man, or anybody, to visit a country considered out of bounds by the State Department and try to provide the public with reliable information. Our travel freedom had not yet been abridged.

The best route, I believed, was to go in from the Honduras side— the back door. Sandino might be suspicious of anybody arriving directly from the North American camp, and I might be unable to get through the American lines.

Credentials to Sandino were supplied to me by Dr. Carlos León, head of the Union of Central and South America, and by Sandino's representative Dr. Pedro José Zepeda, who was relaying the leader's messages to the world, pressuring the Secretary of State and raising money for medicines, supplies, and arms.

What was known about the guerrilla? Next to nothing in those days. Augusto C. Sandino was born May 18, 1895 in Niquinohomo, in east central Nicaragua. He was the son of Gregorio Sandino, who owned three small coffee *fincas,* and Margarita Calderón, a servant in his house. When Margarita died, Augusto's father married América Tifén, a girl of his own class, with whom he had three other children. Augusto was raised by her. Between Augusto and his younger half-brother Socrates existed an imperishable bond of deep love.

Augusto was put through what passed for high school, then he took up farming. He organized a cooperative to make farmers independent of commission merchants and loan sharks and came into conflict with the ruthless loan-agent of the region, José María Moncada.

Forced out in 1921, Sandino went north to New Segovia. Then, with his cousin Santiago Sandino, he went to Honduras where he worked near Ceiba as a foreman on the Montecristo banana plantation. He was wounded in the neck by a chauffeur trying to steal gasoline. When the police did nothing, Sandino brought the man in at rifle point.

He worked briefly in Guatemala for the United Fruit Company, went on to Mexico in 1923, first to Yucatán, then worked in the Tampico oil fields except for a short trip to the United States. It was entirely untrue—as stated by United States Secretary of War Stimson who persistently branded him as a bandit and footpad, that he had been in Honduras making trouble from the age of ten on [he was twenty-seven] or that he had fought with Villa in Mexico. Villa had already quit.

Sandino did participate in several oil-workers' strikes under the Regional Confederation of Labor's red-black banner, which he later adopted as the insignia of his own forces.

He was an omnivorous reader. Even in Honduras he was in contact with writers and intellectuals, among them his fellow Nicaraguan exile Gustavo Alemán Bolaños, who later wrote the hero's biography. Sandino attracted attention because he neither drank nor smoked and was a vegetarian.

He returned to Nicaragua in May 1926 at the age of thirty-one. Within a year he was to win international fame.

He did not get on well with his father Gregorio. Sandino joined a workers' gang being taken to the San Albino gold mines near the Honduranian border. The workday was fifteen hours. Wages were small, paid only in script on the company store, and workers were housed in sheds where they had to sleep on the ground.

Following the Conservative Party armed coup by Emiliano Chamorro that year, Sandino believed in the constitutional claims of the Liberal Party and ousted vice-president Juan B. Sacasa. Sandino was equally opposed to Adolfo Díaz, imposed as President in November 1926 by the United States Embassy and the Marines.

Sandino's travels, reading, and personality gave him ascendancy over his fellow miners, and he gathered together a group of thirty-five to fight against Díaz and the Yankee forces. He spent his last three hundred dollars in Honduras for arms and taught his men to make hand-grenades with dynamite filched from the mine. They blew up the mine and took to the hills.

At El Jícaro, November 26, they attacked the garrison of two hundred men—a swift blow and quick withdrawal—really "a defeat," he admitted, "from which I learned much."

On December 2, Sacasa disembarked in Puerto Cabezas on the north coast near Honduras to establish his claims to the presidency and organized a provisional government. He was recognized immediately by President Plutarco Elías Calles of Mexico, who secretly sent down four boat-loads of arms. At once Secretary of State Frank Kellogg and President Calvin Coolidge branded Mexico's government—and Calles personally—as "Bolshevik" and "Red."

Sandino decided to go down the great Coco River to Puerto Cabezas to get arms to carry on the fight in the Segovias. With half a dozen men, he went down-stream in a primitive *pipante* (dugout canoe), a nine day trip.

But Sacasa's general was Moncada, a turncoat Conservative, with whom Sandino had already had difficulties. Moncada scoffed at Sandino's military abilities. No arms!

The United States rushed down war-vessels. Admiral J. B. Latimer landed Marines and ordered the presidential claimant out of the port. Sacasa refused to budge. Moncada slipped off to nearby Prinzapolka with men and arms. The Marines began throwing confiscated rifles and ammunition into the river.

Under the pretense of a night picnic with patriotic town prostitutes, Sandino and his men went to the shore where some weapons had not yet been dumped, and carried off forty rifles and seven thousand cartridges. He got the cache out of town and joined Moncada at Prinzapolka. The general seized the weapons and ammunition, but two of Sacasa's ministers insisted he let Sandino take the weapons to the Segovias.

Sandino got back to his camp on the upper Coco River on February 2. His forces had grown to three hundred and from then on it was one steady triumph. He drove into town after town, taking even such important places as Ocotal and Estelí. Presently he seized the important center of San Rafael del Norte in the coffee country. In three bloody engagements on Yacapuca—a lofty, freezing mountain only six miles from Jinotega, the capital of the department —he drove back Díaz' forces.

Sandino talked over campaign plans with Blanca Arauja, the pretty young telegraph operator in San Rafael del Norte to whom he had become engaged. They pored over a street map of Jinotega to devise the best way of assaulting it.

His forces moved in from four directions at five in the morning. He looked down on the town. The street lights were still on. "With the first rays of the sun . . . could be seen the cemetery with its white mausoleums, a spectacle that would have made Rubén Darío ecstatic. It was the first time I had ever seen the city. I fell in love with it as one would love a sweetheart, and I have never been able to forget it."

By 4 P.M. the plaza was in his hands, along with a big supply of ammunition and guns. At 5 P.M. forty Marines and Conservative troops, arriving too late to reinforce it, withdrew.

He prepared to strike at nearby Matagalpa, another key coffee city. The Yankee commander there informed him it was a neutral zone (brilliantly defined by Secretary of State Frank Kellogg as a place where no fighting was allowed). Sandino replied that he had understood that neutrality was supposed to aid Liberals as well as Conservatives. Why were the Americans aiding the Conservatives? He demanded that the Yankee forces recognize Liberal civil authorities in all Jinetega province.

Moncada, after fighting through the marshes, the forests, and mountains of central Nicaragua, had by then come close to Managua, the capital. Largely due to his own blundering, he was broken and hemmed in at the foot of the Black Mountain range. Admiral Latimer wired north the joyous news of Moncada's destruction.

Sandino called in dispersed guerrilla bands. General Parajón, a good fighter, who'd been driven out of Chinandega after the bombing, hurried with all of his men to Jinotega from Estelí, arriving on Holy Thursday. More rebel contingents galloped in, and Sandino rode fast to relieve Moncada. His forces overran the headquarters of the government troops. He seized the enemy field hospital full of wounded, as well as several thousand rifles and millions of cartridges. He armed the hundreds of volunteers who showed up. At once Moncada ordered that no commander could have more than three hundred men. He ordered Sandino to join the Liberal forces at Boaca.

This was a deliberate trap since the enemy, not the rebels, was in strong possession there. Sandino occupied nearby El Común Hill. "Our black and red banner floated majestically there on these rugged and cold mountains," Sandino wrote, "until the day Moncada hung the Liberal Party on the Black Thorn of Tipitapa."

Moncada renewed his advance on Managua. On April 24, the Associated Press reported that it was unlikely that the capital could be saved. The combined Díaz and United States contingents could not prevent his entry. Latimer's joyous optimism had been premature.

But the United States must not lose face. The former Governor of the Philippines and a long-time war-hawk, Henry L. Stimson, was rushed to the scene with instructions to keep the tottering Adolfo Díaz in power at all costs.

Although the Liberals had had the overwhelming support of the people from the beginning of the century, fifteen years before the 1927 fight the United States had thrown out elected President José Santos Zelaya and had since kept the Conservatives in power by flagrant bayonet elections.

President Adolfo Díaz had been a petty clerk in a large lumber company in which Secretary of State, Philander P. Knox, had a personal investment. The unknown Díaz emerged with $600,000 to back a revolution against Zelaya and became, thereafter, the fair-haired office-boy for the State Department. I remember him as a dapper, glib, neatly tailored little man uttering incredible falsehoods.

By 1927, unfriendly world opinion against intervention had become appalling. Mexican arch-Conservative Nemesio García Naranjo wrote,

> Never is modern international history has a more tremendous and universal hissing been heard as that which the U. S. has received as a result of its intervention in Nicaragua . . . from Great Britain, France, Germany, Spain, Argentina, Chile, Cuba, Latin America." Something new? "No, just a confirmation of traditional U. S. puritan conduct of always acquiring and conserving absolute predominance in the New World . . . [in the name of] law and liberty . . . Tyranny in the name of justice! . . . A farce! . . . For a year the poor sheep Coolidge scarcely wished to stick a finger in, but now he thrusts his whole body in. Díaz is discredited now throughout the world.

With the Liberal army about to take over, the whole farce was blowing up. Could Stimson win by cajolery what had not been won on the battlefield? He asked Moncada and Sacasa to send delegates to a conference in Tipitapa between the lines.

The Sacasa representatives were hurried in from Puerto Cabezas and listened to Stimson with indignation. In the stern voice of the proconsul, he ordered that Díaz be kept in office until supervised elections could be held. His proposals were hotly rejected. Sacasa deplored that "the United States, departing from the principles of justice and forgetting the true interests of a weak country in order . . . to sustain a regime born of a coup d'etat, has not only violated and broken into pieces the Constitution of the Republic but also the Central American Treaty signed in Washington, D. C."

His Washington representative, Doctor T. Seyday, wrote:

> The Big Stick government is crepe hung in the door of every country of the Caribbean. The next act will see the entrance on the stage of the big banks and the profiteers of the big railroad and other concessions. The Liberals have been disarmed, but nothing can force them to recognize the legality of the Díaz regime, maintained in power by North American armed forces.

What Stimson could not get out of the Puerto Cabezas government, he easily got from Moncada, an extreme alcoholic more interested in his personal fortunes than in his cause. In a conference at Black Thorn, Moncada agreed to submit on Stimson's terms and announced that there was no hope of opposing the whole might of the United States. Stimson informed Washington that Sacasa and the men around him did not matter. They had not done any fighting and would not fight.

Moncada was escorted to Managua to arrange surrender terms. He returned to Tipitapa with a United States Army Gold Cross and secret confirmation that he would be put in as the next president. He obliged his officers to sign on the dotted line. All did so except Sandino who was not present; his name was written in by Moncada.

Adolfo Díaz, on his side, dutifully turned the Nicaraguan constabulary and army over to American officers but never handed over the governments of the departments, as Stimson had promised the Liberals. The entire country was now apparently in the hands of the United States and the Marines. Stimson sent an exuberant wire to Secretary Kellogg: "The Civil War in Nicaragua is now definitely ended."

A marvelous bit of opportunism! Moncada betrayed his Liberals and the revolutionary army, and the United States threw its erstwhile Conservative friends to the wolves. All these years, the tide against the Conservatives had been rising. The public had begun to smell out lucrative undercover deals, bankers' loans, hanky panky over the railroad and the National Bank, all the looting and corruption on both sides. The only losers were the Nicaraguan people and the North American people.

Sandino arrived belatedly to see Moncada. The commander, wearing his shiny new United States Gold Cross on a white ribbon, received him lying in a hammock under a big shade tree. Realizing that he would be seized on the spot if he did not pretend to go along, Sandino asked to be allowed to deliver his arms to the Yankees in Jinotega instead of in Tipitapa.

He rode off with his staff to that city where he was received with flowers and music. Telling his followers he intended to fight the foreign invaders, he sent machine guns and material to the mountains and rode off to San Rafael del Norte with three hundred men.

In the early predawn of May 8, Sandino and Blanca Arauz were quietly married by the local priest. The church wedding bells were answered by a machine-gun salute.

The road of resistance would be bloody and long, but "selling out the country" filled him with shame. "Not wishing my soldiers to see me weeping, I went off alone." In a mountain camp at Yalí, he prepared his first Independence Manifesto: "The Civil War has not ended, Mr. Stimson, it has only begun."

Indeed, the day after Stimson's jubilant May 16 message, eight hundred Liberals under Juan Cabula attacked the Marines near Chinandega. He then surrendered and was murdered by the Marine officer to whom he delivered his gun.

For three months Sandino lay up in Yalí, sending out messengers, recruiting, arming, and training men. His communiqués went across frontiers and electrified all Latin America. According to Washington, however, his insignificant forces were all dispersed. He moved north and set up his headquarters on top of Chipote, a jungle mountain.

After several days, Captain Hatfield of Ocotal sent Sandino an ultimatum to surrender, calling him an outlaw, but reminding him that the great guerrilla Aguinaldo had once hated the Americans but after surrender had become a good friend. Sandino replied from El Chipote —actually at the moment he was in San Fernando close to Ocotal— that the only outlaws were the foreign invaders. "I wish for a free country or death. I am not afraid, for I enjoy the patriotic zeal of those who accompany me. *Patria y Libertad.*"

Hatfield's real answer came at 8 A.M. Sandino attacked Ocotal, with eight machine guns, three hundred men, and four hundred unarmed peasants. After six hours of hard fighting, thirty-six marines and a large National Guard contingent were driven into a barracks in the outskirts. Sandino ruled the town and stationed sharpshooters in the church tower.

Five American planes came over. It was bad weather. Three planes were forced to land in León and two took refuge in Honduras. The next day seven planes came over. By then the Sandino forces, after dynamiting captured barracks and the houses of notorious Conservatives, had withdrawn. The planes bombed and strafed the village, killing about three hundred and wounding a hundred more—many of them women and children. A good body-count.

Whether the Sandinistas were patriots or bandits, remarked *La Nación* of Buenos Aires, the United States had violated the sovereignty of Nicaragua.

> The U. S. troops were exercising supreme power, therefore had ignored the legitimacy of the very government imposed by bayonets and cannon and the Secretary of State . . . Ocotal was assassination . . . No recognition was given the national sovereignty or the belligerents. They are trodden under foot . . . with a primitive treatment used against bandits . . . The U. S. has no police power it can properly exercise beyond its own frontiers.

Sandino issued a manifesto (published throughout the world except the United States) that his Ocotal attack was:

> (1) To demonstrate that our force is organized . . . to defend the constitutional rights of Dr. Sacasa (2) To destroy the idea that we are bandits and not men of ideals (3) To

prove that we prefer death to being slaves, because the
peace of Moncada . . . is that which a slave enjoys . . .
(4) To hunt out and punish the traitors and invaders of
our country . . . The only one to blame for what has occurred, is occurring and will occur in Nicaragua is the
President of the U. S., Calvin Coolidge, since he obstinately
upholds the power of his lackey Adolfo Díaz, an individual
who enjoys the contempt of all good Nicaraguans.

"Ocotal," wrote Solomón de la Selva, exiled poet, "is a vast cemetery
where bands of crows devour the bodies." Major Ross Rowell, American air commander in Nicaragua, was given a medal.

The American Federation of Labor, which had more moral dignity
than it does today, demanded the immediate withdrawal of American
troops. Illinois Governor Edward Deane denounced the Ocotal massacre by United States planes and demanded that General Feland be
stripped of his rank and punished. Democratic Representative H. H.
Knowles spoke of the "defenseless peoples of Latin America."
F. L. Hopkins said that Ocotal demonstrated the brutality to which the
United States will resort to impose its will on small New World nations.
Senator Borah told the Press, Díaz wouldn't last an hour if the Marines
moved out. The overwhelming majority of the Nicaraguan people are
against Díaz and his regime . . . [The Marines are violating] the
great basic principle of independence and free government."

More and more peasants flocked to Sandino's banner, especially
after their homes were bombed or burned and their fields destroyed.
"The planes," said Sandino, "poured death over the people of towns,
villages and the valleys, killed with impunity the defenseless peasants,
machine-gunned rural homes, applied *ley de fuga* to prisoners, shot
them down from trees; some they beheaded. They killed the animals,
too."

A leading Nicaraguan noted that Stimson, in his book on Nicaragua,
stated that one of Spain's mistakes had been not killing all the Indians.
Colonel Fagan, a United States officer in León, said, "Sandino is a
patriot with little judgment. If he would ask that a cathedral be built
any place in Segovia, it would be something possible; if he demanded
ten million dollars, he would be asking the possible, but to believe he
can defeat the U. S. A.—that is lack of judgment."

Actually, wrote a Cuban author, "The U. S. A. has never recovered
from the moral defeat it suffered at the hands of Sandino."

Presently, after studying the underground defenses of the American
forces at Talpaneca (a place of two thousand people) Sandino stationed sharpshooters to pick off every gringo head that showed. He
overran the place, then retired just before the planes came over. His
men sang *Adelita*, the Villa marching song. Sandino remarked, "You
may have noticed that in Nicaragua, it is the rat which eats the cat."

For eight months in El Chipote, he directed operations, issuing manifestos to the people of Nicaragua and the world. His pronouncements were published in all Latin America, in Europe, Asia, and Africa, if rarely in the United States.

Chipote was bombed almost daily. The effect was negligible, for the defenses were cleverly constructed. Chipote became the world's symbol of bravery and human liberty, another Bunker Hill, another Chaupultepec. For months on end, the Marines oversaw sweating Nicaraguan workers build a road to Chipote through the dense jungle, over which to bring up big guns.

I was headed toward this stronghold, Chipote, when I set out from Mexico City that Saturday night on January 7, 1928.

In El Salvador, Sandino's representative Dr. Francisco Zamora provided me with letters to Froylán Turcios, editor of *Ariel* in Tegucigalpa; to Sandino; and to a guide—General Rivas, a regular courier. On our trip to La Unión in eastern Salvador, we were shadowed by a Nicaraguan police spy, and at the port we were detained briefly. Fortunately my money belt was not found, but I lost Zamora's letters, my notes, and loose change.

The Gulf of Fonseca (which we crossed by launch) is one of the world's finest harbors, a true prize of empire, a great purple-green sea, dotted with fair islands and fringed by lofty densely wooded mountains. By numerous treaties, all rights in the gulf had been guaranteed by and for three countries—El Salvador, Honduras, and Nicaragua. But in 1916, the United States had secured from Nicaragua's puppet government a ninety-nine year military lease that violated the rights of El Salvador and Honduras, and those of Costa Rica in the San Juan River.

The Central American Court of Justice and Peace (originally set up at the behest of the United States) outlawed the agreement, but its verdict was ignored by both Nicaragua and Washington, and the Court ceased to exist. A marvelous satire, *La Oficina de Paz*, was written by the Guatemalan writer, Rafael Arévalo Martínez.

In Ampala, the Hondureñan port of entry, Rivas was arrested. He was deported to Nicaragua where to avoid being shot, he divulged to the Marines all he knew about Sandino, about Chipote, and about my own plans. He was shot anyway. His disclosures brought the Chief of Police of Tegucigalpa—the highland Honduras capital—to arrest me. But by then I was already on my way to the frontier.

Froylán Turcios, a former cabinet minister whom I had contacted, was a curious mixture of poet and politician, realist and idealist. He had made his *Ariel* a mouthpiece for Sandino, and the United States Embassy had been unable to get the Honduras government, so dutiful in most matters, to suppress it. We spent agreeable hours in the high garden park above the city—the only safe place to talk.

Turcios provided me with another guide, General Santos Siqueiros, a Nicaraguan. Years before, Siqueiros had been seized by the Marines, put on a battleship, and dumped into Guatemala. Arrogant, irascible, and suffering from a bladder ailment, he was a difficult traveling companion.

In Tegucigalpa we holed up in the servant's quarters of a friendly third-class hotel, sewed our credentials into our saddle-blankets, and slipped out of the capital on Sunday, January 21—two weeks after I had left Mexico City.

We rode through rain and mud, snatching a few hours' sleep in wet clothes in half-open freezing Indian huts. Our half-starved hosts fed us unpalatable fried or boiled green bananas. Beyond the coffee town of Danlí, we evaded all patrols in the night rain. On the lofty Depilto heights, we could hear the persistent around-the-clock booming of United States artillery and planes bombarding Chipote. Inside Honduras, we met refugees from the war zone and listened to their stories of maltreatment, robbery, rape, and burned-out homes.

We put up at the cool sprawling home of a pipe-smoking English mine-manager, married to a Nicaraguan woman by whom he had had five attractive daughters. His eyes popped out of his head. "Crazy men I have known. Now a blond gringo comes out of the sky to put his head in the lion's mouth. Incredible!" Our talk in comfortable rocking chairs on the cool vine-smothered veranda was punctuated with the Greek chorus of the heavy artillery.

"Go back. Go back," my English host insisted. "These Sandinistas will kill every gringo they can. Some are patriots, some are plain bandits, some are riffraff."

"But you sit here on top of your mine."

"Even the worst ones like me. I feed them when they are hungry. Besides, I'm not a Yankee."

Siqueiros and I went on the next morning with Sandino couriers. The Englishman warned me to ride in the center of the group, lest some idiot recognizing I was an outlander take a pot shot at me.

The big guns ceased abruptly. The silence was more terrifying than the previous thunder. Word came from a traveler: "Sandino has abandoned Chipote."

"Where is he?"

"¿Quién sabe?" Nobody knew.

We learned that a bayonet charge up the slopes had been launched. American newspapers played it up as a gallant bloody assault. Sandino's forces had been dispersed. He had fled to Honduras. The war was over!

Actually, all the marines had found were dummies with fake wooden rifles manning the trenches.

Sandino had marched out days before with the bulk of his force very well armed, and gone south into the heart of the coffee country. He had not fled to Honduras, he was headed for his old stamping grounds of San Rafael del Norte.

Our small band made a wide circle inland to avoid the Marines. For a time we had to abandon our horses and most of our belongings— even my medicine-kit—and flounder on foot through mud on the deep jungle trails. Cattle ticks, boring into our skin, made sleep almost impossible.

We reached various camps, one on a mountain crest. The Marines were on the opposite ridge, but it would require days for them to hack through the valley jungle. And so guitars thrummed. We danced and sang.

On nearing San Rafael, I sent my credentials ahead by a courier. A small force led by Captain Pedro Altamirano escorted us to San Rafael.

Altamirano answered all my preconceived notions of a bandit; he was a heavy big-faced lummox who grunted in monosyllables. He had been accused of every depredation. But as we rode along, he gained confidence in me, and I came to appreciate his economical courtesy and his quiet thoughtfulness for my welfare. His men were fanatically devoted to him, and he himself was unshakably loyal to Sandino. Though close-mouthed, with little or no education; he had a razor-sharp mind plus vast courage and cunning. (Soon after, Sandino made him a general. He came to rule over a vast area, outwitting the Marines for years.)

Riding within a few miles of Jinotega—strongly garrisoned by Marines—we entered hill-perched San Rafael, a picturesque tile-roofed place. It was a warm, star-studded night. The bugles sounded, and we rode through the cobbled streets between lines of soldiers. An aide brought Sandino's regrets that he was unable to welcome me in person. He was suffering from the grippe and had taken medicine, but would see me at 4 A.M. in his headquarters at the home of his wife Blanca.

Most of the night I spent with Sandino's staff, answering their eager questions, listening to their guitars and stirring freedom songs. General Girón, a Guatemalan, was a small graying man of fifty. Highly cultured, trained in San Cyr, and a veteran officer of the French army, he had built the able defenses on Chipote which had so aroused the admiration of North American officers, that they believed them to have been built by a captured American aviator. Another Sandino officer was a prominent Costa Rican writer. Our talk that night ranged far beyond the military invasion to international affairs, to Paris, literature, poetry, and art. It was a surprising entourage for a "bandit."

At exactly 4 A.M., Sandino received me at breakfast at a small oil cloth covered table. Short, slender, almost frail, with a light-olive complexion and black eyes, he had a round, jutting jaw, relatively thin

lips, and rather delicate features. He wore khaki, highly polished boots,
a red bandana, and he kept his large Texas Stetson sombrero on even
when eating. He was trim, with a faintly irritating cockiness, especially
when he stood in a spread-leg fashion with his thumbs in his belt. But
his knowledge of what was going on in the country, in the world at
large, was extraordinary. He was earnest and amazingly fluent. His
ideas were organized, his words epigrammatic, precise, sparkling. A
born phrase-maker, and his impact consisted of will, purpose, courage,
and knowledge.

"Your men are always talking about their faithful Con-Con," I remarked.

"A, yes, those are the rifles that came from Mexico on the boat
Con Con." He had an aide bring me one. It was a long-barreled
Russian rifle, originally manufactured in the United States in 1917 to
be sent to Kerensky. Kerensky fell from power too soon, so they were
rushed down to Mexico to help Obregón squelch a military uprising.
Calles sent them on to Sandino in Nicaragua. Now they were killing
not Germans or Bolsheviks, but the soldiers of the country that had
manufactured them.

Sandino also showed me the type of rifles, automatics, and machine
guns captured from the Marines. "If it weren't for the guns and
munitions we've taken from United States convoys, we would be in
a bad way. The more forces they send, the better we can fight. It's
too bad," he added with a grin, "that the pirates have such a big
stature. Their uniform can't be worn by our people."

Later after I reached Managua, General Logan Feland in charge of
the United States occupation told me tersely, "We have lost no convoys." But after I left Nicaragua, he wrote me several times, inquiring
about American prisoners taken in such attacks!

"The American officers are very bitter," I told Sandino, "Because
when they recover a body the penis has been cut off and stuffed in
the man's mouth." *

"It's an old pre-Spanish Indian custom in the Segovias," explained
Sandino. "Four centuries ago the Spaniards also complained of the
habit. It's a ritualistic act—quite as civilized as drinking the blood of
Christ. If the gringos would get out, they wouldn't have their penises
cut off." He looked at his wristwatch. "It's five minutes to ten. The
planes will come over at ten."

We walked down the street. They were empty now, the horses hidden in patios or the woods. He spoke to sharpshooters posted in the
doorways. They were not to shoot unless the planes fired.

One sharpshooter was dancing with impatience. "Let me have just
shot," he begged.

* This was also a Mau Mau custom. The Aztecs used to cut off ears, as U. S.
soldiers in Vietnam have done, to verify the body count.

"You shoot one shot, and I'll have your penis cut off."

To me he said, "This is my town. The planes could hurt a lot of people, as they have in other towns, without the excuse they'd have here. They have bombed or wiped out ninety inhabited places, killing innocent women and children. Their barbarity has so aroused the civilized world that a few days ago they ordered their planes not to fire on any village unless fired upon. Today, we shall see."

His troops, as I had already observed on the way to San Rafael, had known almost to the minute when the planes would be coming over. They tethered their horses, and we lay deep under the jungle trees where the men smoked, played cards, thrummed their guitars or slept. Now, in San Rafael del Norte the planes flew over right on schedule. They scraped the rooftops.

As the roar of the planes neared, Sandino waved me into a doorway. He himself stood in the middle of the cobbled street, his thumbs in his belt, watching them fly over, a contemptuous smile on his face.

Later in Managua, I asked Major Rowell about the sortie. "You flew very low."

"I wanted the bastards to shoot at us so we could knock hell out of the place. We were loaded full up for it."

"You were taking quite a risk."

He shrugged. "Yes, these bastard Nicaraguans are good shots. Our planes have been hit by rifle fire higher than any were in the World War."

Sandino and I were back at the oil-cloth table. I asked bluntly, "Why are you fighting?"

"We want the United States pirates to go home. I want a Nicaragua for the Nicaraguans. A free country. Our own country."

"And you personally?"

"Nothing. I won't ever accept a government position of any sort. The day the gringos go, we arrange to lay down our arms."

"Will your men obey you?"

"They will obey me. I have some plans for them. I am going to ask the government to set up a new Department along the Coco River, at present mostly uninhabited, to be called 'Peace and Liberty.' My boys will get land there and work. The country is rich. Until they get fields cleared and crops in, they can live easily on wild fruits, wild plants, the roots they know. They can make money right away selling wild cacao, bananas, cutting lumber, panning out the gold. We'll build a dam and a power station and make the river navigable for good-sized vessels. We'll work it through cooperatives, I think."

"That is in the future."

"Yes, a man who does not have a handspan of earth, as I don't, on which to die, deserves to be dead unless he fights. I am a Nicaraguan and am proud that in my veins there circulates, more than any other,

Indian blood, which contains the mystery of my being a loyal and sincere patriot."

He was indifferent to the "pessimists, the cowards, the eunuchs who sneer at those who fight for the things they desire. They call me a plebeian. True. I am an urban worker, an artisan as they say in my country. My great honor is to have emerged from the loins of the oppressed, I am the soul and nerves of the race, of those who have lived at the mercy of the shameless lackeys who have incubated the cause of high treason—for seventeen years now . . ."

"Do you want land reform?"

"There are not many big plantations in Nicaragua. What the country needs is cooperatives, so the farmers can get machines, good seeds, fertilizer, electricity, more schools, doctors. It would be so easy if the government and the army would quit stealing from them. This is a rich country."

Sandino leaned forward with a laugh. "You know, the first thieves on this planet were the priests, then the soldiers. I'm a Catholic, and I do not permit desecration of the churches. The Marines usually loot them. I've recovered many holy articles, which I have restored to where they belong—that gold chalice from the Ocotal altar for instance."

"But will Nicaragua be free if the Americans leave behind their own dictator and their armed National Guard?"

"Díaz will soon be out. Moncada is slated to succeed him. He, too, will have to go. Still, if he agrees to celebrate no more Shylock loans and gets back the national bank and the railroad, if he lets us breathe, we'll live with it. What we need is a real election, not with United States bayonets but a free election, with Latin American, not gringo supervision. I've written to most of the Latin American governments about it."

"You mentioned the proposed canal."

"Yes, I have ideas about that, too. This upsets the gringos more than anything else, for I demand that the Bryan-Chamorro Treaty be abrogated, that the canal be built by all the countries of the world, which wish to participate, but with predominantly Latin American capital. That was Bolívar's idea, which the United States destroyed, when it built the Panama Canal. As soon as the Marines go, we'll call a continental conference in Buenos Aires to arrange for building it. It will be the sort of canal that Bolívar wanted in 1826, one that will symbolize the cooperation and friendship of the peoples of the world. The Panama Canal was a chantage, the word "Panama" means "a big steal." It violated the laws of nations and the spirit of the continent. It is a raw red wound across the throat of America.

"Take the Bryan-Chamorro Treaty. It was obtained by force and fraud. United States bayonets surrounded the Chamber of Deputies to insure its adoption. It violated existing treaties and the rights of all the other countries of Central America. It has no real validity. Of course, Nicaragua was supposed to get $3,000,000—enough for each peasant to buy a few sardines and crackers. Better if the money had been used that way; the people would have had at least one decent meal. But Nicaragua never smelled one cent of that money, not one penny. It was kept in New York banks to pay off bankers and loan-merchants. The puppet government timidly asked for a few thousand dollars for several schools. They could not even get that much. Yes, we want a canal and the benefits it could bring, but we don't want another raw wound slashed across our bellies."

Sandino leaned forward intensely. Sometimes he emphasized his points with the edge of his hand on the table top, sometimes stood up and paced, or held that cocky pose, his thumbs in his belt, with an air of ease and confidence.

He had a knack for little homilies—things he told his men: "The bullet always seeks out the coward."

"Everyone dies sooner or later. All that is important is how one dies."

"Independence is not discussed, it is fought for arms in hand."

"We'd rather die for our rights than live on as slaves."

"I have in one hand the symbol of my country, in the other a rifle to defend it . . ."

"The Marines and the State Department men are the 'garbage men' of the tropics, but they make more garbage than they cart away."

I asked about lives and property.

"Every one of my officers is forbidden to abuse the peasants, but is empowered to impose forced loans on national and foreign capitalists. The only condition is that our officers prove that the sums are actually used only for the forces under their command."

He called in an aide and dictated messages to Admiral Sellers (who had had a surrender ultimatum dropped by plane), another to the United States Senate, and a third to the Pan American Congress about to meet in Havana. President Coolidge, Ambassador Dwight W. Morrow, and Secretary of State Hughes were being rushed there to try to stem the rising tide of Latin American antigringo sentiment. Nicaragua and all talk about intervention had been arbitrarily kept off the agenda. "The cat is covering up—the whole world sees the farce," said Sandino. "Who do they think they are fooling?"

His first communique read: "Mr. D. F. Sellers, Representative of American Imperialism in Nicaragua. The only way this struggle can be ended is by the immediate withdrawal of the invading forces from our territory." He demanded a nonpolitical provisional president and supervision of elections by Latin American representatives. He pledged once more to lay down his arms the day the Marines withdrew and never participate in any civil war or to accept any public office.

To the United States Senate, he protested against "continued barbarism . . . such as the recent total destruction of Quilalí," one of many towns, villages and settlements destroyed by air bombardment. The message to the Pan-American reunion was similar.

When I left San Rafael I told Sandino. "You have generously received me, a man of the same tribe you are fighting. I am going now through the American lines to Managua."

"You are free to go anywhere you wish—north, east, south or west."

"I shall be questioned. I do not wish to disclose anything that would injure your efforts."

"You are free to tell them about anything you have seen or heard, the size of my forces, the arms I have, the men and officers who are with me. No strings whatever. Go with God, and come back when we have a free Nicaragua."

He assigned Colonel Santos Rivera, a young defrocked Senator, to take me to the nearest town on the highway. Even as we rode off, he snapped out orders to mobilize his men. He was preparing to ride on into the coffee country, then swing northeast into the jungles again. Here in San Rafael del Norte was the first time the planes had spotted him since he had left Chipote more than a week before. The war was still on.

That afternoon the Colonel shot a fat iguana, which we ate that night at the peasant's house where we stayed. In the morning we rode through Darío, the birthplace of Nicaragua's great poet Darío, of whom I am sure no Marine had ever heard. In the small town beyond, the colonel left me at a store and rode out of town fast.

The store-keeper, a handsome man of fifty-odd, told me accusingly, "That colonel you were with is a Liberal."

"I'm riding around getting stories. He knows the country hereabouts."

"Well, he's one of the better ones," he conceded, "so we haven't bothered him. You're lucky not to have been grabbed by the bandits. I hear they've taken San Rafael del Norte. That's pretty close."

It was only a few hours ride on into Managua. The road was crowded with cars, every one jammed with well-dressed people frantically fleeing from Jinotega, which they feared would be captured by Sandino. Not until the following noon was I able to get a lift in the car of a young woman with her small children. She was hysterical with fear of the "bandits."

After several hours the road-check guards waved us on into Managua. I put up at the little Motel Lupone, brought clothes and cabled the *Nation* editor:

FIRST AND ONLY AMERICAN ONLY FOREIGN CORRE-
SPONDENT EVER SECURING INTERVIEW . . . ANNOUNCE-
MENT IN ORDER.

I borrowed the hotel keeper's typewriter. It soon broke down, and I
had to go out and buy a Royal portable. Two days later an angry army
intelligence officer barged in on me. "How'd you get into Nicaragua?"
he bellowed.

"None of your damned business."

"I have orders to take you to General Feland."

"I hope to see General Feland. If he wants to see me sooner, he can
come here."

He thought it over. "I've been told to warn you not to try to see
Sandino."

"You mean you will forcibly prevent me from getting the news?"

He backed off from that. "No, there's no objection, but you might
have trouble getting through the lines. Likely you'd get stopped at the
front. We wouldn't want you to get hurt. That guy Sandino doesn't
like us."

"Thanks for your concern. This much I can promise: If any time in
the future, I decide to see Sandino I'll let you know."

"*Me.*"

"Yes, in person."

He thawed. I gave him a cock-and-bull story of how I had entered
the country, and got rid of him.

Fearing further molestation I worked all night, finishing all ten
articles. I mailed one set to the magazine, another to my parents in
California, and deposited a third with a shopkeeper referred to me as
a trustworthy pro-Sandinista. I radioed the first one to New York.
Since all messages were monitored by the United States battleships off
shore, I kept the first articles to innocuous travel details. To be sure
that the significant part of my story got through, I had to get to
another country fast. Only in Costa Rica would I be free from molestation.

The intelligence officer returned to my hotel rather sheepishly. "So
you have already seen Sandino."

"Yes. If you hadn't tried to bully me, I might have told you the
truth."

He asked me a lot of questions, then said, "General Feland still
wants to see you. Now get it straight. You don't have to go."

"I'll be glad to see him."

The general received me lying on his spine. He was obviously feeling
the heat, seemingly almost indifferent about his task, and apparently
unconcerned about my having seen Sandino. He wanted me to see all
the bigwigs of the intervention, especially General McCoy, who was

busily working out an election law. It was like feeding a diabetic sugar.

At one point, with a slight show of animation, Feland said, "You don't need to quote me on this, but we can't do the job here with the five thousand men we have. That's not enough even to keep the roads, the railroad, and the towns guarded properly. Even fifty thousand could not do the job—only if by some such lucky chance Sandino were killed or betrayed. People don't realize what fighting guerrillas is like. They can hole up in those jungles for years. They are in their own country. People are loyal to him. They hate us." *

General McCoy sweated for many hours telling me his plans in detail for the elections and for setting up the National Guard. He believed in what he was doing, that a nonpartisan constabulary and technically honest elections—in which voters would be dyed with indelible ink, like chickens—would bring peace and prosperity to a war-torn bankrupt land.**

McCoy's neat election, it turned out, did not cure the patient. It was a lesson, not yet learned by Americans, that democracy cannot be imposed by outside force. Imposed "freedom" is always a bad joke, a platitude for politicians.

I also talked with Irving Lindbergh, United States High Commissioner who doubled as an Associated Press correspondent, and Clifford P. Ham, Collector of Customs (to see that the bankers got most of Nicaragua's revenues) who doubled as a United Press correspondent. Now I could understand better why the United States public was not getting *all* the news.†

* Years later, in Columbus, Ohio, where I was giving a talk at the Athletic Club, Feland looked me up. "I can't get to your lecture tonight, but I want to tell you what I could not tell you that day in Managua. We had no business being in Nicaragua at all. Before we sent in troops, no American lives or property were in any danger. After we came, many American lives were lost. It was just a miserable effort to get hold of Nicaraguan property, to satisfy the bankers and the politicians. I could not say so those days, and can't say so openly even now. I was a soldier obeying orders. But you were wholly right, and I admire you, as I did then." Feland was greater than the forces which moved him.
** The head of the constabulary imposed by the Marines, Anastasio Somoza, was a man with a police record in the United States. He hardly waited for the Marines to leave the country, before he bombarded the Palace and took over—the Somozas, father and sons, have ruled Nicaragua ever since—but with little respect for the freedom and democracy we said we were establishing.
† When I mentioned this later in reviewing a book by Karl Bickel (head of the United Press) in which he crowed that the American press was free and not subsidized like Reuters or Tass, Bickel asked me to lunch. He admitted that I had caught him where his hair was short.
Our agencies didn't need to be subsidized. They were then—and still are—little more than mouthpieces for the State Department. Bickel said it was either play ball or not provide *any* service. Recently he had published a statement by Senator Borah, head of the Foreign Relations Committee, about an unholy con-

The dreary Nicaraguan struggle went on for years. The Marines held most towns, which the guerrillas sometimes raided; the Sandinistas held the forest, the mountains, and the rivers nearly everywhere.

Besides telegraph lines, Sandino utilized century-old means of communication: smoke signals, mirror flashes, pedestrian mail-carriers, whistles and cries imitating birds and animals. The apparent natural grouping of rocks or the odd position of a tree became messages. The guerrillas knew how to lie in wait, patient as cats, rifles pointed at the prepared spring-back of a tree trunk or branches set to dig into a face, possibly gouge out eyes. The rifles rang out. They covered over spiked pitfalls with fallen leaves. They turned aside streams with trunks and stones to confuse men marching according to maps and lead them into ambush.

"He knew every inch of Segovia, his followers even better," wrote Alemán Bolaños.

> Every tree, every thicket, every rock was a possible hiding place for a rifleman or a patriot spy. The invaders knew it and traveled only on known roads or in open fields, pistols or rifles ready to fire . . . Even so they were uneasy, for at any moment, without warning a fusilade came from different points . . . and when the North Americans reacted and counter-attacked, the tracks disappeared into the jungle where it was even more dangerous. After firing and killing their usual "tenths" of the gringos, they [the Sandinistas] retired in good order as silently as they had come." Sandino did not have great supplies or many weapons; it would have slowed his men up. "The small band is slippery, difficult to locate; it dissolves toward distant predetermined points.

At Havana, President Coolidge, Ambassador Morrow and other high dignitaries strove unsuccessfully to frustrate the mounting tide of antagonism to our aggression. Presently a continent-wide boycott of American goods began to hurt. A combination of depression and international opprobrium caused President Hoover to order the withdrawal of Marines from Nicaragua, Haiti, and the Dominican Republic. Presi-

---

cession in Colombia. The United States bank involved was furious, and in order not to have the United Press kicked out of Colombia, Bickel had had to permit all news sent to Latin American papers to be pre-censored by the bank.

My first article was published February 22, 1928 in the *Nation* and the *Herald Tribune*. The series was also printed by other large dailies and by leading journals of Europe, including *El Sol*, the most venerable daily in Madrid; in the U.S.S.R.; in all Latin-America—except Nicaragua, though in due time they appeared there, too. Newspapers on five continents printed them, also small rural periodicals and most weekly and monthly magazines. In the Orient, they were published everywhere. They were translated into Chinese, Japanese, German, French, Arabic, Polish, Italian, Slavic, etc.

dent Franklin Delano Roosevelt carried this out, getting praise for his
"good-neighbor policy."

Meanwhile in Managua, even the hand-picked Congress gagged at
adopting the McCoy election law and national guard law that set
aside the constitution. Adolfo Díaz had to put it into effect illegally
by decree. With a North American heading the electoral inspectors in
each booth and surrounded by armed guards, "treacherous" Moncada
was duly inducted into office.

After similar elections four years later Sacasa, who had been a good
boy after being kicked out of Puerto Cabezas, was put into the presidency. That was January 1, 1933. The next day the last Marine embarked. The long nightmare—so it seemed—was over.

Time correspondent, the Canadian William Krehm wrote in his book
on Central America,

> For seven years, practically without any aid whatever, fight-
> ing with rifles captured from the enemy and hand grenades
> made from sardine tins filled with stones, Sandino with-
> stood the airplanes and modern equipment of North Amer-
> ican Marines and the National Guard . . . His most bitter
> enemies have paid tribute to his fantastically well-organized
> espionage, a sure sign that he enjoyed the sympathies of
> the population . . . Some long-time American residents
> . . . were sure that the Marines were never anxious to wipe
> out Sandino; he provided too good a pretext to utilize his
> country as a [military] training ground." *

The Marines folded their tents; they departed. At once Sandino
offered to lay down his arms. Meetings were arranged by Solforino
Salvatierra, Sacasa's Minister of Agriculture, and Sandino went to
Managua. Agreement was quickly reached—not particularly in
Sandino's favor. He was to retain a permanent guard of one hundred
men and was granted virgin lands for his men along the Coco River.
Sacasa balked on setting up a new department and side-stepped
Sandino's suggestion that an international conference be called in
Buenos Aires to build a canal by all nations. (Later, he reneged on his
promise to Sandino to make no further financial deals with the United
States.)

There on the Coco River jungles, the Sandinistas cleared the jungle,
built houses, planted crops and started industries. But before long,
provocative raids were made by the National Guard, headed by our
man, General Anastasio Somoza. Sandino protested and told his followers he preferred to leave Nicaragua rather than engage in more
civil strife. But Sacasa, by then fearing Somoza and the National

* Retranslated from the Spanish edition.

Guard, wished a counterforce and pled with Sandino not to leave the country.

A year later Sandino, who had a number of development projects in mind, was invited to the capital as the guest of the President. He and his brother Socrates, among others in his entourage, were provided hospitality in Minister Salvatierra's home. But after dining at the National Palace, he, his two aides, and his father Gregoria, were stopped near the Guard barracks while riding in Salvatierra's automobile and taken inside.

Their captors had already consulted with Somoza. Fresh from the United States Embassy, he told them that the Ambassador had informed him "Sandino should be eliminated." This may have been a lie, but it caused acid comments throughout Latin America.

Sandino and his aides were taken to the airport and murdered. Other National Guardsmen machine-gunned Salvatierra's home, killing Socrates Sandino and a small boy. All the bodies were thrown into an unknown grave.

Shortly after, United States Ambassador Lane appeared at the barracks and took Salvatierra and Gregorio Sandino under his protection.

The names of all the assassins were well-known and were given, shortly after by Gregorio, who fled to Salvador for his life. Gleefully, the killers displayed their trophies of death—the gold teeth, the hair, clothes, and trinkets from the victims' bodies. No effort was ever made to punish them. Somoza toured the country making speeches, lauding himself for the elimination of the "bandit."

Ere long he turned his guns on the National Palace and drove Sacasa out. He installed a provisional president just long enough to have himself awarded the Cross of Valor, the Medal of Distinction, and the Presidential Medal of Merit, then took over the presidency in person. For twenty-five years thereafter, he maintained one of the most brutal and thieving dictatorships in the history of the Americas. He was lauded by American Ambassadors, Congressmen, Presidents, correspondents, and businessmen and was aided bountifully by the United States government. He turned the country into a personal plantation, a prison, and a cemetery.

Several decades later, Somoza was gunned down when visiting Panama. President Eisenhower had tears in his eyes as he spoke praise for the dictator and angry words for the killers and sent down a personal physician to try to save the ruffian's life.

The country thereafter remained in the hands of his two sons; Tacho, head of the National Guard; and Luís, who became President. Luís' first act was to stage a fake trial of Conservatives and newsmen accused of conspiracy in his father's assassination. To arouse patriotism and be more sure of the outcome of elections, he seized part of

Honduras' territory, long ago awarded her by an international arbitration commission. So ended the decades of Marine training in democracy—an experiment long ago destroyed by its chief pupil. It is still Somoza-land.

But if Sandino failed to bring the freedom to his people which he hoped would result, the world-wide condemnation of American military invasion influenced the withdrawal of Marines and custom collectors from Nicaragua, Haiti, Salvador, and the Dominican Republic. The resultant Good Neighbor policy insured the cooperation of nearly all Latin America during World War II. The Latin American people made tremendous sacrifices, sending raw materials at prewar prices, providing military bases and other help despite fantastic inflation that brought misery to millions. Had it not been for our more liberalized policy in the Western Hemisphere which grew out of Sandino's resistance, we could not have embarked on the war against Nazism with clean hands.

Sandino's resistance was instrumental in bringing about an outlawing of unilateral armed intervention in the Western Hemisphere. More liberal treaties with Panama and other countries were celebrated, and the one of the most enlightened international systems in the history of man was created—on paper.

If that system was later violated in spirit and in fact many times by the United States and some other New World countries, it still set a pattern of international conduct and law superior to that in much of the world. Sandino's resistance led to a new awareness of the rights of colonial peoples everywhere. We learned all about freedom fighters in Nicaragua long before Hungary and Vietnam and Alabama. Sandino, a great and noble guerrilla, was one of the architects of a free world and a genuine hero of the Americas.

6

ABDEL KRIM AND THE RIF

The battle of Anual in northern Africa in July 1921 was the most disastrous colonial defeat ever suffered by a European country prior to the French surrender at Dien Bien Phu. It was inflicted on Spanish troops by young Abdel Krim, in many ways the most remarkable of modern guerrillas. Nineteen thousand Spanish soldiers were annihilated in the Rif in three days of running battle by several thousand tribesmen. Their unburied mangled bodies were piled high in the army posts and along the trails. Sixteen thousand perished; three thousand panic-stricken soldiers finally managed to reach the Spanish port of Melilla or struggled into French Morocco to the south. General Silvestre (who threw himself on his own sword) and all his staff died at Anual.

"He was a brave soldier," said Abdel Krim, "but he had no political sense at all." It was an over-generous statement.

Silvestre had pushed outposts into nondefensible places, with little control over communications. Water had to be transported to them every day. Food was scant, medical care almost nonexistent. His men were ragged and hungry. There was little morale.

General Navarro tried to make a last-ditch stand but he, his officers, and all his men had to surrender, and he was chained to a sergeant in a dungeon. In all only 570 prisoners were taken, of which only 274 were still alive when ransomed eighteen months later for 4,000,000 pesetas. Spanish officers led one fleeing contingent (of which three-fourths had been killed or had died of hunger and wounds) into the French Zone, where they abandoned their units and began carousing with the whores in Taza. Every Spanish garrison in the Rif was wiped out. In one swift blow, the Rif joined the ranks of free republics.

Spain itself was filled with dismay, fear, recriminations. The government fell. Postmortem investigations revealed the horrible plight of the Spanish soldiers who were ragged, hungry, sick, and unable to fight; the ineptitude of arrogant officers; the incredible graft and corruption. Partly to suppress these findings (which threatened to implicate the King himself) and to stave off revolution, the armed coup of General Primo de Rivera, subsidized by Catalán industrialists, occurred two years after Anual. Spain became a totalitarian dictatorship —in fact and in name. It still is.

Abdel Krim could have pushed a baby go-cart into Melilla. There is no explanation of why he pulled back to the boundaries of the Rif. Later he admitted ruefully in his *Memoirs*: "That was the greatest blunder of my career."

At the time of his stupendous victory, Abdel Krim was thirty-three, the wealthiest man in the Rif and the best educated. His father had been Caid or headman of the Beni Uriaghel tribe, the most important of the jealous quarreling groups of the Rif. The Caid had started to organize his people for revolt against the Spanish advance into the area only the previous year. He died suddenly, and young Mohammed [Mohand] Abdel Krim stepped into his shoes. By his side was his younger brother, Mahammed Abdel Krim, a Madrid-educated engineer.

The ancestors of the Abdel Krim family had emigrated to Morocco from Yambo near Uedjaz on the Red Sea in the third century of the Hegira (i.e. about 900). The family entrenched itself in Ajdir on the lovely and strategic Mediterranean Bay of Alhucemas, midway between Melilla and Tetuán, the capital of the Spanish zone. Thus the Abdel Krims had been Moroccans and, above all, Rifs for a thousand years. "It is our country," Mohand said simply.

For most of those thousand years the high rugged mountain world of the Rif had been sealed off from the outside, except for trade through Ajdir and the mountain passes. The Sultans of Fez had been content with token allegiance. The French had never tried to invade the Rif. The Spaniards edged into the shore country west of Melilla and won over interior Caids. A little while before Anual, General Silvestre sent Madrid a glowing account of the ease and success of his advances. But after the disaster, it was evident that it would take years, bloodshed, and money to subjugate the Rif. But the stakes were big: rich mining concessions and glory.

The cold rugged mountains and desert wastes were good country for resistance. There were some forests, some olive groves, almonds, grapes, but little grain. The tribesmen raised many goats and donkeys. Food was not abundant.

Si Mohammed Abdel Krim, "Mohand," born in 1888, was sent to the famous University of Fez, then studied in Melilla. A brilliant student with an attractive personality, he secured good employment in the Bureau of Native Affairs and edited the Arabic section of the newspaper *El Telegrama del Rif*.

His wealthy father, Abdel Krim el-Khatabi, was engaged in extensive trade and business enterprises. Aware of the Rif's untouched iron, manganese, copper, zinc, and lead deposits, he sent his younger son, Mahammed, to Madrid to study mining. The British, French, Germans, and Italians secured small concessions. A pack of German agents smelling around for mineral riches found a valuable ally in the elder Abdel Krim.

By agreement with England, the French won a free hand in Morocco as a reward for getting out of Egypt. Germany did not accept this high-handed carving up of North Africa, but was mollified with territorial rights in West Africa. The northern zone of Morocco was handed over to Spain. In 1912, the boundaries of the two zones were tentatively traced across desert, rivers, and mountains with little regard for native tribal boundaries or geographical sense—the sort of boundaries always being drawn by diplomats in far off places and nearly always eventually ending in war (as in Poland, Czechoslovakia, Greece, India, Korea, and Vietnam). But the cession soothed Spain's pride, badly wounded by the loss of Cuba, Puerto Rico, and the Philippines—at least it soothed the generals and colonial bureaucrats, deprived of their authority by the loss of the empire.

The newer, more progressive Spanish generation looked upon this belated African adventure with dismay. This meant not modernization of Spain, but the Africanization of their own feudal country.

Spain, unable to provide the necessary capital, initiative, or technology to develop Morocco, favored German entrepreneurs, then and all during the World War. The Germans began arming the interior Moroccan tribes and incited them to raid into the French Zone. More than once the Fez-Algiers line was cut. Agents were given gold to propagandize the tribes as far south as the Atlas. Spanish officials and tribal Caids profited enormously, and Abdel Krim père became a millionaire.

After the defeat of the Reich, the German-armed tribes threatened Spanish rule itself. As Spain turned to the British and French victors, Abdel Krim's relations with Madrid cooled. When Spain began garrisoning the Rif, he secretly helped organize and equip a group of well-armed irregulars.

Already in western Morocco, the great Caid of the Jibalás, Raisuli (who had at first flirted with the Germans and taken their money without helping them much) had broken with the Spaniards. Originally he had been the ally of the Spaniards when they landed on southwest Laraiche in 1911. But when they began advancing north to Arzeila, where he had built a handsome palace over the sea, he rallied the Jibalá to resist. The infidels entered the city, imprisoned him briefly and confiscated his properties. After World War I, he began ambushing Spanish convoys and troops. He battered them badly in several serious clashes. His sway extended from Tangier to the southern border.

From bad prison treatment and lavish living, he suffered from serious ailments. He had to spend a good deal of time on his back with his feet and legs hoisted in a sling to relieve excruciating pain.

His curses at such times were singularly ferocious. He was a huge
bearded man with small devilish eyes, and his great bellylaugh rumbled
when he heard of punishment meted out to any Spaniards unfortunate
enough to fall into his hands.

The Spaniards, fearing that trouble with Raisuli and the Jibalá
might be duplicated in the east, arrested Mohand in Melilla. This was
an insult not easily swallowed by a proud man like Abdel Krim père
or, for that matter, by his son. Mohand escaped, and he and his younger
brother Mahammed joined their father in organizing the military
strength of the Beni Uriaghel.

By then the Spaniards had pushed far into the Rif, setting up 130
military posts and bribing tribal chiefs. They advanced into all of Beni
Said, and soon into the rich Temsamán plain next door to Ajdir.
Clearly their goal was much-coveted Alhucemas Bay.

After Mohand Abdel Krim stepped into his father's shoes as Caid,
the first hint to the Spaniards of trouble was an attack on the Abarán
outpost overlooking the Agermus Valley on May 30, 1921. The native
"police" killed their officers. On July 18, the Igerribén outpost was
attacked. The garrison escaped in headlong flight, with considerable
loss of life.

General Silvestre hurried to Anual, the main strong point. Other
posts fell, and before he could move, an avalanche swept over every
Spanish garrison in the Rif. The villagers poured down out of the
mountains. Those unarmed snatched up rifles discarded by the fleeing
Spaniards. Whole garrisons were massacred. Two thousand, six hundred dead were piled up in Monte Arruit alone. Everywhere panic
sent the Spanish soldiers scurrying in sobbing fear across the hot,
barren ravines. In four days the Spanish lost the Rif.

The name of Abdel Krim flashed around the world. The news of his
great victory swept through a horrified Spain, through an exultant Rif,
through all Morocco.

Overnight the Rif Republic was formed: a government with customary cabinet ministers was set up. Mohand's lean bespectacled
brother, who had unusual military talents, was made Minister of Defense and was sent to Paris and London to negotiate for recognition.
Adhesion was demanded of all the Rifian Caids. Only three heads of
strong tribes, long at odds with the Beni Uriaghel, refused to join up.
Mohand Abdel Krim quickly seized and executed them. His political
and strategic acumen was as great as his military talents. He knew his
people well, he was an indefatigable organizer, and his diplomatic
talents were superb.

Though a calm, thoughtful character, when aroused he became a
bundle of fury. Though heavy set, he was a magnificent, agile horseman. His typical Berber moustache and fringe beard—which made his
broad face seem even broader—gave his countenance a ponderous,

implacable quality, though he always wore his turban at a jaunty angle. His brother often wore European dress; Mohand Adbel Krim never did.

Ironically, the Spanish government sent aged General Valeriano Weyler (the "butcher of Cuba" who had helped lose that island) to report on events in Melilla. He pulled no punches. Several ministers resigned and disclosed the inefficiency and graft, the misery of the Spanish soldiers. "We buy barley at double the market price . . . The hospitals are pitiful, everything is hopeless!"

Public temper grew ugly. Morocco was "the grave of Spanish youth." It was "the bottomless pit where Spanish wealth disappeared." The colossal theft of money and supplies and the selling of munitions to the enemy apparently involved the royal palace itself. Talk of revolution threaded every café *tertulia*. Market women openly jeered and spat at the gray-and-red Civil Guard. Premier Eduardo Dato was assassinated. Generals Berenguer and Cavalcanti were put on trial.

The top brass and the cliques around the King could not tolerate the scandalous trial of high-ranking generals. Spain was ruled by the Army, the Church hierarchy, and the corrupt bureaucracy. A military coup was staged in Barcelona September 13, 1923 by General Primo de Rivera, in connivance with Catalán industrialists and the King. The Cortes ceased to function. Spain's rachitic institutions of representative democracy were wiped out.

The crisis deepened. Abdel Krim was getting hold of more and more arms to supplement his vast arsenal captured at Anual. They were bought openly in Tangiers; they were landed everywhere along the coast. In May 1924 he began attacking Spanish positions and supply trains between Tetuán and the Holy City of Sheshuán, fifty miles to the south.

Xauén, known in English as Sheshuán, the center of the Akhama tribesmen, was largely autonomous. It was a Holy City, nominally under the Sultan and the Moslem church. Before the Spanish had seized it in 1920, only three "infidels" had ever trod its sacred soil, and one of these was poisoned.

It is a charming place with red-tiled roofs and tilted, winding streets, set in a spur of the almost barren Jibel Mezzet mountains. Hardly Moorish-looking at all, it resembles towns in arid north Mexico. On one side great precipices rear up, but on the other side, over a hill where I spent many agreeable hours, are a stream, a small lake, and a stretch of irrigated fields and fruit trees—an oasis in an almost sterile region. Yet in winter, the town is high enough to be laced with snow.

Mostly, though, it is balmy, massed with flowers nearly all year— geraniums, roses, bougainvillea. The air buzzes with bees, and in the open-air cafés, where people sit on mats or ottomans, tea had to be served with wire coverings to keep the insects out. The society of the town is polygamous, for the rich people had enormous harems. Various pleasant geisha-type cafés exist. The muezzin calls came from the minarets. Long robes kneeled on prayer rugs. Spanish bugles rang from the barracks. A tepid beer could be obtained at a small Spanish shop with a garden-trellis over the entrance, the only place any alcoholic beverage was purchasable. A very plump girl in bright red rocked at a doorway and batted her big black eyes. A Berber-boy, sweeping the dirt floor of the little Spanish inn, raised a cloud of dust. Only yesterday this city had been a place of death, flowing with blood. Already it had slipped back into its ancient, easy-going life.

The Spanish foothold in Sheshuán, won with considerable loss of life, was precarious whenever Rif guerrillas came over the mountains. The fifty miles or so between it and Tetuán, over a scarcely defined road twisting among bald, ochre hills, was rough, treeless country without water where Abdel Krim and Raisuli guerrillas could ride in and out—or, if necessary, take refuge in the high peaks of the Beni Said and Beni Hassan country. All about were hostile anti-Spanish Akhama and Jibalá, also the Beni Idir, Beni Aros, and Beni Gorfet tribes. To the north the Beni Lait, astride the road, were magnificent raiders. The community was cut off repeatedly. Many Spanish supply convoys were captured. The 135-mile route from Laraiche on the coast running through little known Jibalá country controlled by Raisuli was even more difficult and unprotected.

By 1923, Abdel Krim forces converged on both Sheshuán and Tetuán to the north and even harrassed the area about Tangier. Briefly the rainy season held up Krim's drive, but it was resumed in February, 1924 with additional *harka* or tribal warriors from the powerful Ghomara, east of Sheshuán. They kept the holy city under constant assault.

By May, Wad Lau outposts on the northwest coast, a major Spanish holding, were put under siege. Tangier was surrounded, and Tetuán was bombarded with artillery fire. From the air the Spaniards dropped six hundred bombs on villages around Tetuán, killing mostly women and children for the men were at the front. This resulted in the torture and murder of every Spanish prisoner who fell into Abdel Krim's hands. Primo de Rivera rushed over and even visited Sheshuán.

Spanish troops attempting to relieve Wad Lau were routed and slaughtered. By August there was a general uprising of all the tribes, and native units of the Spanish army began deserting en masse. Three Spanish columns had to retreat. Even Laraiche on the west coast was menaced. A garrison on the Tangier-Tetuán road was attacked, and more convoys were captured.

The almost isolated garrison in Sheshuán was in bad straits. Nearly all the 90,000 Spanish troops were pinned down in Tetuán, and rains and fever incapacitated at least half of them. Primo de Rivera hurried back to Spain to round up six thousand more men for the battlefront.

The manpower and financial strain on Spain began to tell. The raw troops sent over did not even know how to fire a rifle. The enemy was mobile, and determined, and the roads to Sheshuán and Wad Lau remained firmly in Krim's hands. Telegraph lines were cut. Bullets whined through the Tetuán streets. The hospitals were full and over-flowing. Many wounded had to be taken to Ceuta.

Troops under General Riquelme were cut off at Sok-el-Kriba, half way to Sheshuán. General Quiepo's relief column managed to get a few survivors back north to Dar ben Karich, just outside Tetuán. All posts in the Sheshuán area had to be abandoned. On September 8, warships managed to evacuate twenty-nine officers, seven hundred forty men and six pieces of artillery from Wad Lau.

Primo de Rivera announced withdrawal to a new holding line—a small strip from Tetuán to the coast along the northern slope of the mountains to the Fondak of Ain-Jedida (this was by an arrangement made with Raisuli) and a narrow strip along the Atlantic coast as far as the French zone.

Forty thousand troops in three columns were assembled to cut through and bring out the Sheshuán garrison and outpost troops. They had orders to burn all native villages, kill all cattle, destroy all crops, and plunder all supplies. A fourth force was held in reserve at Dar ben Karich.

The eastern column was soon driven down into the road. Badly mauled, the joint force finally reached Sok-el-Arba. Rear forces were being attacked everywhere as far north as Dar ben Karich. Fighting every foot, the main force finally entered Sheshuán on September 30. The sick and wounded were piled up. The heavy rainy season would soon begin, and escape from Sheshuán would then be almost im-possible. The Spaniards hurried to send the wounded north, but on October 1, forty trucks were destroyed. Troops trying to keep the road open suffered repeated attacks.

Even to the west, Abdel Krim scored victories over strong forces. Every post in the Jibalá mountain area—180 in all—had to be abandoned. Numerous garrisons were rescued by the payment of large sums. East of Tetuán also, all was lost. By November 15 there was not a Spanish soldier left between Tetuán and Ajdir.

Sheshuán was wholly evacuated by November 17. The wet and miserable Spanish force reached Dar Akoba the next day and pushed on with the sick and wounded through a sea of mud, fording streams flooded to their high banks toward Sok-el-Arba. The rear guard was wiped out in a narrow defile. Two generals were badly wounded, and one thousand casualties were reported. The whole force turned into a broken rabble with all morale gone. Hundreds of stragglers were killed; the entire valley was strewn with dead. The advance guard managed to escape from Sok-el-Arba and reach Dar ben Karich in pounding rain, but the main body in Sok-el-Arba was surrounded, apparently doomed.

Planes bombed the hills on either side, but Rif reinforcements and the Beni Said *harka* were coming in from the Beni Idir. Jibalá were coming up from the Oued Ras. The defenders, little more than refugees, fought free after numerous hand-to-hand battles with clubs, guns, and bayonets, and finally reached Tetuán.

Primo de Rivera greeted the bedraggled, beaten soldiers with customary double-talk. "You enter Tetuán in triumph through a long valley, the hills on both sides . . . held by the enemy . . . A new trail of blood marks the track of civilization . . . [sic]. There is still much work to be done to dominate the fires of rebellion lit behind our lines . . . The punishment will be quick and severe."

The defeat was almost as terrible as that of Anual. Nearly as many soldiers had lost their lives. Primo was appalled by the sort of material he had to use for soldiers. They had to be taught everything, how to mount guard, perform the simplest duties, even how to march and patrol—things the Rifs knew years ago and always. "Incredible!" he exclaimed, that Spaniards had not learned these simple lessons in their prolonged, unhappy experience.

Primo de Rivera finally established his holding lines fairly well and went back to Spain. He entered Madrid with a barrage of fine phrases about victory, under triumphal arches. He had brought peace to Morocco, he proclaimed. But even the little corner Spain still held was far from secure.

Abdel Krim rapidly extended his control over the Jibalá region. Except for a corner, he was in possession of all Spanish Morocco. But the unpredictable Raisuli was still helping the Spaniards. Krim sent an ultimatum to his headquarters in Tazrut to fight the Spaniards "as a Moslem should," or surrender.

Though unable to stand on his feet because of dropsy, the wily old leader fought Abdel Krim's attacking forces from his home, then took sanctuary in the adjoining mausoleum of his ancestors. He offered to surrender. If his life were spared, henceforth he would obey all Abdel Krim's orders.

He was carried prisoner across the mountains in a huge litter born by half a dozen tribesmen. He suffered greatly. His body was swollen and covered with open sores. On the Ghomara coast he was transferred to a motorboat. At Ajdir he was scarcely able to greet Abdel Krim, who looked down at the bloated figure with a certain compassion. "Such is the end of the great," Abdel Krim said, turning away. Raisuli died early in April, 1925.

Trouble for Abdel Krim struck next from the French zone. There, by the time World War I broke out in 1914 after seven years of bloody resistance, Marshal Lyautey had strengthened French controls sufficiently to be able to send native troops to Europe and partly check German infiltration into Morocco. After the war, France was occupied with putting down resistance in the middle Atlas in the south and below Taza in the northeast. Lyautey did not attempt to occupy the unexplored areas near the northern border line, which remained a vague trace cutting through tribes and territory. But by 1923, the French reached the Wergha River valley.

On the fertile north side, Abdel Krim maintained nominal control. He collected taxes in money and kind and levied man-power and food for his guerrilla fight. The rich black soil there was among the finest in all Morocco; the bountiful grain harvests were shipped north to the Rif to feed his army.

This was cut off in 1924 when the French crossed the river and fortified the parallel hills north and west as far as the foot of the rocky, wooded seven thousand foot Tazrut range.

Southern caravans to the north had long since learned of Abdel Krim's overwhelming successes. They had enjoyed the spectacle of white prisoners, hungry and ragged, toiling on the roads, a humiliation that exalted the supremacy and glory of Allah and Abdel Krim. The invaded tribes now looked to him for help. He sent strong protests to the French government. The French curtly reminded him that the disputed area was in the French zone. They kept digging in on the south slope of the high Tazrut range and threw out a strong outpost network about their main fortification, two thousand feet up at Tanaut, from which could be seen vast stretches of country as far as the snows of the southern Atlas.

Abdel Krim had little reason to have faith in European good intentions.

He answered sharply he had not been a party to the French-Spanish border treaty of 1912, and whatever arrangement made about territory never under their control where they had no subjects and no morale or material interests, was "an arrogant improvisation." Europeans, he said, talked of law and order as justification for any and everything. Over most of Morocco, he had established law and order superior to what the Spanish or French were able to maintain, and he should receive thanks, not hostility. By crossing the Wergha, the French had introduced anarchy into a region he had thoroughly pacified. French protestations of unselfish intentions were belly-wash.

Both sides strengthened their forces. On April 13, 1925, Abdel Krim moved thirty-five hundred experienced guerrillas against the pro-French Derkawi sherif at Amjat. Simultaneously numbers of tribes on the French side rebelled. Amjat was seized and burned. The Rifs and

Jibalá moved up to the French lines on the Wergha, easily overrunning all outposts. Soon rebel groups were operating within twenty miles of Fez.

The French rushed in four battalions from Algeria. Altogether they had eighteen battalions, six cavalry squads ,and heavy artillery units. But they faced four thousand Rifs in the front lines and four thousand in reserve. Rif warriors appeared everywhere, exciting tribe after tribe to rebellion, providing them with Rif irregulars, arms, and artillery. They burned the villages and crops of those who refused to join up. Propaganda by letters, printed matter, word of mouth was distributed. Abdel Krim had agents penetrated everywhere.

The French had believed their defenses invulnerable, but they crumpled like paper. Their forces flew about trying to relieve outposts or withdraw them. As a result Abdel Krim captured more convoys of food and arms than ever got through. The French were beaten at all points. As is customary, they suppressed all news of the disasters.

Political discord at home increased. Widespread anti-imperialist movements got under way. Matters in France itself were serious—financial troubles, a falling franc, the grim problem of Syria. Loud wrangles went on in Parliament. Sentimental Socialist Foreign Minister A. Briand was solemnly telling the Chamber that his government was "passionately in favor of peace"—the usual official double-talk. Some deputies even urged the Rifs to fight on and expressed hopes for French defeat. They demanded immediate withdrawal. But imperialists are historical illiterates, and for now, funds and blood continued to pour out blindly to try to prevent what time would bring about anyway.

The French did manage to reclaim some posts, such as Bibán the Fez-Algerian highway and a few others south of the Wergha, but only by fierce bayonet and knife fighting and the loss of many lives. Bodies piled up in all the French outposts hit by heavy artillery.

By June the Rifs were operating far below the Wergha, and Taza on the Fez-Algerian line was endangered. All women and children had to be evacuated. In the center too, the Rif continued to advance. Sidi Mahammed Abdel Krim, Rif Commander in Chief, moved to the front with well-trained, well-armed reinforcements. All villages loyal to the French were burned and the people shot. Convoys on the Fez-Algiers road were ambushed. The Rifs advanced to try to join forces with the Atlas Berber rebels. Everywhere armed Rif guerrillas were filtering through the French lines, pushing tribe after tribe into revolt. These mobile columns were breaking up the whole French rear. Abdel Krim had boasted he would be in Fez to celebrate the great Eid-el-Kebir (Abraham and Isaac) feast day of July 2nd. The faithful feared to make their usual pilgrimage.

To reassure the people, the Sultan arrived for the fiesta at the in-sistance of the French. But Abdel Krim had acquired such fame as a miracle worker, he was momentarily expected to appear. The Sultan talked bravely about the blessings of peace and ordered more levies on the tribes for troops and money. Then the powerful Tsul and Branes tribes revolted.

The French had won no decisive victory. Whenever the Rif were driven out at one point, they reappeared almost immediately there or elsewhere. The sixty thousand French troops on the scene were inadequate; a large percentage were sick. More troops and another experienced general were rushed in, but more outposts near Wazzán were lost.

The news of French defeats filtered back to Paris. Opposition became worse. Not until July 15 did the government issue its first fairly frank communiqué. The Rif were closer to Fez than ever, Berber revolt was increasing, the enemy mobility made the front like water. More reinforcements had to be sent quickly.

The Rif cut communications between the garrison at Ain Aichá and Fez, and more strong posts fell. French casualties were alarming. Marshal Pétain rushed over from France to inspect the front.

"The brutal fact is," he reported honestly (which is unusual for generals) the French were being "attacked unexpectedly by the most powerful and best armed enemy we have ever met in our colonial campaigns." The Rif fighters required so little they had no need for the French-type convoys, "which so hamper our columns." Even so, the Rif forces were abundantly supplied with machine-guns, common and ammunition. However, Lyautey had stemmed "the onrush of the barbarians [sic]," and Abdel Krim failed to reach Fez. Lyautey's efforts had won "the admiration of the entire world [sic]." From now on public opinion should be kept "properly informed."

But the French were driven out of more posts. French farms were pillaged and burned, and French forces, tanks, and armored cars had to be rushed to save Wazzán itself. Gradually they drove Rif besiegers from surrounding heights.

The Tangier-Fez road was again cut, and the Rif tore up the rail line between Fez and Taza. The Ain-bu-Aissa post could be succored only by air. By the end of July it was destroyed; only fifteen defenders managed to reach Teruel, itself beleaguered. The French managed to provide besieged Tafrant with food. Authority was restored in Tsul where a French column had been isolated for two weeks. Many French soldiers were prostrated by the heat.

Abdel Krim was continually visited by European newsmen. His words were printed far and wide, and foreign sympathy grew everywhere for a people fighting against great odds to maintain its independence. Large political followings were aroused in England and France.

Abdel Krim was constantly growing stronger, capturing adequate supplies or getting them through Tangiers where the Rifs openly bought ammunition, some of it from Spanish soldiers, officers, and speculators. He was sweeping all before him.

In September, Pétain launched a tremendous artillery barrage all along the Wergha Valley front. (Big noise and wasted ammunition always delight generals.) However, Bibán was reoccupied on September 15. The eight and a half months' fight thus far had required 150,000 troops and had cost 11,419 French casualties.

A serious blow to the Rifs was struck far in the rear. The previous January the Spaniards had retaken Alcazar-Sorier across from Gibraltar by putting six thousand men ashore in lighters. After consulting the French, Primo de Rivera decided to strike at Ajdir by sea. It required half a year of preparations. The experiences of the World War attack on Gallipoli were carefully studied and some of the matériel used in that unlucky incursion was acquired. Landing troops were given special training in Ceuta, Tetuán, and Melilla. On September 1, Primo de Rivera visted his officers in Tetuán and six days later, before boarding the Warship *Alfonso XIII*, he issued a proclamation: "We can be proud of being a superior race, of constituting a strong people and of belonging to an organized well-governed nation, [sic]."

Abdel Krim caused a diversion by attacking near Tetuán and Melilla. Landing operations by many Melilla soldiers had to be abandoned. Two Foreign Legion battalions of the assembled landing force had to be rushed to prevent Rif assault on Tetuán. The Legionaries proudly returned to Tetuán displaying trophies of war: heads, hands, ears, and legs.

The flotilla for taking Alhucemas numbered one hundred vessels, but many were decrepit and dangerous, some were merely small launches. A feint was staged at Wad Lau with full-fledged bombardment and landings. When the maneuver was given up, the Rif spread word of a major Spanish defeat. The flotilla moved on to Cebadilla, just west of Alhucemas Bay, but owing to strong currents and bad timing, a surprise landing had to be postponed. Instead, the whole bay shore was bombarded.

A landing was finally made. But the water at Cebadilla was too shallow for the lighters to reach shore, and the soldiers had to wade in a long way up to their chests. The Rifs had never imagined that any sane invader would pick such a silly point. Three Rif guns on surrendering heights, inadequately defended, were captured.

A second landing could not be attempted until ten days later, and then a strong east wind almost wrecked the enterprise. In the end about twenty thousand men were put ashore, but few supplies could be landed.

The Rif shifted to the heights around Cebadilla. Spanish air cover hit

them during the day, but at night the Rif bombardment of the cluttered
Spanish force was intense. They were barely able to drive off two
fierce Rif attacks. The Spanish forces, hungry, mouths swollen from
lack of water, clung to the cliffs like flies where they were picked off
by Rif guns.

On September 12, Primo de Rivera appeared in person. A few mules
and horses and some water were landed, and an advance was made
with Moroccan mercenaries. They were met by a withering fire from
rock-entrenched Rif troops and fled with great loss of life. The whole
Spanish expedition was thrown into panic. If anything was to be
saved, a full-scale assault had to be made at once.

The following day, a desperate three-pronged attack was launched
—actually a slow cautious crawl under deadly fire, with much hand-to-
hand fighting. Many attackers were blown to bits by land mines. As
the Spaniards reeled back, the Foreign Legion (the only competent
fighters in the Spanish force) aided by a powerful bombardment from
the warships, saved the day. They reached the top of Mount Malmusi
where they found only one wounded Rifian whom they stabbed to
death. They clung there in a continuous rainstorm, making no further
advance until the end of the month.

They finally advanced to Ajdir, the capital, and found it and all surrounding villages abandoned. They were angry that there was little
left to loot. But, it was a serious blow to Abdel Krim.

In July 1923 he had replied haughtily to a Spanish demand for
surrender that the Rif would defend its independence against tyranny
by every means within its power. "Imagine your own feelings if your
homes were in the hands of foreigners, intent on possessing your
property. The Rif and all its people are ready to die, and believe me,
they will die in the cause of truth to the last man. They will defend
their homes until the end."

Early in 1925, the French and Spanish, by then in bad shape, drew
up new peace terms, insolently informing Abdel Krim they could be
obtained in Tetuán or Melilla. They offered as much autonomy to the
Rif as would be compatible with existing international treaties—customary double-talk. Other items were: release of all prisoners, full
amnesty, delineation of the districts to remain under Rif control, an
agreement on police forces, and commercial freedom in the Rif. All
arms traffic was to be abolished, but a Spanish base was to be maintained on the coast.

After the loss of Ajdir, his rear threatened, Abdel Krim's star began
to decline. His tribal allies grew restless, some deserted him. His
magic seemed to slip away. Soon he would be thrust back again into
hit-and-run guerrilla warfare.

No resistance was made to a new Spanish advance on Sheshuán.
The men were away in the fields, and the Spaniards entered a city of

women and children. Their eyes were poked out or they were killed.

In the new mountain capital in Taurirt, Abdel Krim called a meeting of the clans. Delegates came from far and wide, dressed in narrow white turbans and brown woolen *jelabas* that fell to their knees over long white skirts.

The wealth of the Rif mines, he declared to the world, were at the root of the whole matter. "The cupidity of the Rifians themselves, and the actions of foreign financial interests had resulted in the sacrifice of a vast number of Rifian, Spanish, and French lives."

More tribes surrendered to the French or Spanish. The powerful Beni Uriaghel around Ajdir alone remained loyal, willing to fight on, but he could not even get to them.

By then Abdel Krim, who would never surrender to the hated Spaniards, began making overtures to the French. They demanded the immediate delivery of all prisoners.

"This we cannot do," said Sidi Mahammed to his fellow officers. "Too many are dead, and the condition of the rest would horrify Europe."

Abdel Krim abandoned Taurirt and took refuge in friendly Snada, asking the sherif there for protection for himself and family. Spanish planes bombed the outskirts, killing three, and the French continued to advance. Finally on May 23, 1926, seeing all was lost, Abdel Krim agreed to surrender. On May 27 he and his family were escorted to the French lines by a small guard of Spahis under French officers. As he mounted to ride away, weeping Rifians kissed his stirrups. The party reached Targuist at sunrise. Five years of war were over.

Other weary refugees went south, some with no possessions, others driving their cattle to the French lines. All prisoners were taken two hundred miles to Taza.

Besides his wife and children and other relatives of hers, the hero was accompanied by his uncle and his foreign minister. On June 5 they were taken on to Fez and lodged in sumptuous quarters. The Spaniards demanded that he be punished. The French refused.

In Spanish Morocco 17,000 rifles were delivered. Confiscated lands were returned to their former owners. Guerrillas wishing to join Spanish forces were taken in.

On August 28, Abdel Krim, twenty-eight members of his family and his entourage were taken from the Casaba to Reunion Island. He slipped off the ship at Cairo, and lived there to a good old age— long enough to see all Morocco, with both zones reunited, become independent.

7

TITO: THE JUGOSLAV EAGLE

The best-dressed man among the rulers of nations, it was said, was Marshall Josip Broz Tito of Jugoslavia—"a haberdasher's dream." He was accused of aping top Nazis, but he was no Nazi and no popinjay. A visiting writer objected that a bust of Tito had a Napoleonic pose. The artist protested hotly—he had been inspired during guerrilla days, while secretly watching Tito pacing for hours alone, usually at night, in front of old religious catacombs that served as a shelter when Nazi bombers flew over. Even in the most trying days in the forests and the snowdrifts, Tito's uniforms were nearly always spotless, his boots polished. He never let down.

Tito's passion for good clothes was a rebellion against his ragged boyhood attire. In his teens, lacking good clothes, his great dream was to become a tailor's apprentice. Too sedentary for an active lad like Josip, his schoolteacher said.

His love of fine apparel was further instilled in him after he became a Comintern agent. Well-dressed affluence made the Royalist police deferential, and officials scarcely examined his false documents. During part of his underground activity, he lived as a prosperous engineer in Zagreb in a handsome villa "with a grape arbor," drove an expensive car and wore expensive clothes.

In Eastern Europe, he once escaped arrest by going to Istanbul, where he posed as a wealthy Turk merchant of Greek origin from Paris. Among his forged papers was a Turkish passport, and he was a remarkable linguist. With a small deposit—his money was almost gone—he secured passage on the international express to Gibraltar, ostensibly to board a vessel sailing for the United States. At Zagreb he abandoned his baggage and took a cab to his villa—as Babic, the engineer. He provided the Serbian and international police with an unsolvable mystery—possible kidnapping or murder of a wealthy merchant who had vanished into the blue.

In the *v globo ilegalpost* (the deep underground) he had been known as "Rudi," who had endured long imprisonment after defying the judge. But from 1937 on, he took the name of "Tito," which meant "You do this"—the expression he used when ordering comrades to

113

carry out assigned tasks. Whenever he went to Moscow or Vienna, he altered his facial makeup, the color of his hair and his gait, and he often traveled with a Czech passport, bearing the name of an engineer named Tomak.

If any one had a right to wear fine clothes, it was Tito. He had struggled up from abject, peasant poverty; he had organized the people of Jugoslavia to resist the monarchy; he led the great *borba*, or struggle, to drive out the Nazis, with little aid from anybody. Most of the time he was opposed by both the Western Powers and the Soviet Union. Afterward he established a federated "socialist" republic. He sat in the Palace and enjoyed the fanatic adoration of his people.

This popularity was never expressed more frenziedly than after his 1948 break with the Soviet Union when Stalin, trying to subordinate him to imperialist Soviet demands, called on the Jugoslav Communist Party to repudiate him. At the party convention in Belgrade, Tito tried in vain to calm the prolonged chant of "Here Tito! Here Tito!", the din of twelve hundred clapping hands and thundering feet. It was the most enthusiastic ovation (*skandiraje*) he had ever received. Gio Bilainken, an early biographer, described him:

> Tito was slimmer and smaller than pictures suggest. The voice, gentler than I would have expected from his power-ful shoulders, strong chest, was resonant, but low, almost musical . . . The light blue eyes, deeply set, immobile at will, were gay at times . . . [or] suddenly far away. The expressive, lively hands, conveyed restlessness . . . one of the two rings on the left hand . . . nearly dazzled me . . . he smoked many cigarettes in an L-shaped holder . . . [he] looked really taut but once, when he spoke of [how] the Nazis entered the wards of a Jugoslav hospital and slashed every visible throat, 320 in all.

Louis Adamic, a Jugoslav emigrée, reported that Tito was hand-some, agile, free-wheeling, nothing "fraudulent or dictatorial in his manner," except he was "over-neat . . . too dapper . . . clothes too carefully pressed." He was jaunty with a natural cockiness. In his prime, fifty-seven, his curly blond hair beginning to gray, he was almost "too good-looking, with wide-apart gray blue eyes and sym-metrical features. . . ."

The New Jugoslavia was then rising with new schools, hospitals, cities, new industry, better farming, and increased production. Enor-mous brigades of volunteer youth were marching out singing to help build public works. The Western World looked dourly on this eco-nomic and political liberation and attempted to thwart its progress and growth. The Soviet Union was no better disposed. It wanted the country's rich resources—particularly its minerals—at low prices and did not want the country industrialized. It acted in the best "Western" tradition.

The federated Jugoslav "nations," were no longer denied their rights by dominant Serbia. This had created new euphoria and great devotion to Tito. They were a sturdy people who loved folklore and poetry, music, art and the dance. About this time, a hundred thousand Jugoslav peasants turned out for the village funeral of one of their poets. In the United States it would be a baseball hero, a Hollywood star, a politician, or a general—Only among "crazy people" like Jugoslavs could a poet be so honored. This craziness was never understood abroad, least of all by leaders in Washington or London or Moscow. All three had tried unsuccessfully to restore the king and the cruel prewar system. For both the West and the Soviets were attempting—before, during, and after the war—to use Jugoslavia and its suffering people as a pawn in the great power game. What little help Tito got later was not for his people, but to get his aid in the Cold War. However much financial aid was later taken from the West, Tito never deviated from his avowed purpose of building up an independent socialist commonwealth.

"Broz" was a Croatian name that went back for centuries. Josip's mother, Marija (Mica) Javoresec, tall, blue-eyed, and very beautiful, was a Slovene from across the border. Franjo Broz, Tito's father, brought her as a bride to a nine-acre farm in the little village of Kumrovec in the Zagreje—Beyond-the-Mountain Province—in northwest Croatia. Handsome, boastful, able to sign his name, he was a clever horse and grain trader; he supplemented the yield from his farm, on which Mica did most of the work, by renting out a span of horses. One day he came home from a trip without his horses and without a penny. He had been robbed, he claimed. From that hour on, he went downhill until he became a drunken idler. The farm shrank to five acres. When Josip was still a child, his mother had to hire herself and his two older brothers to work in the fields of wealthy kulaks in return for a few dinars, a little flour, a handful of beans, and bacon fat.

Josip was born May 25, 1892, the seventh child of fifteen children, of whom only seven were still living in 1950. He was an agile daredevil, stealing cherries and plums or battling neighbor gangs. "Never get caught," was one of his early mottos. He rarely told anybody about his plans or his doings. He was determined not to be a farm drudge. When he was thirteen, Mica wove him two homemade shirts. He managed to get shoes and went to Sisak, near Zagreb, where he became a busboy. The obsequiousness necessary to win tips was distasteful, so he saved enough to buy a pair of workmen's jumpers and get taken on as a metal-worker apprentice for four years.

He and his six fellow apprentices slept in a loft and were super-

vised by Karl Schmidt, a young German socialist, who read Marx and
Engels, taught Tito German, and inspired in him love for reading and
knowledge. Josip was adept and soon was running a drill press. Since
the loft was dimly lit, he used to read while working, hiding his book
whenever his employer Karas came near. But one day he became too
absorbed and a drill snapped off. Karas was so angry he struck Josip.
At once—though he had only two months to go to get his machinist's
certificate—the youngster got his clothes from the loft and left Sisak,
going to Zagreb, from where he walked home.

Three days later the police took him back to Sisak. His employer
came to the jail, put his arms around him and said they had both
been foolish. Karas sent Josip good food and got him released to
finish out his apprenticeship. He got a machine-shop job in Zagreb.
Hard times hit, and for three and a half years, he wandered through
Austria-Hungary, Switzerland, and other countries looking for work.
He learned Czech and more German, read Goethe and Heine and a
story of the French revolution—a theme he kept on reading about
for the rest of his life. He joined a *Turnverein* and became an expert
fencer. In the spring of 1913, he was conscripted, made a sergeant,
and was sent to the Galician front.

When war came, his regiment deserted to the Russians. Badly
wounded in the armpit by the lance of a Circassian cavalryman, he
spent some months in hospitals. A pretty school girl taught him
Russian. Soon he was reading Gogol, Dostoevsky, Chekov, Kupirin,
and Turgenev—nearly a hundred books.

He was sent to Ardatov as a prisoner-mechanic in a grain mill. He
borrowed books from schoolteachers and made contacts with the
local anti-Tzarist group. Sent to Kungur in the Urals to administer
the prison camp at a railroad project, he plotted to get the prisoners
to break out in an anti-Tzarist insurrection, but was jailed. "Kungur
was the worst prison I've ever been in," he said years later.

In May 1917, he escaped and walked a thousand versts to get to
Petrograd. Everywhere he heard the word "Bolsheviki" and Lenin's
name. Everybody (except the Allies) was aware that the Kerensky
regime could not last. The Russian people were "smelling freedom.
Wonderful people!" Arrested several times, Broz talked his way
out, for he spoke Russian, as he put it, "better than most Russians."

Petrograd was jammed with deserters from the front who had killed
their officers. Still starving, they scrounged about for food, stole,
brawled, and rioted. Broz watched the demonstrations and battles
in the streets by Tzarists, Cadets, Kerenskyites, Mensheviks, Bolsheviks and other factions. Kerensky was hysterically orating to the multi-
tudes. The Bolsheviks' leaders harangued the factory workers, the
soldiers, and sailors. There was little food and no sugar, but lots of

newspapers, pamphlets, and leaflets exhorting the people to support this or that party. Presently there was no electric light or fuel.

Josip made his way to Finland, where revolution was about to erupt. He was arrested, but he had a white-card (i.e. of a man too ill for military service). Back in Petrograd he was arrested again and sent with a hundred other prisoners on a slow train bound for Siberia. He jumped off fifty miles from Omsk and reached there on a regular passenger train. He had no ticket and no money, but the conductor shrugged and smiled. The Bolsheviks had seized power the previous day and ruled Omsk.

At the Maryanovsky station, everybody was closely questioned by Red Guards. Broz was taken to a courtyard where Austro-Hungarian and German prisoners were organizing a Red Guard unit. He served with them until the summer of 1918, then was kept busy in the railroad yards repairing railroad trains. Czech deserters seized the yards as the Kolchak White-Guard army closed in, Broz fled across the Steppe.

He got work as a mechanic at a Kirghiz flour mill. His employer, Hadji Isai, had a vast estate, three thousand horses, a score of wives and a hundred or so children; he did not know exactly how many. He did not like the Reds. He had not liked the Tzar either. As for Kerensky—*Puf!* Mohammedanism, though he had once made a hegira to Mecca, was horse manure. But he did need a good mechanic. He liked Broz, partly because Broz loved horses and knew how to handle them. Become a Kirghiz, he suggested, and offered Josip his pick, any four or five, of his best-looking daughters as wives. No! A girl in Omsk? "Well, every man has a right to his own folly!" Several times Isai hid him from the Kolchak guards. They also searched the house in Omsk of Broz' sweetheart, Pellagia, whose brother was a Red Army Guard.

Disguised as a bearded Kirghiz, Josip had risked visiting Pellagia. (He wanted to return to Jugoslavia, but she refused to leave her family.) Twice arrested, he could speak Kirghiz well and easily won his release.

By November the Bolsheviks retook Omsk, but train-traffic to the west was not restored until 1920. Broz had several hundred rubles saved and persuaded Pellagia to marry him and go to Jugoslavia— now made independent by World War I treaties. Her brother got him put in charge of Austro-Hungarian prisoners being repatriated. They rebelled in Stettin, Germany, and the outfit broke up.

Josip and Pellagia entered Jugoslavia in November 1920 at Maribar, Slovenia. They were arrested and were quizzed for a week. At his Aunt Ana's home in Pedsedra, he learned that his mother had died two years before. He turned pale, sat down, then asked for details.

"When they were leaving," said Aunt Ana, "he put his arms around me without saying anything . . . I'll never forget it." Pellagia, she thought, looked much like his mother; tall, lithe, blond, and blue-eyed.

He got a machine-shop job in Zagreb and joined the Communist Party, where he was looked up to as an authority on the Soviet Revolution. His work kept him busy from ten to twelve hours a day, but he put in many hours in party duties. He handed out pamphlets. "Here, read this," he would say. He was described as "a good fellow with a lively sense of humor who liked good food and good clothes." Generous, he helped others. When his father showed up asking for money, Broz always gave it to him, even if he had to borrow.

"Don't blame my father for having turned into a bum," he said after Franjo died. "If you knew the trials and hardships of Croatian peasants, you would understand how it could happen, how it happened to so many. He was a good man."

Josip helped organize a strike and was black-listed. In a Croatian village he organized the workers, led three strikes and was jailed seven times. His son, Zarko—who later lost an arm in the defense of Moscow against the Nazis in World War II—was born in Bjelovarin in 1923. For the next two years, Tito moved from pillar to post getting jobs until thrown out.

In 1925 he got work in Kraljevica, a small boat-building town on the Croatian litoral, just south of Susak and Fiume, where they rented a small shack. He was thin and pale, and explained his visit to the coast as due to ill-health. His hourly wage was fifteen cents. He organized the men and pulled a strike which within two weeks won a wage increase. The gendarmes escorted him out of town. He moved on to a French-owned factory in Smederevo Palanca in Serbia, where again he organized the workers. Three of his fellow-workers were killed by the police, and again he was ordered out of town. Back in Zagreb, Croatia, he was elected Secretary of the Metal Workers Council. His position was dangerous, not merely because of King Alexander's police but also because of the Stalin-Trotsky feud. Underground factions hated each other so bitterly that some became police informers. Broz refused to join any faction. Arrested with eight others in 1927, he was taken in chains to Ogulin prison, a dank filthy place full of vermin and rats. The prisoners went on a hunger strike.

There was a bit of publicity. The other eight were released, but Broz was held. The security police refused the judge's demand to produce him. His Honor came to the prison. He was shocked by the filth and stench. A leftist paper told the story of his trial.

"Are you a Communist?" he asked Broz.

"Ask the Security Police. It's their business to find out."

The judge said it was silly for Broz to endanger his health by a hunger strike.

"My health would be more endangered if I ate the slop they serve as food."

The judge saw to it Broz was given decent food, sending in meals from his own kitchen, and soon let him out for lack of evidence.

He worked harder than ever for the cause. Due to the police terrorism during the 1919–1922 strikes, leaders had moved away or were in hiding. How about the peasants? Broz went to Kumrovec. But the peasants there (partisans of Stejepan Radic, a Croatian member of Parliament) proved indifferent, even hostile.

Returning to Zagreb, Broz was hunted by the police. He never dared sleep more than two or three times in the same bed. Once he escaped by jumping from a second-story window and was saved from being hurt by landing on several freshly slaughtered pigs. Frequently he changed his facial makeup, so cleverly even some of his closest acquaintances were fooled. He spent three weeks in jail, but his identity was not discovered. The following month he was captured and handcuffed but escaped, and a comrade filed off his irons. Party strength kept on declining because of arrests, police beatings, and killings. "Nationalism . . . Peasant revolt—these are our best slogans," Broz kept saying.

Radic and three other Croatian deputies were shot down during Parliamentary sessions by one of King Alexander's trigger-men. The streets filled with angry peasants and workers. Broz distributed hand grenades, a few guns and leaflets, calling for insurrection. "I was very naïve those days," he later admitted. Five agents took him handcuffed to the Glavnjaca Royal Police Headquarters. He was slapped, abused, and hit in the chest with a stool, causing him to spit blood for three weeks. After two months in solitary, he admitted he was the head of the Metal Workers' Council, that he had distributed leaflets calling for an uprising, but claimed the revolver he was carrying was for self-defense. Pellagia and Zarko were also arrested. After he was sentenced, they left for the Soviet Union.

The trial of Broz and his fellow "conspirators" November 7–11, 1928 was attended by students. The reporter of *Novasti* wrote, "Without doubt Broz—'Rudi'—is the most interesting figure in the case. His visage suggests steel. His eyes have a cool, energetic, calm look. Whenever a question was put to him the spectators became still in order to hear his answer."

JUDGE: Guilty? . . . .

BROZ: Of course, I'm guilty. Actually I am not *guilty*.

JUDGE: In precisely what way do you consider yourself guilty?

BROZ: I have urged the proletariat to resist injustice and to study the scientific theses of Karl Marx, which spell out a better future for all mankind. I do not recognize this court.

JUDGE: The law is for the Protection of the State . . .

BROZ: It's a transitory affair; it doesn't interest me.

JUDGE: The law forbids Communist propaganda.

BROZ: Yes, but it's a transitory law.

JUDGE: It's the law in force now. It was initiated by the people to protect them against you Communists. Anyone caught breaking the law goes to Lepoglava prison.

BROZ: It will be an evil day when the CP permits a "law" like this to frighten it.

JUDGE: Tell us something about your life.

(He told about his days as a metal worker in many countries before and after the war, his life in the Soviet Union, the poverty of Kumrovec.)

The judge stopped him in midsentence. "The court is not a platform from which to spout propaganda. Sit down."

BROZ: What did you expect me to do? Spout propaganda for your Serbian Radical [ultra conservative] Party?"

The guards rushed him out. To the spectators he shouted, "Long live the Third International." On November 14 he was sentenced to five years. A student who attended the trial and who later died as a Partisan fighter, sent the clipping from *Novasti* to his brother in Belgrade: "The first free man I have ever known." "Rudi" became a byword in every part of the country.

On January 6, 1929 King Alexander ordered the army to extirpate all leftists. "White terror" descended on the land. Twelve thousand oppositionists passed through various *glavnjaca*. A thousand, said to be Communists, were sentenced to from one to fifteen years. Leaders were brutally killed.

Broz was lucky to be already in Lepoglava prison. The warden had been a fellow conscript, with whom he had spent several months in a Russian hospital. "Dr. Bohacic gave us good food and allowed me to work on the town's electrical installation." Broz was thus able to meet with underground leaders.

In all prisons the inmates set up study classes in Marxism and in underground tactics. The first was started in Metrovica prison near Belgrade by Mosa Pijada, an artist and writer who later became a leading guerrilla and a top member of Tito's government. In 1920 Pijada had founded the newspaper *Sebordna Fec* (Free Expression). Arrested five years later, he had been given a twenty-year sentence, reduced on appeal to twelve years. But two more years were added because he sang the *International* in his cell. He staged hunger strikes and used his free prison time to paint portraits of his fellow prisoners. He painted Tito when they were in the same prison, and completed the first Serbian translation of Marx' *Das Kapital*. Then, hearing of the Mao Tse-tung insurrection in China, he began studying Chinese. In 1930 he was transferred to Lepoglava prison. Broz got him made his assistant at the power plant.

Because of an escape attempt by a fellow prisoner, Broz was transferred to Maribar, the toughest disciplinary prison in the country, where he had to sew flour bags. But it was well-run, and years later when in power, Tito put the aged ex-warden on the government pension list. The prisoners got Engels' works and *Das Kapital* (bound in the cover of the *Arabian Nights*) smuggled in and started study groups. From 1932 on they began getting the *London Economist* and learned English by reading it. Broz read everything he could lay his hands on—about the Quakers, Pavlov's conditioned reflexes, above all the French revolution.

In 1934 (he was then forty-two) he was released with orders not to leave his native Kumrovec. He stayed in his hometown for ten days, then disappeared into the underground.

The Jugoslav party was discontented with the leaders in exile in Vienna and sent Broz to size things up there. He was outfitted with fashionable tourist luggage, good clothes, money, and a false passport. Communist Party leaders in all countries had to be approved by the Moscow Comintern and were on the payroll. Most lived not in their respective homelands but comfortably in adjacent countries. Secretary Gorkic, who headed the Jugoslav party in Vienna, never seemed to lack money.

Broz was received coldly by the comrades. He sized them up as lazy, immoral spendthrifts. Gorkic stroked his reddish moustache and showered him with abuse. Broz said conditions under the Alexander dictatorship were scarcely as rosy as those enjoyed by the leaders in Vienna. The Vienna comrades should come home and find out what Jugoslavia Fascism was really like. Gorkic backed water, saying his abuse was just a tactic to test Broz. In the week that followed they had long talks, and Broz was made a member of the Jugoslav directorate in exile—subject to approval by the Third International Presidium. Broz said he wished to visit Moscow to see his wife and son. Gorkic promised to arrange it. Meanwhile Broz was to serve as liaison between Jugoslavia and Vienna.

Broz made three more visits to Vienna that year, using a different passport each time. He did not trust Gorkic, never let him know his assumed name, and always went by a different route and train than the one he said he was going on. Later Gorkic was exposed as a

Royalist Jugoslav spy, *provocateur*, an agent of the Warsaw Pilsudski government and of British-French interests, and (not proved) of the Jesuits! His wife was also suspected of having been a Serbian spy.

On his return to Jugoslavia, Broz met new young underground leaders in Llanca and Belgrade. Most of them later died in the war against Hitler or in Nazi prisons. He heard a great deal about two young Montenegro poets—Milovan Djilas, sentenced to three years, and Alexander Rankovic, serving six years. He sized them all up. If a man acted like a bureaucrat or was a glib phrasemaker, he had little confidence in him.

King Alexander was assassinated on October 9, 1934 in Marseilles. New police terror and assassinations—in jail and on the streets—engulfed Jugoslavia. Victims were thrown out of upper story windows. Bodies were thrown into the streets or the Danube. Broz hid out in the woods near his Aunt Ana's house in Podsreda until he could be provided with a new wardrobe, money, and a false Czech passport. The passport was crude, but he bought a first class ticket and went boldly by train. At the border crossing, he created a humorous diversion by pretending to be urinated upon by the child of a young lady in his compartment, and his passport was stamped without examination.

He remained in Vienna six weeks in a small room rented to him by a Jewish woman with three daughters. One attempted suicide. Broz revived her by artificial respiration, then got out of the house just as the police were coming in. He took the night train for Prague.

In the Soviet Union he found Pellagia ill and moved her and twelve-year-old Zarko to the Hotel Luz where the government housed visiting Communists under assumed names. The three of them lived there until the summer of 1936.

Broz took over the Jugoslav desk at the Comintern, headed from 1935 on by Georgi Dimitrov, Bulgarian hero of the Reichstag fire trial. Broz came to know Togliati of Italy, Peck of Germany, and other party leaders, but did not meet Stalin until World War II—in 1944. Broz worked for the full independence of the Jugoslav Communist party from Comintern control. More than ever, he distrusted Gorkic and his clique then in Moscow, and they clashed bitterly. Broz was not overly surprised when Gorkic was exposed.

Rodoljab Colakovic, a friend from Maribar prison days, described Broz.

> I liked to drop in on him. He would greet me with a smile and a funny remark, then clear a chair of books and papers for me to sit down. He continued to be interested in the French revolution, as he had been at Maribar. "Rocke," he would say, "The more I dig into the entire *problematika*

[of Jogoslav Communism] . . . the more I know how little
I know . . . [but] I'm beginning to see daylight."

He studied the Soviet system thoroughly and was particularly impressed by its industrial accomplishments, such as the huge Dnyperstroi
dam and Magnitogorsk, the great new steel city. Often he cried "There
is the answer. Industrialization!"

Leaving Pellagia and his son in Moscow, Broz returned to Jugo-
slavia as a well-dressed Austrian tourist spending a few weeks in a
Dalmatian resort. He got in touch with Franc Leskovec, a friendly
Social Democrat.

"At first I was worried," said Leskovec, "he was so well groomed.
But later a letter of introduction identified him as Rudi. So now he
was in my house. He was outspoken."

Broz had come to gather volunteers for the Civil War in Spain and
had sent thousands across, though six hundred were intercepted on
one boat and arrested. He himself never got to Spain—as was customarily believed. Many Spanish Civil War veterans became experienced leaders in the subsequent guerrilla battles against the Nazi
invasion of Jugoslavia.

From 1937, Tito (his new name) worked hard to reorganize the
party. He fought against personal feuds. A man could not hate other
comrades and at the same time love the cause. "These . . . traits . . .
are brought into our party from a petty-bourgeois milieu." Jealousies
and irresponsibility in secret work had resulted in comrades' being
beaten to death by the police. Braggarts had no place. "Modesty is
the first quality of a Bolshevik. . . . Those who put on airs are merely
ridiculous and puerile." His attitude was Puritanical and monastic.
He demanded obedience, self-sacrifice, and absorbing devotion. "Avoid
swearing . . . scolding and abuse. . . . The party . . . must pay attention to the private life of every single member." Heavy drinkers
and women-chasers had to be kicked out. Bourgeois charges that
the Communists wished to destroy the family had to be discredited.
He warned against "revisionism" of Marxist-Leninist doctrines, a
charge which he made in 1948 against Stalin. The scrofulous word
was hurled back at him by the Stalinists in the usual meaningless
growls of doctrinaires. To this day "revisionist" is a horrendous charge,
be it in Guatemala or in Cuba.

From 1936 on, Jugoslavia was overrun by Nazi agents posing as
tourists, who wormed in close to acting King, Regent Paul. In January
1941, President Roosevelt sent Colonel William J. Donovan (later of
the O.S.S., precursor of the C.I.A.) to "stimulate" resistance to the
Germans. Mr. Cordell Hull sent a warning message, and F.D.R. cabled
the Jugoslav government that the United States was against its align-
ment with Germany. But Paul held a secret session with Hitler and,

hoping to fend off Nazi invasion, signed a friendship pact. After Greece's rout of Mussolini's Army, Ivan Subusic promoted a military coup against Paul (Subusic was a crafty plotter, according to the *Saturday Evening Post*). Paul was put across the border, and the seventeen year old son of Alexander was crowned Peter II, as a Western puppet.

It was premature and disastrous, for it forced the Germans to invade at once. The United States was still supposedly neutral and was in no position to interfere. "Wipe out Belgrade," Hitler told his air commanders. They hit on April 16, destroying a fourth of the city and killing ten thousand. The storm troopers began marching. Peter and his government fled to London.

As early as 1937, Tito and other underground leaders had begun laying plans to fight expected invasion. He formed a military committee to arrange operations against any Hitler move. The Hitler-Stalin alliance came as a traumatic shock to him. Nevertheless, the Jugoslavs had little love, either, for the West's last-minute betrayal of the Soviets. Tito believed, correctly, that Stalin's move was a time-saving subterfuge.

Tito left Belgrade right after the bombing and held a plenum session in Zagreb. It sent two delegates to General Orlovic, demanding arms for the workers to fight the oncoming Germans. The general threatened to arrest them. But his troops disintegrated, and he surrendered. "As we left the conference in the backroom of a milkshop on Herzogovatsk Ulic," said Tito, "German tanks were driving through the city." The slaughter was terrific. Whole villages were wiped out. At least one hundred civilian lives were taken for each German killed, a death toll said to have reached eight hundred thousand.

The Germans were aided by local quislings (*Ustachis*). General Milan Nedic organized remnants of the Jugoslav army into a force to help the invaders. Another was Ante Pavelic, involved in the Alexander assassination, who set up the independent pro-Nazi State of Avaka. A basket on Pavelic's desk was apparently filled with oysters. "How about a nice oyster stew?" the Italian minister asked facetiously. Pavelic replied, "It is a present from my loyal *Ustachis*—forty pounds of human eyes."

In May, at a secret national reunion for resisters to Hitler in Zagreb, Tito was named Commander in Chief of the Resistance. Stalin and the Comintern, still tied to the Germans, were furious. However, Hitler's invasion of Russia began a few weeks later.

Tito returned to Belgrade boldly by train, as engineer Babic, and took a big house in the outskirts not far from German headquarters. From there, well into September, he brashly sent orders and issued a bulletin *The High Command* ordering sabotage and blowing of trains, power stations, etc. The Germans were killing all leftists they could lay hands on and had a dragnet out for the mysterious man named "Tito." Also they were after his close friends and collaborators, among the most brilliant men in the country—young Vlado Dedijer, an enormous man of "child-like devotion"; young Milovan Djilas, who gave Tito the nickname "Staryi" (the old man); and Alexander Rankovic (all of whom held high posts after Tito seized control). All house doors had to be kept unlocked, so that German agents or soldiers could walk in whenever they chose. When Tito heard the neighbor's dogs barking, his housekeeper would lock him in a closet with a trap-door behind a washstand. But the Nazis arrested Alexander Rankovic and tortured him to try to make him disclose the Resistance com-mander's whereabouts. Tito made an armed sortie and took Rankovic out of the hospital bed to which he had been strapped.*

After numerous narrow escapes, Tito left Belgrade in the company of an Orthodox priest to join the Partisans operating out of Krupanj, a small western Serbian town. His guerrilla life began in earnest.

In the south, Partisans had suffered costly setbacks. Tito sent out word to restrict operations for the present to demolition of telegraph and telephone lines, railways, bridges, factories, shops, and munition stores. Any foodstuffs captured were to be distributed to the people. He sternly forbade Partisans to loot. "I am not going to be the Supreme Commander of a plundering army . . . but kill enemy officers, Ges-tapo men, Black Shirts, etc. and their domestic agents."

He called the first guerrilla war council; fighters from Belgrade, Bosnia, Herzegovina, Montenegro, Slovenia, and Croatia. They met in the Stalac mine, adjacent to Krupanj. For the moment the chief objective was to get the Germans out of West Serbia, but headquarters were set up in all departments. The assemblage voted in favor of a broad nationalistic front, to include if possible Colonel Drazo Mik-hailovic, head of the pro-Royalist Cetniks, the only other sizable force in revolt.

Tito arranged to meet Mikhailovic in the neutral village of Stru-ganic, not far from the latter's headquarters at Ravna Gora. For once, Mikhailovic, a far-gone alcoholic who was long considered to be a British agent, was sober and did not seem too unreliable, though he argued that it was not yet time to fight the Germans. His chief aide Draisa Vacic, a haughty Pan-Serbian and a go-between for the West-ern powers and close to private British interests, was openly disagree-

---

* After the revolution had succeeded, they split. Djilas was sent to a long term in the penitentiary (where he was held until early 1967) for his writings—mostly about Stalin and the corrupt Soviet bureaucracy, though Tito himself had pre-viously denounced both. Dedijer, the chronicler of the long guerrilla war against the Nazis, was punished for protesting the imprisonment of Djilas and was sent into exile. In Stockholm, he acted as chairman of the 1967 Bertrand Russell War Crimes Tribunal against Johnson, Rusk, and McNamara.

able. He hated Croatians more than he hated Germans, and Tito was a Croatian. He blamed the Croats for recent wholesale massacre of Serbians. (This had been perpetrated by Croatian *Ustachi* on Himmler's direct orders.) Even so, Mikhailovic agreed not to put any obstacles in the way of Cetnik guerrillas who wished to fight alongside Tito's forces.

Tito moved his headquarters to Uzice, a southwest Serbian town where the townspeople turned over to him about 50,000,000 dinars ($100,000) abandoned by a Royalist general who had surrendered to the Germans. He used part of this to get a rifle and cartridge factory going again. Soon it was turning out 420 rifles and 80,000 rounds of ammunition a day.

In Bibac, Montenegro—"the capital of Liberated Territory,"—Tito organized a popular front, the Anti-Fascist Council of National Liberation, known as AVNOL. Delegates of all the nationalities came from all over the country. Elections were held in all places not occupied by the Germans, and a Parliament of 572 delegates was convened. Councils were set up everywhere, particularly in Serbia and Macedonia.

The German offensive was resumed in October 1942. To get aid in stopping it, Tito went to see Mikhailovic, leader of the Cetniks, who was being visited by British agent Captain William "Marko" Hudson. Hudson was connected with British mining interest, sent to warn him not to help Tito but to aid the Germans in destroying him.*

Already, when Tito came to see him, Mikhailovic had been secretly collaborating with the Italian Fascist commanders in Dalmatia, Herzegovina, and Bosnia. He was also getting large sums of gold from Peter's British-backed government in exile in London. King Peter named him Minister of War. The Soviets, who also had direct relations with Peter's exile government, were urged by the British to support Mikhailovic and stop Tito. The Soviets responded that they did not wish to mix in Jugoslav domestic affairs.

Tito, knowing nothing of all this, asked Mikhailovic for immediate help to block the Germans who were advancing on Uzbec. Mikhailovic promised men, provided Tito would share his arms, supplies, and funds. Tito, much better equipped, at once handed over what was demanded—money, his best rifles, and much artillery.

---

* According to Mikhailovic's later postwar trial testimony (corroborated by documents in his files) Hudson had been sent to inform Mikhailovic that the struggle in behalf of Jugoslavia must not become a struggle of Communists in behalf of the Soviet Union. Mikhailovic was told to get in touch with the Germans to help plan for Tito's annihilation. Mikhailovic later admitted that all during the long war—the *Borba* or struggle—he had acted on British orders to help the Germans eliminate the Partisan forces.

Mikhailovic pretended to attack the Germans at Kralijevo, but it was merely a fake battle cooked up by Hudson. Then, in connivance with the Germans, Mikhailovic's Cetniks captured five hundred Partisans, tortured them, and drove them naked into the snow to be murdered by the Germans, who also killed seventeen nurses and a doctor.

As the Germans attacked Tito, a large body of Cetniks attacked his forces from the rear. After gory fighting against both Cetniks and Germans, Tito had to pull out the remnants of his guerrillas in a raging blizzard. Only three thousand Partisan fighters were left, one fourth of them women. Tito led them into the rugged mountains of Montenegro and Bosnia where the cumbersome equipment of the Italians and Germans would be useless.

The northwest was extremely cold at this season of the year, deep in snow and with little available food. But there were few *Ustachis* in the area, and they would have the support of Montenegran Partisan guerrillas, commanded by the faithful Mosa Piljade who had escaped from a Royal concentration camp in 1939. Now a grayish man of fifty, he was called *Cika*, Uncle, by his affectionate followers.

And so that December 1941, Tito's followers moved through the snow-spangled forests in near zero weather. At night Tito often slept under a tree in the snow with only a German officer's greatcoat for warmth. Most of the night it was too cold to sleep, and he was alone with his somber thoughts. Invariably at dawn, without breakfast, he would order the advance.

In a warmer sunlit valley, he called a halt. He walked among his men. Many had dropped in their tracks and were asleep. Others were picking lice off each other or wrapping their bloody feet or mending clothes. Several were bathing in an icy creek.

"We don't want the king back," one told him.

"He won't be permitted back without the consent of the people."

Then and there, he created the First Proletarian Brigade, a special force to wear a red star in their caps. He named Koca Popovic, a Belgrade banker's son long active in the underground, as commander. Soon other proletarian brigades were formed. They became his most ardent fighters.

The Soviet authorities were furious. There must be no "Proletarian" Brigades. A revolutionary movement would upset Britain and the United States. "Resistance to the Nazis, but no Red Stars." When Tito did not obey, Moscow angrily announced to the world that Jugoslavia, ergo Tito, had stuck a knife in the back of the Soviet Union.

Tito saw no reason to drive out the Germans merely to get back the prewar terrorist system. There *had* to be a social revolution that would recognize the rights and freedom of all Jugoslav ethnic regions —a federated system, free of arbitrary Serbian rule.

He set up his headquarters in Bosnia at Jajce—"capital of Free Jugoslavia." There the following November, two hundred forty national delegates, meeting in an abandoned tunnel—"used as a bomb shelter and school house, where dances and theatricals were staged"—drew up a constitution.

Radio news from London and Washington informed Tito that Mikhailovic was the hero of the liberation. For the most part, Mikhailovic merely lay drunk in Ravna Gora, taking money and arms from any and everybody. The Cetniks looted and abused the people in the villages, trying, with the Germans, to destroy the Partisans.

It took the British three years to realize the truth. On May 25, 1944, Churchill finally told the House of Commons. "We have ceased to supply Mikhailovic . . . he has not been fighting the enemy . . . some of his subordinates have made accommodations with the enemy . . . [and have engaged in] armed conflicts with the forces of Marshal Tito." As a result, there has been "loss of patriot lives to the German advances." On July 8, Peter's Royal government in exile reluctantly dismissed Mikhailovic as Minister of War.

After the Germans were beaten, Mikhailovic was tried for treason on July 17, 1945. The evidence against him was overwhelming, and, despite Allied efforts in his behalf, he was shot. The commotion in the Western press was enormous. Tito was denounced as a "murderer."

Almost to the last, Tito remained a mysterious unknown in England and the United States. "Some say Tito is a woman," was the brilliant comment of the *Daily Express*. Queried by the House of Commons about "that man Tito," Mr. Eden said awkwardly, "I understand he is a Croat, but I hope I shall not be held to be wrong."

He was much better known to the Germans. As early as September, 1943, Goebbels had written about Tito: "The Slovenians had gone almost entirely over to his Partisans." On October 14, war-reporter Lutz Koch wrote, "The Partisans are a festering sore . . . [they] are armed to the teeth . . . millions of rounds of ammunitions, countless lorries, tanks, armored reconnaissance, cars and aircraft. We are advancing from Fiume to attack Tito's tanks."

The sixth German offensive was launched seven weeks after Italy's collapse, with sixteen German divisions, seven thousand *Ustachi* quislings, Cetniks, Bulgarians, and Hungarian troops, and Jugoslav and Soviet deserters. It had some success along the Adriatic littoral, but Tito's territory continued to expand. In spite of German—and Allied—efforts, great stores of Italian arms and supplies fell into his hands.

In April 1944, a seventh (and last) Nazi offensive was started—a force of twenty-five divisions, directed by General Rommel, the desert fox of Africa—not against Mikhailovic but against Tito. Toward the end, Tito received a few American supplies via the Partisan-held island of Vis, and nonofficial aid from a group of sympathetic

American officers in Cairo. The material included a large shipment of shoes—all left ones. By then he was buying weapons from smugglers on islands along the Adriatic.

The peak of the Nazi offensive came on May 25, 1944, Tito's birthday. Daring paratroopers made an effort to capture him in Drovac. The Partisans believed this was arranged by a treacherous British mission that had visited them a few days earlier: not a single Allied plane (usually thick in the skies) challenged the German parachute attack.

Nor did the Soviets do anything to help Tito. Instead, he was reprimanded frequently. As early as February 1942 Tito made an appeal for medical supplies. Arms, legs, hands, and feet were being amputated and torn bellies sewn up without anesthetics. Moscow promised to drop supplies by plane on the night of February 23 in Junco Do at the foot of Mount Durmitor. A beacon was to be lighted.

Tito sent Ciko Jankov with seventy-four men. They had to fight through six feet of snow from Zablyak to Junco Do. The peasants gave permission to burn one of their four haystacks as a signal. Fifteen men waited there; sixty were scattered over the plateau. The first one to sight a plane was to fire his gun so that the haystack could be set on fire at once. They shivered there for thirty-five days with their ears and faces, hands, and feet, tingling from the intense cold. No plane came.

Instead of sending supplies, Stalin began objecting to Tito's tactics. Proletarian Brigades, he insisted once more, were to be disbanded. Tito was endangering the Soviet-British Alliance; why didn't Tito set up a Popular Front? We already have a national Popular Front, said Tito. Stalin asked for a Jugoslav manifesto to the peoples of all Europe to rise against the Germans. Tito obliged, but asked again about the medical supplies. Stalin ignored the appeal and said Tito's manifesto was too revolutionary. Seven versions of the draft were hammered out; in the end Stalin suppressed it.

Meanwhile Ciko Janko and his men strained their frost-bitten ears for five weeks for the expected plane. On March 29 a watcher fired his rifle. A plane came over, circled. Everybody shot off his rifle in wild joy. In the excitement all four haystacks were set on fire. But the sound of the motors faded away. It was a British plane returning to Malta. Word came from Stalin that same night. "No plane. No supplies. Technical difficulties too great."

After German collapse in 1945, Stalin, Roosevelt, and Churchill (to show their great love of democracy!) ordered Tito to join the government of exiled King Peter. Tito must accept Ivan Subusic and other royalist leaders (who had sat out the war safely in exile) as part of his administration and put his victorious forces under the Royalists—the very ones who had persecuted him and his followers before and during the war. Actually, Stalin and Churchill, ignoring the United States, made a secret deal to divide control of Jugoslavia fifty-fifty.

Neither the exiles nor London nor Washington nor Moscow had the faintest conception of the actual workings and aims of the new revolutionary Jugoslav government, forged in the sacrifice and bitterness of war. The three big victorious powers were trying to sit on top of the world for their own interests. In Jugoslavia, besides the one and three quarter million lives lost, the war had wiped out 750,000 homes, destroyed every truck, car, boat, tractor, and most horses and cattle. In numerous villages the Nazis had slaughtered everybody.

Once the villages were in hands of Tito's Liberation Front, local committees everywhere established their own police forces and the Liberation army, a popular militia, as the Royal police fled or joined the pro-Nazi quislings. It was a mighty upsurge of the people. Huge mass meetings were held everywhere three or four times a week. Even while fighting was still going on, they carried out programs to combat illiteracy, to initiate reforms. They provided food for the Partisan fighters. On a higher level, the Partisan OZNA, later VIDRA (a secret security organization) was built up by Tito's aide Alexander Rankovic.* Soviet G.P.U. made unsuccessful efforts to absorb it. This was one of the chief reasons for the open break a few years later between Stalin and Tito.

By the time the Soviet army marched into Belgrade, completing the liberation, Tito had 300,000 armed men plus a million more for whom arms were lacking. The Anglo-Americans, as anti-Tito as was Stalin, sent in Royalists and pro-Nazi collaborationists (who had earlier fled to Italy) to plot against him. On Italian soil they helped organize a Royalist army to restore the prewar status quo. The British set up a secret "Slovenian Government" in Ljueljar. Tens of thousands of Nazi collaborationists and Royalist Cetniks hurried to that city. Tito rushed in armed forces and stopped the nonsense.

A republic was declared November 29, 1945. On January 31, 1946, it became a Federated Republic in which all the autonomous nationalities and regions participated with equal rights. The old Serbian terror system had been uprooted.**

But Tito was having serious trouble with the Soviets. The Soviet technical and military missions lorded it over their Jugoslav counterparts. They earned four to ten times as much (which Jugoslavia had to pay) and insisted on special privileges. A Soviet Lieutenant-Colonel was paid three times as much as a Jugoslav cabinet member. When

---

* He was ousted in 1968.
** The moves in Jugoslavia were paralleled in nearby Albania. A similar pattern occurred in Bulgaria, where guerrillas had wrecked King Boris's regime.

Tito tried to bring Soviet salaries into line, Moscow jeered back. "How do you expect a Russian to live on what a Jugoslav earns?" Tito then reduced the number of Soviet officers. The Soviets angrily yanked out its missions and all technical aid; arrogant notes showered in from Moscow.

Tito replied in a conciliatory tone, asking for a proper investigation of all charges. The Russians merely exaggerated the accusations and called on the Jugoslav people to seize control of the Communist Party. Meeting in a great convention, the party gave Tito the biggest ovation of his life. The big pictures of Stalin were yanked down from buildings, homes, and meeting places. Tito was obliged to turn to the West for the equipment needed to restore the war-ravaged land, and labor for his fast-moving industrial and agricultural program.

The debate over freedom still goes on. Djilos was finally released in 1966. The attempt at collective farming—unsuited for Jugoslavia's topography—was abandoned early. From the start, the federated system which guaranteed much local autonomy has had a leavening influence. Industry is not state-owned in the Soviet sense, but each unit is administered by its own workers and management. Until 1965, 70 percent of the profits went to the state, 30 percent to the workers' council. Since then the ratio has been revised. Decentralization has steadily progressed in nearly all fields. For some years, industrial production and living standards have increased approximately 10 percent annually. By and large Jugoslavia has the freest system of any country in the communist world.

8

THE AFRICAN GUERRILLAS

Even before his recent and voluminous anti-American book on neocolonialism, Kewane Nkruma indicated the reasons for Ghana independence. In precolonial days Ghana had been the head of a great empire. He described, much as earlier writers such as Lenin and Parker Moon, present-day imperialism in these terms:

1. The export of capital to sources of raw materials.
2. The frenzied struggle for monopolistic control of these sources of raw materials.
3. Exclusive markets for manufactured goods of the imperialistic powers.
4. Making colonial peoples nonmanufacturing dependencies and prohibiting their trading with nations other than the "mother country."
5. Exploitation of colonial cheap labor . . . exploitation and oppression to squeeze out superior profits.

In colonies under foreign rule, the battle is not for the recovery of rights, but for independence and the establishment of rights not previously known. The leader of the unsuccessful 1945 Algerian revolt, Ferhat Abbas, issued a manifesto in 1943:

> Politically and morally . . . colonization can have but one concept, that of two mutually alien societies. Its systematic or disguised refusal to allow the Moslem Algerians into the French community has discouraged all those who have favored a policy of assimilation . . . The policy appears today, in the eyes of all, as . . . a dangerous device in the hands of colonialism.

A new power doctrine: Algerian Power.

Berbers and Arabs could vote, but it took nine of their votes to equal one Frenchman's vote. There and in much of Africa the native people had few if any civil rights and, until last-hour concessions, no representation whatever.

Algeria is an incredibly rich and beautiful wine, grain, and fruit country, with vast potassium deposits, and in the sixties extensive oil reserves were discovered. (I crossed the whole country before the last guerrilla struggle began. Algiers is one of the most handsome and modern ports in the world).

British writer Norman Lewis, an on-the-scene observer of Algerian guerrilla tactics in the sixties, quoted a rebel major, white-haired at thirty-two, on the military reasons for rebel defeat of an army at least eight times its numerical strength and supported by abundant armor and by an air force of a thousand planes:

> We have the whole of our civilian population behind us. They keep track of enemy positions for us, so . . . we're never taken by surprise . . . The French have to keep to the roads. We use the goat tracks and move three times as fast . . . Take the celebrated Operation Brumair in 1958, and there've been a dozen more like it.
>
> The French plan was to knock out the headquarters of our Third Wilaya [military region]. They threw in three divisions—tanks, heavy bombers, everything they had. Of course we got word that they were on their way, and by the time they got their 105mm howitzers into position, we'd moved our headquarters ten miles. We ran rings around them, shot up their rear, ambushed their reinforcement columns as fast as they came up.
>
> Before they had enough of it and pulled out, they burned every village in the area . . . We drive our people hard. A forced march in our army means sixteen hours at a stretch. The French are welcome to their tanks and howitzers. Light antiaircraft, machine guns, howitzers and mortars—that's all we need for our kind of war.

The struggle in Morocco was stepped up after the war. Independence was achieved under a monarchical regime, and the Spanish province was turned over to the new independent government by Dictator Franco for unification with the previous French zone. The most outstanding leader, Ben Barka, went on to organize an all-African movement and became an organizer of the Cuban Tricentinental Congress in 1966. Later he was murdered in Paris by the Moroccan secret police in connivance with French secret police, a scandal that shook all France and led to a recall of ministers and the direct involvement of De Gaulle in trying to cover up revelations—which according to leading French newspapers and writers involved the CIA.

Colonial liberation in Africa moved massively after World War II. Within a decade, a large number of new independent countries were born, many by means of guerrilla resistance.

Nearly everywhere in Africa the ousted imperialist power endeavored to continue neocolonialism by installing reactionary governments or helped so-called pro-Western elements to seize power soon after independence. In numbers of instances independence has led to a period of peace, but in most the struggle for popular freedom and justice continues bitterly. Many countries are doomed to a long twilight of neocolonialism and disillusionment.

Armed coups and/or guerrilla war since independence have occurred in, among other places, Algiers, (Socialist Left coup) 1966, Ghana (pro-Western coup) 1966, Upper Volta (military coup) 1966, Uganda (Leftist) 1966, Dahomey (Right military coup) 1965, Central Africa (military coup) 1966, French Congo (Leftist) 1966, Burundi (Leftist, military, tribal) 1967, Ruwanda (attempted Watusi invasion) 1963, Camaroons (Left guerrilla war) 1955–68, Rhodesia (native guerrillas) 1967–1968. Tanganyika and the United Republic of Zanzibar joined as Tanzania, following 1964 leftist coups.

On January 15, 1966 in Nigeria (which had taken the British twenty years and more than three bloody wars to conquer), Major General Johnson Aguiyi Ironsi, somewhat of a Leftist, broke the terrorist rule of British-imposed Sir Abubakar Tafawa Balewa supported by heavy U.S. arms shipments and military instruction. Aided by his Ibo tribesmen and the Sawaba Party, he seized power over the 35,000,000 Nigerian people. But by May, guerrilla warfare and mass riots broke out in the entire north. By July he was dead, and Colonel Yakubu Gowen, backed by the northern Jawa Tribesmen, had taken over. Disorders were still serious in 1966, and in the fall of 1967, civil war abetted by oil companies and outside governments, plus tribal antagonisms, broke out. Lieutenant Colonel Odurieguri Ojukwu, backed by a British army officer, revolted and set up the independent republic of Biafra in the eastern coastal area—a bloody struggle that was still going on in 1968 when Britain, getting new oil guarantees, abandoned Biafra and supported the central government already receiving Soviet arms. In May, just before peace talks were to be held in Uganda, the government troops captured the airport, five miles from Port Harcourt; and wheeled up artillery to fire into the city of 350,000 people. The great oil installations were set on fire, and starving people were sent fleeing along roads bombed from the air. However, Colonel Benjamin A. Adekunle predicted at least nine months more of guerrilla warfare in the interior. By December, 10,000 people were dying daily of starvation, and Biafra had been reduced to 60,000 square miles.

Ever since independence, the Belgian Congo, a vast area of over 900,000 square miles with 15,000,000 people, has been the theatre of repeated coups and almost continuous guerrilla fighting, briefly pacified partly by a United Nations expedition and United States interventions.

This whole empire was once the private property (and hell-hole)

of King Leopold II of Belgium, whose horrors were so vividly revealed by Mark Twain. Later it, particularly Katanga, became the
happy hunting ground of Belgium, British and American mining
companies, which after independence contributed to popular unrest
and secessionist movements. But the Congo knew guerrillas well
before independence. Since the murder of Independence-hero Patrice
Lumumba, it has continued to be troubled by tribal, regional, racist,
and political armed movements complicated by the same selfish political and economic meddling of foreign corporations and foreign powers
(these included briefly the Soviet Union, but particularly Belgium and
the United States). The incomparable Senator Thomas Dodd of
Connecticut, previously heavily subsidized by Dictator Ydígoras of
Guatemala, briefly became spokesman for the Katanga revolt which
the United Nations finally suppressed.

In September 1964, Belgian paratroopers, air-lifted in American
planes from a British base, were dropped into Stanleyville, which had
been taken over by guerrilla leader Gaston Soumialot, head of the
National Committee of Liberation. Ostensibly the intervention was
to save European and American lives. But the guerrillas, negotiating
for the liberation of the prisoners, at once murdered scores of Americans and Europeans and made the United States Consul eat an
American flag. The paratroopers there and in other guerrilla-held
towns mowed down some three thousand Congolese, mostly civilians.
Later, Moise Tshombe, who had taken over in Leopoldville, brought
in mercenaries from hated South Africa and Rhodesia, Belgians, and
anti-Castro Cubans. The tab, it was said, was picked up by the United
States. The brutalities—sportive shooting of women and children and
burning of peaceful villages—has been gleefully told by several mercenary leaders.

The chief Congo guerrilla movement, reorganized in the east and
northeast, is still headed by Soumialot, who visited Cuba in 1965–1966
with half a dozen followers. Che Guevara went over to help him,
before going to Bolivia. Two other allied Congo guerrilla fronts were
under the command of Pierre Mulela and Laurence Kabila. Little
news about them has since come through.

When in Cuba, Soumialot told a news conference "Our struggle
started in difficult circumstances; we began with the most primitive
equipment, machetes, clubs, stones. Soon we outfitted ourselves with
arms taken from the enemy. That is our source of weapons and ammunition." A few outside countries, he said, were sending in medical
supplies. By 1968 guerrillas were fairly quiescent, likely the lull before
a new storm. Leopoldville has been taken over by the pro-Western
head of the army.

Noise is a guerrilla weapon. Stuart Cloete, in his *Gazella*, quotes
a romantic old Negro warrior of eastern Africa. The mistake of his

people, he said, was trying to fight white men with white men's weapons.

> The *assegui* is our weapon, the short spear that T'Chaka taught us to use. "O King," I said to Lobengula, . . . "attack by night. Let no white man sleep. For twenty nights make noises, spear a few watchdogs, set grass fires, raid a few cattle, and then, when they say: These Mathabele never attack, they only try to disturb us—then . . . eat them up, for they will be tired from lack of sleep" . . . Whenever we go near them, we must make noise, much shouting; we must take girls and women with us. It goes hard with man's sleep if he has heard a woman scream. The high voice pierces his heart and will not let him rest.

In the daytime, the attackers were to be beyond reach, but ready to decoy the invaders out and ambush them. He told the king:

> Other nations . . . will learn that the best weapon in the hands of the weak is that of noise and disturbance . . . the strongest becomes weak when he has no rest . . . when the eye is red from lack of sleep the hand that holds the rifle trembles. . . . The white man will destroy himself with his ignorance which he mistakes for wisdom. He will be swallowed up in a vast sea of black men.

Noise has always been a terrorist weapon—famous Japanese *Banzai* attacks, the new American "Screaming Eagles" are examples. But those who have used it have not always been able to get rid of it after their success. In Cuba, in 1957—then after 1959, when Castro had taken over—I was in a number of public places where tiny noise bombs were exploded in theaters, hotels, and cabarets, creating panic. One bright American sergeant has suggested that our buglers —an amusing archaism—play Chinese calls to confuse the North Vietnamese. Of course, the Vietnamese Nationalists do not even know Chinese bugle calls.

At present, the main foci of African guerrilla fighting are in the Portuguese colonies of Angola, Mozambique, Guinea, and the Cape Verde Islands—areas containing in all, more than 15,000,000 people. As the drain on the mother country has increased, the colonial revolts have found more backing in Portugal itself, both to overthrow the long dictatorship of Salazar and to shed the colonies. It was dramatized a few years ago in Venezuela by the capture of the large ocean-liner *Santa Maria,* its crew and passengers by Henrique Galvas, and more recently by the exiling of Catholic priest José da Felicidade Alves.

Guinea, facing the Atlantic, is a country slightly larger than Mary-

land, with 550,000 inhabitants. There the guerrillas (African Independent Party of Guinea and Cape Verde, PAIG) headed by Amilcar
Cabral, an agrarian engineer, began fighting in 1961 and have become well-armed since. Despite 20,000 Portuguese troops sent in
by January 1966, the guerrillas controlled the south and part of the
north, and by December, were reported to be only 25 miles from
Bissau, the capital. Photographs show specialized corps, flamethrowers,
antiaircraft sharpshooters, machine gunners, artillery men, and trained
women nurses and women militia in perky uniforms, armed with rifles
and machine guns. Cabral, a semibald man with a grim but animated
face, attended the 1966 Tricontinental Conference in Havana as the
representative of the rebels in all the Portuguese colonies. All through
1968 and 1969 he reported more progress, by then Bissau was surrounded, "The fact is the Portuguese soldiers are surrounded by the
patriot force in fortified camps from which they venture less every
day." He said farm production has increased, that they even had
enough now to exchange the surplus for clothes and medicine. Health
care had improved. They now had two hundred schools. "In January
1968 a hundred coffins had been shipped to Portugal, and the number
of bodies rotting in the patria was far greater." The day of liberation
is "close at hand."

Angola, one of the most backward areas of the world, has been
ruled by Portugal (itself a backward, Fascist-type dictatorship) for
over four hundred years. Fourteen times the size of Portugal, it is
larger than France, Germany, Belgium, and the Netherlands combined. Of its 5,000,000 people, only 300,000 are white settlers. Eighty
percent of the land is owned by the Companhia Agrícola de Angola,
a Portuguese-American corporation. Iron mining is owned by Krupp.
An international consortium has a monopoly of diamond deposits.
The foreign-owned railways are vital for overseas shipments of nearby
Rhodesia's products. A system of forced labor exists, large foreign-
owned plantations took over the best land and ruthlessly lashed the
farm workers. Infant mortality has reached 60 percent; medical care
is almost nonexistent; illiteracy is 98 percent.

After several years of clandestine organization and propaganda,
guerrilla revolt was begun February 24, 1961 by the Movimento
Popular de Libertaçã de Angola (MPLA). When the prison in the
coast city of Luanda was stormed, the city was quickly taken over.
Soon sixty thousand square miles and many towns were held by the
rebels. A provisional government was set up, land distributed, and
schools and health services were started. In a patriotic ceremony,
vast sums of Portuguese currency were burned in the public square.
Later the gains were lost, and in 1963, 80,000 Portuguese troops
began using scorched earth tactics, inflicting a death toll of 130,000.

In the Matalange cotton area of Northern Angola, the plantation laborers refused to work, and 5,000 were killed. A million Angolans have been driven into the Congo. But the fight goes on.

According to Commander Benedetto, the guerrillas at first had only *catanas,* or can-cutting knives, a few crude homemade wooden lances, clubs, and Molotov cocktails or bottles of palm oil or gasoline with short wicks. Now, among other equipment, they have modern rifles and machine guns from Nigeria, Algeria, Egypt, and the Congo. Much was captured from NATO material and American armaments supplied to the Portuguese.

The movement had setbacks when the leadership abroad split. The more militant set up the Angolan Revolutionary Government in Exile (GRAE) headed by Robert D. Holden, who was promptly recognized by all members of the Liberation Committee of the Organization of African Unity (OAU) and by the Congolese and Algerian governments. The MPLA was all but expelled from the Congo. It set up headquarters in Brazzaville (French Congo) and opened a new front in the northern Calinda district of Angola.

Military coups in Algeria and the Congo, where American backed Mobutu took over, further slowed up the activities of GRAE. MPLA, with headquarters in friendly French Congo, amassed the more vigorous groups and set up a provisional government there. By mid-1966 it was claimed that fifty thousand guerrillas were strongly entrenched, especially in northern Cabindu. For several years, the freedom movement has been firmly established in the Dembos and Nambriangogo regions and along the Zambia frontier.

Late in 1965, the Congo's foreign minister protested to the United Nations Security Council, accusing Portugal of helping Tshombe organize armed forces across the border in Angola to invade the Congo and possibly Zambia also. Armed clashes between these mercenaries and the Angola patriots occurred.

By November 1967 the MPLA claimed that more than 2,000 political-military cadres had been trained and sent into Angola. Attacks—among others in ten military posts—had caused the death of 1,160 Portuguese soldiers, secret police, and traitors. There were more than 1,500 wounded, more than 700 Angolans freed from strategic villages, more than 150 Angolan workers released from forced labor, 4 planes shot down, 9 launches and 10 bridges destroyed; large quantities of Belgian, Israeli, West German, and American arms and equipment captured. Eighty thousand square kilometers (four times the area of Portugal) are allegedly under MPLA control, where it has started schools and a newspaper, built homes, an arms plant, stores, and so on. They are handicapped by Mobutu's refusal to permit propaganda or transit.

On January 3, 1968, the MPLA moved its provisional government from Brazzaville to Eastern Angola. The OAU switched its support from GRAE back to the MPLA. The shift of headquarters to Angola proper, executive committee member Daniel Chipenda says, will end many divisions in authority, and give the movement "a more clearly defined political content and bring the struggle to the decisive stage." Fighting has been pushed into the center of the country.

In Mozambique, the Liberation Front (FRELIM) headed by Edward Mondluene, a powerful, long-faced, semibald man, for a long time a well-known professor in the United States, was organized in 1962. All countries at the Pan-African Congress in Ethiopia pledged themselves to send arms.

Mozambique, where the Portuguese began settling in 1508, is about the size of Thailand and considerably larger than Texas, with nearly 7,000,000 people plus a few whites. The first guerrilla strike came September 25, 1964. According to the leader Marcelino Dos Santos—an intense, light-skinned man, forehead bald, with straight heavy eyebrows and enormous black sunken eyes—war material is cached in Tanzania, some in Malawa. Heavy shipments have been obtained from Egypt, Ethiopia, Czechoslovakia, the Soviet Union, and China. By the end of 1965, some 200 attacks had been made on barracks, bridges, police stations, and other installations, more than 1,000 Portuguese troops killed. The rebels claim that two provinces in the north (Cabo Delgado and Nyassa and their 817,000 persons) have been "liberated." The Portuguese have sent in 70,000 NATO-armed troops and, with American aid, are hastily building jet-air strips and new ports. The FRELIM representative in Algiers, Pascual Macumbi, admitted in late 1966 that the Portuguese still had a few military outposts in the rebel areas, supplied with great difficulty by airplanes, but that the soldiers were completely isolated from the bulk of the people. In March 1966, the Johannesburg *Star* reported that in the previous three weeks large shipments of American artillery and Sabre jets had arrived at the port of Berra and its nearby air field. In November 1966, the Portuguese planes began using napalm obtained from the United States. "The U.S. needs Mozambique's ports and air strips intermediary [to Asia] and won't let us down," said a high Portuguese official. The guerrillas had little additional success through 1967, but still held on to a considerable territory—and more firmly. But in the spring of 1968, they began making new advances in new areas. In late March, according to a Hsinhus news agent, the guerrillas killed thirty Portuguese soldiers in ambushes and destroyed about ten trucks in the Cabo Delgado Province. In February 1969 Mondluene was assassinated in the Tanzanian capital. The movement, however, continues actively.

By the end of 1965, trouble was boiling worse than ever in Southern Rhodesia (Zimbabwe), another Black country ruled by the iron hand of a small governing group of whites. The African rights movement there was founded as the African National Congress in 1957. Soon outlawed, in 1959 it was re-organized as the National Democratic Party. To try to stave off trouble, the British provided the 1961 constitution which gave some hand-picked Black representation in Parliament, but income and educational requirements for voting were set so high that scarcely a score of blacks could enjoy suffrage. Soon "Reservations," or segregated black ghettos were established and the independence party outlawed.

Today the movement is called the Zimbabwe African Popular Union (ZAPU), headed by Joshua Nkomo who since 1962 has been imprisoned in an abandoned gold mine, as are thousands of other patriots. It is against the law for any one even to mention his name.

Following the break-away from Great Britain in late 1965 by Ian Smith's racist government of several hundred thousand whites (owning forty-eight million acres and all industries), fresh terrorism descended on the four million blacks who toil in plantations and in asbestos and chrome mines for a few cents a day. At the beginning of 1966, thousands of "patriots" were arrested. Even so, guerrilla and sabotage counter-activities increased all through 1968.

The situation, not told about in the American press, was described by guerrilla leader Edwardo Nodluvo. He rose in his long robe and enormous leopard skin headdress to tell the Havana Tricontinental Congress in 1966 how his people at first were armed only with determination against powerful modern weapons. Preparing for the break with Great Britain, the Ian Smith government had obtained the latest arms and a fleet of army planes from South Africa, the United States, West Germany, and Portugal via Mozambique—also by seizing arms en route to independent Zambia. The guerrillas fought only "with stones, lances, hatchets, clubs, fire, and even bare hands. We poison the food and the wells of our enemies, derail trains, destroy roads and bridges . . . all their crops and plantations . . . tear down fences." But little by little they captured arms and now got arms from neighboring republics.

He told of the big demonstrations, workers' strikes and student manifestations . . . Workers have been dragged from their homes by white soldiers at pistol point . . .

> Factories, textiles, furniture and small businesses have been destroyed. Some monopoly businesses have been obliged to shut down. In Salisbury [the capital] two big tobacco factories employing 8,000 workers have been closed. Two radio and two textile factories have been bombed. In Bulawaye, the main industrial center, five big textile factories, employing 15,000 workers have closed their doors

. . . four factories have been burned . . . In Umtali on the Mozambique frontier, the four thousand oil-refinery workers are obliged to sleep and eat within the heavily guarded barbed wire fences, unable even to visit their families.

He reported:

Sixteen demonstrating workers were killed November 14 and 15, 1965. Many patriots . . . are being brutally murdered in the prisons, jails and slave centers . . . Our boys have been beaten so savagely that most have permanent scars on their backs . . . Though these and other activities have not been revealed by the colonial regime, the authorities admit having jailed 73,000 African patriots . . . The number of prisoners increases every day as the struggle . . . grows more intense.

In March 1968, the world was shocked by the public execution of patriot leaders. Queen Elizabeth had pardoned them. The Pope protested, other governments (but not the United States) sent pleas. Through 1968 the guerrilla war, now openly aided by neighboring Black republics assumed formidable proportions though more ferocious counter-terrorism has been perpetrated. During the year, some six invading guerrilla outfits were broken up. In November, the leader Moffat Hadebe and two other guerrillas were put on trial for their lives. Five others had already been given life sentences. In May 1968 the Ian Smith government was subject to absolute United Nations economic sanctions, even to the point of barring travel abroad. Without the aid of South Africa, his government would find it difficult to survive.

Of the sixteen and a quarter million people in the Union of South Africa, only 3,700,000 are whites. Though slightly smaller than Angola, the Union is rich, producing nearly half the mineral wealth of Africa. However, mines are mostly owned by British and American corporations. Eighty-seven percent of the land—the most fertile—belongs to the white minority. Black income averages about $70 a year; infant mortality is 40 percent for blacks, under 3 percent for whites. Only a small percentage of black children receive as much as four years' schooling.

South Africa has a long history of violence. On April 6, 1652, the first Dutchmen set foot on the southern tip. After diamonds and gold were discovered, Europeans rushed in. Negro lands were seized, and native rights steadily deteriorated. Under the present cruel Apartheid ghetto segregation, the black people have no bona fide political rights and few other rights. On March 20, 1960, thousands of unarmed Negroes gathered in the streets of Sharpesville without their obligatory passbooks and demanded higher wages. They were machine-gunned; seventy-two were massacred. Tension and repression have steadily increased since then.

During harvest season, Negroes are stopped by the police who tear up their passbooks, then jail them for not having them. They must then spend months as convict laborers on private estates, not even receiving the customary pay of a few cents an hour. In the last ten years, nearly 4,000,000 blacks have been arrested or rearrested for not having their identity cards on their persons.

In defiance of United Nations orders, South Africa also holds a mandate over Southwest Africa—an enormous area of 317,725 square miles but with only 564,000 inhabitants, of whom 74,000 are whites. In 1959 the Southwest Africa National Union (SWANU) was founded by Jariremdo Kozonquizi, a big-faced bearded man who visited Cuba in 1966. Also in 1959, the Southwest Africa Popular Organization (SWAPO) was founded by agile San Nujoma. Some armed revolts have occurred, but no open call to arms was made until early 1966. South Africa still defies the United Nations' orders. Guerrilla fighting increases.

In South Africa proper, a secret Ku Klux Klan called the Broeder-bond, founded in 1918 to maintain white rule Apartheid, is the inner power of the official South African Nationalist Party. It perpetrates terrorism against all Negroes and any whites opposed to segregation. Negro guerrilla outbreaks have invariably been put down with whole-sale massacre. Even so, the liberation effort, organized in 1961 chiefly as the Congress of National Africa (CNA) steadily gained ground though its leader (the lawyer Nelson Mandela) has been in jail for life since then along with 155 other leaders, 50 of whom have been executed. Some 8,000 political prisoners are serving terms from five years to life. Many are on Robben Island, where Mandela breaks stones.

According to Dennis Biritus—a poet, teacher, and sportsman who served eighteen months on the island, some of it in the hospital after beatings—inmates have to lie on the floor without mattresses. While he was there, they were allowed to use the beds only during an inspection by Dr. George Hoffman, an International Red Cross official who whitewashed all the prisons he visited as "spotless." White editors who exposed the abuses have been sentenced to long terms.

Since 1961, *Umkbonto We Sizwe* (*Voice of the Nation*) has directed secret sabotage: arson, destruction of property, particularly govern-ment buildings and works.

But it is not overly effective, and the last few years a great deal of new American capital and arms have flowed into the country. (The Chase National Bank, headed by David Rockefeller, has been harassed by various New York protests including pickets.) However, most outside aid to South Africa has come from West Germany. *The New York Times* estimated that in 1965, more than six thousand West German businessmen, scientists, engineers, and technicians had gone there. South Africa has the greatest concentration of uranium and lithium in the West, and in 1963 the German firm of Gewerkschaft Brunhilde completed a nuclear pilot plant outside Johannesburg. I. G. Farben specialists are setting up plants to make virulent war gases such as tabun, soman and sarin—of which a single plane-load, it is claimed, equals the lethal capacity of a 20-megaton bomb. West German firms are also aiding with rocket research and testing—one such undertaking has been financed by the German General Staff—and it is estimated that South African missiles will soon be able to hit any part of Africa. "We—the South Africans and West Germans—are all working on the task of shaping life according to the same principles," Ludwig Erhard told the German South African Chamber of Commerce, shortly before he became chancellor. Many undertakings are being promoted by Hermann Abs, who financed Hitler and the Nazi party and was convicted as a war criminal—but who is again a powerful figure in the West German Government.

Sooner or later, the big outburst will come: guerrilla warfare in the hills and in the cities and the mines. The black South Africans sing a folksong of many years standing:

> No matter how hungry we may be,
> No matter how persecuted we see ourselves,
> No matter how oppressed we find ourselves,
> Those who make fools of us are playing with fire,
> Those who abuse the sons of Great Africa
> Are playing with the tail of a lion.

9

THE GREAT DRAGON: MAO TSE-TUNG

Mao is the leader of the Chinese guerrillas, a leader of armies, the Republic, and of the Communist State. Among others, he made two blunders, though both in the long run may have been beneficial to his cause and his supremacy in the revolutionary movement.

The first blunder—which he himself admitted had been unnecessary—was the terrible Long March that took his army on a whole year's desperate struggle deep into the hinterland of China. The second was his failure to shoot Chiang Kai-shek when he was a prisoner.

Years before, at dawn on February 4, 1929, he led his four thousand ragged, hungry, poorly armed guerrillas from the high "Mountain of Liberty"—Chingkanshan, not far from his birthplace in Shao Shan in northwest Honan Province—through the forested, snow-covered mountain range along the western border of Kiangsi province. They were harassed hither and yon for almost a year. Two thousand died in a single battle. Their numbers were reduced to a few hundred, but they finally established themselves in two mountain towns on the Fukien frontier. Before long they numbered thousands.

The causes of Chinese guerrillas are to be found deep in the long history of China, which has known many such upheavals over the centuries and in the more recent disruptions of its feudal society by industrialization and foreign interventions.

Lionel Max Chassin, a French military man, comments in his remarkable book on China, "Three new factors appeared in the nineteenth century; the end of China's isolation; the growth of its population; and the industrialization of the western world. In the face of such an assault, the millennial traditions which had for so long maintained the framework of Chinese society were suddenly swept away." The result was Civil War, the Boxer revolution, and continued upheaval which in turn broke down the decrepit mandarin system no longer able to govern decently.

On the heels of national fragmentation, the Sun Yat Sen revolution in China occurred seven years before the Russian Communist revolution. (Like the Mexican revolution, it predated the Russian. In northeast Brazil, the peasants first began organizing well before Castro rode atop a tank into Havana. Revolt occurred in Vietnam, in Morocco, in Algeria, and in the Middle-East long before Lenin and Trotsky took over Petrograd.) Chiang Kai-shek, who organized the Kuomintang Army in 1927—by then acting almost as an American agent—excluded all leftists from his government and sent Soviet agents Borodin and Rabindranath Roy flying back to Moscow. All popular organizations were outlawed. A strike in Canton in 1927 was drowned in blood, and the leaders including Mao and General Chu Teh fled with their famous nine hundred survivors to the mountains to begin guerrilla war. Twenty-two years later they took over the entire country.

Powerful annihilation campaigns—five in all—were waged against the Mao guerrillas in Kiangsi and Fukien. The first attempt, with 100,000 troops, was completely outmaneuvered. In December 1930, by clever retreats and counterattacks, hitting first this and that division, Mao threw the enemy completely off balance. Once his forces whirled back into an abandoned town, and on New Year's night took nine thousand prisoners and a Kuomintang general. Chiang Kai-shek offered $200,000 ransom for the general and his staff. The offer arrived too late. He had already been executed. In retribution Chiang Kai-shek at once killed all jailed Communists in Peking.

More important to Mao was the capture of 8,000 rifles plus machine guns, trench mortars, telephones, medicines, huge amounts of provisions, several radio transmitters, and the entire payroll of three divisions. Three thousand more enemy troops were captured and killed in the hills, and 4,000 were lost by surprise attack on a full division. Though the rebels had lost 7,000 men, they soon were back to 30,000.

Four months later, Chiang Kai-shek sent 200,000 men to wipe them out. This time, the forces advanced more cautiously, establishing blockhouses. Soon Mao hit fast and relentlessly, first at inexperienced North Chinese troops on the enemy's left flank. Then he swept on to drive the Eighth Route army out of Nangfeng. Moving on swiftly, he hit the Fifty-third division. It broke and fled through Kienning to the bridge across the Min River, only to be mowed down by Red forces on the other side. Mao rushed his men back to destroy two hundred miles of enemy fortifications as far as Kiang. At Tungku, the Fifth Army was cut to pieces with the loss of the supplies and weapons of two divisions.

At once Chiang Kai-shek grimly launched his third annihilation campaign—early in July 1931. This time, with a staff of trained German advisers, he personally led his main army of 30,000 men, 200 cannons and 100 planes. They drove out of Kwangsi into Kwantung province. Mao's forces were pushed out of Kwanchang and Tungku, their headquarter towns. Tungku was put to the torch and every man, woman, and child massacred. Planes bombed every concentration of rebel forces.

Leaving four thousand men in the mountains, the Kuomintang concentrated all their forces on the banks of Kan River. The Maoists, trying to surprise the rear reserve, were discovered and had to take refuge in a small village, wet, bedraggled, and worn out after a month of continuous fighting.

Mao tried to push through a twenty-mile gap only to run afoul of two divisions moving south. After a fierce two-day battle, he routed them and marched for three days to destroy a third division. A few days later, they destroyed the army of Hunan province, then drove on west to devastated Tungku.

Mao, who had strong partisan contingents in the surrounding mountains, was deliberately inviting encirclement. But he was attacked by the powerful Nineteenth Route Army and had to disengage. The guerrillas climbed over high mountain paths to a lofty village from which small groups dashed down to harass the enemy by hit-and-run tactics. The hard rains set in, and Chiang Kai-shek ordered a retreat.

All the way to Kiang his forces had to fight fierce rear-guard actions. One whole divsion was lost. Thirty-five thousand Kuomintang soldiers deserted with their rifles and machine guns, and the whole area was taken over by Mao. In all, seventeen of the enemy's thirty-three divisions were lost.

One Kuomintang general lamented, "Wherever we go we are in darkness; wherever the Reds go, they are in brightness." The reverse was literally true: the Kuomintang forces were always visible to the rebels, whereas they themselves moved swiftly and freely in darkness. It was a tactic of circling around the enemy, constantly threatening him, filling him with doubts and suspense, then hitting him where he least expected an attack. At first the enemy scarcely realized a blow was being struck, then suddenly everything collasped in confusion.

These three campaigns were carefully studied by Mao. The previous guerrilla rules, for campaigns to avoid encirclement, for strategic offense and defense, which he had set forth for his little band on the high Mountain of Freedom, had served him well.

The Chiang Kai-shek defeats and desertions saw the rapid increase in partisan forces. The savage destruction of places like Tungku left the peasants no refuge but the Mao army. The resentment against Kuomintang savagery and corruption had contributed to Mao's success. New "Soviets" were being set up all through the province and elsewhere. Full guerrilla victory seemed close.

An outside blow hastened the Chiang Kai-shek debacle: the Mukden incident (September 18) and the beginning of Japanese occupation of Manchuria. Nearly all government troops had to be withdrawn from

Kiangsi province. Even so, attempts to halt the Manchuria invasion failed ingloriously. The country was hit by floods and crop failures. China was cracking up; the Red Army was more enormous than ever.

In 1932 Mao even occupied Changchow in Fukien for six weeks. More towns were now being attacked and seized. More Kuomintang desertions occurred. Captured airplanes were burned, since Mao had no gasoline and no pilots. Presently 80,000 regular Red soldiers were operating, supported by about 50,000 village militiamen. There were guerrilla pockets in seven provinces.

Despite the Japanese seizure of Manchuria, from April to October 1933 Chiang Kai-shek launched a fourth annihilation attack against Mao. The partisans knew the area like the palms of their hands, and two of the three Kuomintang columns driving south were cut to pieces, the third driven back. But Mao knew his tactics lacked previous brilliance. The partisans had set up arms factories, and this had lessened combative spirit, for there was less need to capture supplies from the enemy.

Arranging a truce with the Japanese, Chiang used his great resources and manpower to launch a fifth anti-Mao drive on January 23, 1934. A naval force landed at Fuchow ended Mao's independent foothold in Fukien Province. Chiang now enjoyed the advice of German General von Falkenhausen, who instituted a "Wall of Fire" strategy. He pushed small fortified garrisons into Mao territory, then burned every intermediary building and village and crop. It was a clever, brutal scorched-earth policy, always featured in a certain stage of antiguerrilla combat. The peasants turned to the Mao army for support, but their hysteria and misery built up into panic among the Mao forces. Quarrelling broke out. New sects and dogmas appeared.

The Kuomintang ruthlessly killed more than a million peasants. Many starved to death as the fiery wall advanced.

While Mao was telling the Second National Soviet Congress what still needed to be done in the rebellious areas, Chiang Kai-shek declared in Nanking that he would have all guerrillas out of Kiangsi by June. The Communists were isolated by a ring of troops.

But the war dragged on through autumn. The rebel forces, totalling 180,000 at the outset of the campaign, were reduced to 100,000. A whole division of Kuomintang forces were driven back from the model village of Hsingkue, mostly by women fighting with spears and sabers against "English tanks and armored cars, French artillery and American airplanes."

The ring grew tighter. "The enemy's supreme command was farsighted in its strategy; we thought only of what was under our nose" admitted Mao. "We panicked and fought stupidly." In the Kwanchang battle on the Fukien-Kiangsi border, 4,000 partisans were killed, 20,000 wounded.

This sort of positional fighting had been against Mao's better judgement; it meant the abandonment of previous, agile zigzag tactics. The rebels still held on to Juichin, but with a growing sense of catastrophe.

As Mao's position and the morale of his forces worsened, he felt close to despair. Some months later, he launched upon the frightful Long March. Years later, he admitted that there had been better alternatives. He could have consolidated his forces in Kiangsi and Fukien and thrown all their strength in a drive on Shanghai.

The rough-hewn rebel military genius, General Chu Teh, always deferred to Mao and did so now when the latter decided to break through the iron ring. Their arsenal machinery was taken to pieces and buried in the forest. Records—everything they could not carry with them—were destroyed. A huge mule train was loaded with whatever would help on the journey. Every man was ordered to take only his rifle and twenty pounds of food (fifteen *chin*).

The Long March began from Yutu on October 18, 1934, with eighty thousand soldiers and about thirty-seven women, including Mao's pregnant second wife. Mao himself was sick with fever; his eyes seemed enormous in his pale emaciated face.

In his *Memoirs,* published in Peking in 1957, quoted by Robert Payne in his *Mao Tse-tung* *, his orderly described the departure.

> Around five in the evening, Mao and about twenty others left Yutu by the north gate and turned left toward the river which was all yellow, roaring and foaming . . . Soon the sun set and gusts of bitter cold wind chilled us. Chairman Mao wore a grey uniform and an eight-cornered military cap, but no overcoat. He walked with enormous strides along the river bank.

Up ahead, the myriad torches of troops, resembling firedragons, were already crossing the river on a pontoon bridge. Laughter mingled with shouts and songs. Once across, they captured Kupo and Hsingtien. The salt works in these places were most welcome, for the army had been without salt for a long time.

But the breakthrough cost them twenty-five thousand men. Chiang Kai-shek's forces belabored them from all sides. A huge force drove down from Szuhuan province to intercept them. They had to skirt Hunan and march up toward Chunking, then back south through Kweichow province and on into Yunan which lay on the borders of Tibet; week after week of marching. However, clouds and mist hung over the area so they were no longer harassed by planes, except for one clear day. Mao's young pregnant wife Ho Tzu-Chien was hit

* pp. 147–8.

by shrapnel fragments and almost died. She suffered from the wounds even after the Long March was over. Three of their younger children had to be left behind in the care of peasants, never to be found again. Only the oldest went along. The new child was born en route.

Determined not to let Mao escape into Tibet, Chiang Kai-shek flew down to Kunming to take charge of his troops.

It was necessary for Mao's guerrillas to cross the great Yangtse, the Golden Sands River. Three columns crossed the open plain. A fourth wove back and forth before Kunming to prevent the Chiang Kai-shek forces from blocking the crossing.

The first column covered 45 miles in a single day. They found only a single boat on the south bank. A group dressed as civilians crossed over and told a tax-officer all boats were to be loaded with fuel and food and sent across for approaching "Kuomintang" forces. He hastened to obey.

All night the Red forces kept crossing over unmolested. At dawn they climbed a mountain and surprised two government battalions sleeping at Tungchow. Rifles and machine guns were captured.

Thirty thousand rebels had been lost on the march, but thanks to new recruits, they now totalled sixty thousand. Everywhere they expropriated land, tore up the old deeds, and gave the peasants arms to defend themselves.

Ahead their great enemy was the mountains: a rugged landscape, few trees, little vegetation, hardly any houses, and scant food. At Anshugang they captured the regimental commander with his maps, codes, and deployment orders. They hoped to get to the ancient iron bridge at Luting-Chiao before it could be destroyed, for that was the only way to get through the narrow gorge. They made forced night marches along narrow stone ledges high above the river roaring below. In some places the stone walls were only a few feet apart. The nights were freezing cold.

They found the bridge well defended. Built in 1701, it consisted of thirteen massive linked-iron chains fastened to the cliffs. The planks had all been removed. A hundred men volunteered to try to get across.

The strong wind blew many of them off into the torrent below. Of that brave hundred, only one man got across, but he threw his grenade so well it wiped out resistance at the bridgehead. Fifteen guerrillas then rapidly made their way across. Others followed. The planks were relaid and the entire Army got across.

They climbed on over the Ma An-shan Pass, marveling at the wild red rhododendrons, the waterfalls, the charcoal huts. The Great Snow mountain was a hellish torment of snow and ice. Their lungs ached from the 16,300 foot altitude. Their feet were bleeding. So few people had ever come this way, they could scoop up unwary fish from the streams with their hands.

They were welcomed by the large guerrilla army of Szechuan Province. Only 40,000 men were left. They rested for nearly a month. At the end of August, Mao ordered the march to go on. He wanted to reach Shenshi province before winter.

Thirty thousand set out, constantly harassed by government troops. The rebel chieftain of northern Szechuan quarreled with them, so they had to take a desolate unmapped western route and fight through hostile tribesmen. August was a month of constant downpour and fog. The Great Plain was as terrible as the mountains—only grass and swamps, treacherous footing, few trees, no villages. The foul mud made their legs swell with red blisters. Tribesmen picked them off from hiding places, sometimes with poisoned arrows. Sometimes their guides led them into ambushes.

They had no protection from the driving rain night and day, no fuel for cooking food or keeping warm. Hailstorms hit them, then snow, and swirling winds buffeted them. Many died of cold, starvation, or drowning. Their rice was gone, and they lived on green wheat carried in sausage-shaped bags over their shoulders. Turnip-like roots proved poisonous. The Manzu tribesmen hid their cattle and sheep. All their pack animals were lost; all their medical supplies were lost. Whole columns lost their way.

Later, Chu Teh recrossed the Great Grass Plain three times gathering them all together. Mao was amazed at his energy and fortitude. "I myself could hardly get across it once." Only twenty thousand, mostly late-come recruits who had never set out from Kwangsi, reached Shenshi Province in October 1935.

If the Long March had been a mistake, Mao forever after exulted over the successful termination. He called it the first of its kind ever recorded in history. "For twelve months we were under bombing . . . by scores of planes; we were encircled, pursued, obstructed and intercepted . . . by a big force of several hundred thousand men . . . but by keeping our two feet going, we swept across a distance of more than 20,000 *li* [kilometers] through the length and breadth of eleven provinces."

There had, of course, been other great marches. General Pío Tristán, the last Spanish viceroy of Peru, had marched from Buenos Aires across all Argentina and Bolivia and over the lofty passes of the Andes to Arequipa, Peru. Later a great army was led over the Andes by patriot leader San Martín. There was Simón Bolívar's tremendous march from the mouth of the Orinoco across all Venezuela and through the Andes to the Colombian highlands to break the Spaniards at Boyaca. There had been the long, long march of modern guerrilla Luiz Prestes of Brazil, hither and yon through thousands of miles of jungles, till the force finally escaped into Paraguay and Bolivia.

Mao set up headquarters in caves in the little, walled village of Pao An. The caves also harbored schools and arms factories. Little by little it became the real capital of China. Guerrillas from all over the land came in, many of them his own lost men.

The exploit, blunder or no, had made him a mythological creature; a man of iron, patience, courage, daring, and success. He was the undisputed leader of the revolution. His fame grew and grew while he sat there doing "nothing." For some years, he did little more than study and plan. While he became a mighty legend that assured his leadership of China, new peasant uprisings shook the country from end to end.

The second possible blunder—though this he never admitted—was not to have had Chiang Kai-shek executed when he was captured along with his entire staff and a swarm of officials and secret service men in Sian, not far from Pao An on December 12, 1936. Chiang was preparing a new attack against Mao, but was seized by an able local war lord, young Marshal Chang Husueh-liang who had led Manchurian troops fighting the Japanese. He sent an airplane to Yenan to request that three responsible Mao officials be sent to participate in the Generalísimo's trial.

Chou En-lai, Yeh Chien-Ying, and Po Ku flew to Sian. But at a specially called rebel Executive reunion in Yenan on December 15, Mao said the arrest of Chiang was an act of the local war lord who had no backing in the rest of the country and was a piece of "pure mischief." The war lord was the one who should be arrested.

His reasons for not killing Chiang Kai-shek were many. The Japanese, preparing to strike China, would likely hasten their invasion. Mongolia and the rebel forces would have to bear the brunt. Mao himself was in no position yet to establish the rule of his party over all China and its unruly militarists. He feared that worse elements than Chiang Kai-shek would seize the government and make dirty deals with the Japanese. Chiang Kai-shek, Mao believed, was the only man who could and would put up a fight against the Japanese. Since he had the confidence of the western powers, he would be helped with arms and supplies.

Chang Husueh-liang had made eight demands on the Generalísimo as a price of liberating him. Chiang refused all eight. Chou En-lai held three secret conferences with the imprisoned Generalísimo and on Mao's instructions, made only one demand—the immediate cessation of civil war. When this promise was made, Mao urged that Chiang be released unharmed and backed it up by threatening to seize Sian.

And so Chiang Kai-shek went back to Nanking and, per agreement, Chou En-lai went there as a resident representative of the rebels.

Mao bent every effort for a real *detente* with the Kuomingtang to prepare for fighting the Japanese. He made four promises: to abandon the agrarian revolution, not to overthrow the Kuomintang by force, to reorganize the local government on a democratic basis, and to reorganize the guerrillas as a national revolutionary army.

Mao predicted almost to the day when the Japanese would fail, how many men they would send, and how much it would cost the Japanese. He foresaw that they would not try to penetrate beyond central China. Even so, their war effort would require a million men and a billion and a half dollars. After a period of semistabilization, the massive resources of China—manpower, production, cultural renaissance—would rise with overwhelming force.

What he did not fully foresee was that had the Kuomintang leader been executed, the United States would not have sent massive aid to Chiang's fight against Mao after the war. This, in turn, might have saved the United States from the distorted Asian policy that led to the Korean and Vietnam wars.

On the other hand, the amount of American armament, guns, artillery, planes and tanks sent to Chiang after the war was colossal, and nearly all this material fell into Mao's hands. Without it he could not have conquered China as swiftly as he did. But the loss of life of his own troops was greatly increased.

Besides being a phenomenal military leader, Mao was a great scholar, a philosopher, and one of China's best poets. He counted every day lost—even in the midst of battle—in which he did not read at least sixty pages. He knew Chinese literature, all the classics and many minor writings, and quoted from them throughout his life. He would quote the entire volume of Sun Tzu on war and guerrilla fighting, published about 600 B.C., and he incorporated many of its passages about strategy and tactics almost verbatim in his own book, *The Strategic Problems of China's Revolutionary War*.

He read the great novels, starting on them before he was ten years old. He re-read his favorite, *All Men are Brothers*, the story of bandits who took refuge in the hills, many times. He studied the texts of the Taoists and the Buddhists and found them deficient. He read Confucius, and if disliking his fatuous precepts of virtuous obedience to the feudal lords, gleaned many quotable passages, particularly from the *Book of Rites* that envisioned the brotherhood of man and God, a society of love and compassion in which people worked not for their own privileges, but for the common good. Confucius' vision of the era of "Small tranquility, then the Great Unity *(Ta Tung)*" provided a passionate lifelong philosophy for Mao.

He studied the two-thousand-year-old peasant White Lotus revolt, and the great Taiping Christian Rebellion that burst out of the Yangtse Valley in the middle of the previous century. It had taken a toll of 40,000,000 lives before it was suppressed. It had been led by a Kwanchtung peasant who called himself the "younger brother of God" and the "Prince of Heaven," who published five new gospels of revelations and set up "the society of the highest God" largely based on missionary and Biblical teachings. His three thousand followers let their hair grow long and wore red turbans. They descended from the hills armed with spears and pitchforks; captured small villages and converted the peasants. "The Little Children of God" would see heaven if they died in battle. "Only a small knife," the leader said, "was needed to open China."

In 1850 the Prince of Heaven's power was augmented by a peasant revolt against taxes. He appeared in the market town of Yunganchow in an imperial robe embroidered with five dragons and proclaimed a society of justice. Women were given equal rights, in the army and out. Opium was outlawed. Private property in land was abolished. Fields were to be tilled in common. His movement centered in Honan province (where Mao was born). The Prince of Heaven had fifty thousand troops when he reached Changsha, a city later captured by Mao's forces. The Prince of Heaven then embarked his forces in vessels down the Yangtse, and by March entered Nanking where they butchered twenty thousand ruling-caste Manchus. They were driven back from Peking by a pro-British Mongol general, but still held nearly all south China. The Prince of Heaven remarked after one victory, "The commander of the imperial forces thinks he can put out a bonfire with a thimbleful of water."

United States Ambassador Humphrey Marshall, a small-minded Kentucky lawyer and a former Confederate Army general whom Robert Payne called "pitifully vain, dictatorial and ignorant," defied State Department orders to contact the Taiping authorities, helped the Manchus, and thereby ruined the United States image in China for half a century. For more than a decade, the Prince of Heaven continued to rule over the rich Yangtse Valley, instituting tremendous peasant reforms and social benefits. Basically these were what Mao put into effect a century later.

The foreigners struck against the Prince of Heaven—the Americans under Frederick Townsend Ward and the English under General Gordon. Gordon accepted the surrender of the Taiping princes at Soochow, who, promised safe-conduct, duly appeared in yellow robes wearing royal crowns, their long hair flowing down their backs. They were murdered.

Nanking finally fell, and the Prince of Heaven committed suicide by poison and was secretly buried by one of his wives. His infant

son was caught and murdered, and everybody defending Nanking
or connected with the Prince of Heaven was dismembered. The last
survivors—a small army led by the "Helping Prince"—took refuge in
Tatu Gorge near Tibet, which Mao was later to traverse on the Long
March. There they were hunted down and destroyed. Mao studied
this revolt and its achievements in detail, noted the mistakes, the
victories, the program, the accomplishments.

Both the Taipings and now the Mao Partisans derived their strength
from the Chinese peasants. Sun Yat Sen, before army-head Chiang
Kai-shek took over the Kuomintang government by force and treachery,
declared that the revolution had come into existence to complete the
work of the Taipings. But in his *China's Destiny* Sun Yat Sen called
the Taipings ignorant, stupid men wholly outside current Chinese
history. Mao was to prove this was not true. He and his land program
have already lasted longer in the seats of power than the Taipings
and their dynasty—in the face of far more powerful foreign intervention.

Even so, Mao believed that help for China must come from both
Western Europe and the Soviet Union. China simply had to depend
on outside capital for knowledge and the wealth to develop its
great resources. His one reservation was, "Everything foreign must
be well-digested. That which remains becomes part of China; that
which is not useful will be sloughed off." But China must never
accept foreign aid on the basis of imperialism. It had to come in on
China's terms. His nationalism, which had developed during the
war with Japan, became bitter and implacable only after he was
hindered by the United States. It then turned into blind angry
chauvinism.

All his life, Mao has written poetry, some as fine as any Chinese
poetry ever written. One book of his poems has sold 57,000,000 copies.
He wrote poetry even before he ran away from home and his hated
father (a rice grower and trader) to attend a school some fifteen
miles away. His father, who had put him to work in his rice fields at an
early age, stubbornly refused to assist him. At the school attended by
well-to-do children, Mao was scoffed at for his rags and his hunger.
But he stuck to his studies doggedly, surviving by odd jobs. He read
night and day, carefully conserving the melted wax from his candles
to make new ones. There, and in the preparatory school he attended
in Changsha for six years, he began reading what foreign literature
had been translated into Chinese. A biography of George Washington
impressed him greatly, how the American revolutionist had survived
with ragged freezing soldiers and had finally driven out the British.
He read Marx and Kautzky and Bakunin. For a time he considered
He made one close friend, a son of a well-to-do farmer who be-
himself an anarchist.

came his boon companion. They became nudists and walked the hills in sandals and shorts—in good weather and bad. This was so shocking that the military debated arresting them. They loved to swim. For Mao it was almost a sacred rite.

Whenever he was deeply moved, he wrote poetry. During later Party or military conferences, even in hours of battle, he would often dash off some verses which usually he tossed aside. Now and then some admiring supporter would retrieve them. After reaching the caves of Po An he wrote a great deal of poetry. Often he wrote about the Long March and the stupendous scenery en route.

> No one in the Red Army fears the hardship of the Long
>   March,
> We looked undismayed on the thousand peaks and the ten
>   thousand rivers.
> The Five Mountains rose and fell like rippling waves,
> The Wu Meng mountains were no more than little green
>   pebbles.
> Warm were the sheer precipices when Gold Sand River
>   dashed into them,
> Gold were the iron-chain bridges over the Tau River.
> Delighting in the thousand snow folds of the Min Mountains,
> The Three Armies vanquished the great pass and smiled.

In a Poem of Farewell, at the beginning of the Long March, he wrote:

> The north wind sweeps over the land, twisting and breaking
>   the frozen grass,
> The barbarian weather brings the fluttering snow of early
>   August,
> As though overnight a small wind made thousands of pear
>   trees blossom . . .
> The evening snow swirls thick on the gates of the camp,
> And the wind is unable to move the frozen red flag,
> At the north gate of Lun-tai I bid you farewell
> You who will go on through the drifts of Tien Shan's snow.
> I lost sight of you when you turned beyond the cliff,
> Leaving only the hoofprints of your horse behind.

All during the Long March through the mountain defiles, the high snows, across the treacherous Great Grass plain, in the hours of battle, he never let his heavy knapsack out of his possession. It was filled, not with clothes or food, but with his books and papers. In the caves at Po An he was mostly a scholar, leaving military manners to his faithful army general Chu Teh—a powerful, dogged, wise individual.

There in the cave Mao wrote his five books *On a Prolonged War; The New Democracy; The Chinese Revolution and the Communist Party of China; The Strategic Problems of China's Revolutionary Wars;*

and *Coalition Government*. His pen danced across the pages. The books are full of historical learning and an intimate knowledge of the classics. His thought is graceful, yet intricate and logical, though he becomes almost clumsy when he passes from the proverbs of Confucius and the set Marxist symbols and writes with the crude common sense of the peasants. He is full of pithy apothegms that cut to the core of human wisdom, of human valor, and the virtues of war and peace.

In the first book, he assessed the Japanese war and predicted its cost in men and money, its possible accomplishments, its mistakes and its duration—prophecies uncannily correct. International aid to the Chinese, he said, would be stepped up. During the unbearably long stalemate period featured mostly by guerrilla war, China's efficiency and military power would increase; there would be a mobilization of the whole people and their culture; an increase in small industries, and much agricultural expansion. One grave error (he pointed out five) of the Japanese was their failure to take prisoners. The Chinese had learned that a captured Japanese could be useful in many ways. He enumerated the Chinese mistakes: (1) failure to mobilize the political awareness of the people; (2) passivity, "Our task is to make the enemy passive"; (3) lack of adequate Chinese propaganda abroad; and (4) the failure to secure enough foreign aid.

"Those who believe we can win a speedy victory are as incorrect as those who say we cannot win," and he added, with passion, "We want to tear out the hearts of their officers; throw them into confusion and drive them mad."

In October, 1938 he wrote that the war had reached the stalemate stage. "China's ultimate victory does not lie in Nanking or any other large city . . . [but] in the stout hearts of the people all over the country."

His words toward his long-time domestic enemy, the Kuomintang, became flattering; he even labelled it "the party of brilliant revolution." The "United Front" should be continued. It should have a membership of five million, Communist membership limited to a million. The class struggle that had been the first casualty of the war should be adjusted for the sake of national unity. But he still dreamed of peasant revolt. It could not be successful in any small country, but China was a vast semicontinent with untapped resources.

Greatly concerned about the impact of Western civilization, he wrote that there should be no unconditional westernization. China had already suffered by blindly accepting foreign ideas. Not even Marxism should be slavishly adopted. The Chinese revolution had first to be Chinese and nationalist.

A year later Mao produced *The New Democracy*. The Communists had assembled a vast army, but their program should avoid exasperating Kuomintang liberals. He saw the solution in a unique New Democracy—a long transition period between feudalism and socialism. In short, he was proposing "gradualism" and inveighing against those who demanded Socialist dictatorship immediately. What really had to be avoided was any intermediary bourgeois dictatorship. Before Chiang Kai-shek's day, the Leftists had cooperated closely with the Kuomintang and had held high offices in the organization. So had Mao. That happy period should be revived.

His concessions were not as real as he set forth. In no basic way had he ceded ground. Since the great powers and the imperialists were the out-and-out enemies of China, the country could not do without the aid of the one socialist country (i.e. the Soviet Union), and the international proletariat. "There are only two decent ways open to all decent people in the colonies and semi-colonies. They must go over to the side of the imperialist front and take part in the world counter-revolution, or come to the side of the anti-imperialist front and take part in the world revolution. . . . There is no other choice."

Thus, like the anti-Communists and imperialists, he arbitrarily divided the world into black and white, no shade in between. Yet the Soviet Union had actually worked against a Chinese Communist take-over. Nor did he foresee any proximate possibility that any new Socialist States might appear in the so-called Free World. Yet guerrilla warfare was already going on in Jugoslavia, Bulgaria, and other states. Mexico, Guatemala, and Bolivia were beyond his ken. (Even today, Cuba seems a bit fantastic to him.)

Not until later did he realize that a third-force "neutralist" world would limp along between the giants. (The liberation of Africa was not yet visible, and he must still be amazed, even though he has since tried to meddle with the tribes of Ghana, Tanzania, and Algeria.) The zigzag course of the United Arab Republic has scarcely been pleasing either to Mao or so-called United States policy-makers. His hostility to Tito is hard to understand. He seems also to have misjudged Indonesia—before, during and after its independence.

His *Chinese Revolution and the Communist Party of China*, written in November 1939, was more theoretical. His treatment of the Chinese ethos exasperates and confuses western sociologists. In passages of poetic eloquence, he considers the many Chinese revolts in the past and examines the class forces involved—all within the framework of Chinese grandeur. He looks toward the greater new China. He throws no more sops to the Kuomintang, for by then the Japanese had occupied all coast cities and Chiang's capital had been moved far south to interior Chungking.

He described prefeudal Chinese society, communistic and without classes, that had endured for thousands of years before feudalism

converted the country into a society based on serfdom—a period
that had lasted for five thousand years. Now for a century, feudal
society had been breaking down under the impact of the West. Ever
since the 1840 opium war, China had become semicolonial and only
semifeudal. "The invasion of foreign capital broke the economy of
Chinese society, destroying its self-sufficient economy of town and
rural handicrafts." The destruction had opened markets for capital-
istic commodities and had enabled the capitalists to exploit the
cheap labor of the ruined farmers and artisans. "The chief enemies of
the Chinese revolution are still the imperialists and the feudal caste
. . . sometimes still allied with the native bourgeoisie and part of
the upper bourgeoisie." But he was not against capitalism and private
property, only against imperialists and feudal monopolies. That was
why the Communist revolution first must try to establish bourgeois
democracy, a "New Democratic Revolution." Such a revolution must
nationalize "all large capital interests and all large enterprises of the
imperialists, traitors and reactionaries . . . distribute the large estates
among the peasants. But rich [i.e. intermediate] farmers should not
be disturbed. Help should be given to private middle and small
industries." Such a "democratic" revolution would clear the way
for capitalism, but also socialism. Since China was so backward, much
of capitalism would survive under the New Democratic Revolution.

In the meantime, since cities were always occupied by imperialist
invaders and their subservient Chinese armies, the revolutionaries
turn the backward remote areas into strong bases, making them powerful military, political, economic, and cultural strongholds. That required intensive education of the peasants and continued guerrilla
warfare. "The struggle against such powerful urban foes was bound
to be prolonged and bloody."

The Strategic Problems of China's Revolutionary War appeared on
thick brown paper in February 1941. This dealt with the essence,
the tactics, the strategy of guerrilla warfare. "There is no mystery
whatsoever in the strategy of defeating superior forces." Revolutionary
forces could defeat twenty times their number. He explained, with
maps, the five annihilation campaigns on the borders of Kiangsi and
Fukien, his mistakes and successes.

Again, his chief source here is Sun Tzu, who wrote circa 600 B.C.
and whom he often paraphrases. He made an intensive study of
the Han Dynasty and examined closely how the Russians cleverly
avoided a positional war with Napoleon in 1812. He praised the
French for their strategic withdrawal on August 21, 1914.

He takes up the innumerable forms of guerrilla campaigns; command, camouflage, concentration, deployment, night fighting, anti-
aircraft defense, feints, ambushes. The chief purpose of guerrilla
warfare is to obtain useful loot. The aim is not war of attrition, but

quick mobile thrusts and the annihilation of enemy troops. "It is absurd," according to an ancient fairy-tale proverb, "for a beggar to match pearls with a foreign dragon." One of his notable slogans is "Our strategy is one against ten; our tactic is ten against one." How happy the guerrillas are, he crows, to observe the vast armaments being put into the hands of Chiang Kai-shek! They would be guerrilla armaments in due time.

Mao frequently pointed out that Sung Chiang, one of the heroes of the novel *All Men are Brothers,* was twice defeated trying to capture a given village. Then he studied the topography and sent in infiltrators. His third attack easily succeeded. (It was advice repeated later by Che Guevara.)

"How long can the guerrilla fight go on?" the peasants asked.

"As long as we have space to move in," replied Mao.

China was big enough. "When night falls in the west, the day breaks in the east." Besides providing time and space, the country was mountainous nearly everywhere, making modern implements of war largely worthless. The canyon defiles were too tortuous for artillery transport and tanks. Airplanes had taken a heavy toll in the fourth and fifth annihilation campaign—until the guerrillas learned to scatter quickly. After that, the planes did not greatly trouble them.

The very nature of Chinese civilization—the division between people, between provinces, between war lords, all the violent social contrasts —provided a basis for revolution. The uneven political and economic development, the frailty of the capitalist economy, and the prevailing inefficient feudal economy were obvious—a few industrial and commercial cities lay in a vast sea of medieval, rural stagnation. There were only several million proletarian workers, but hundreds of millions of peasants held under decaying war-lord regimes. Transportation was a strange hodgepodge of river boats, motor roads, and railroads, but mostly field trails and wheel-barrow paths where even a pedestrian could hardly walk. Yes, China was ideal for guerrilla success.

In *Coalition Government,* published in 1945, Mao returned to his thinking of the "twenties" when he himself had collaborated with the Kuomintang and had much influence in its inner councils before Chiang Kai-shek had made his grab for power. He analyzes critically both the Kuomintang and the Communist Party.

By this time, he was leading from strength. The Red forces had played an important part in driving out the Japanese and could no longer be treated as bandits. They had become armies. They could fight back successfully against any new annihilation campaigns. In 1937 there had been 2,000,000 people under Mao's rule. By 1945 there were 95,000,000 spread over 300,000 square miles. He held some of the main ports. The Kuomintang could no longer hope to absorb them, but must deal with them as equals. He offered a program of peace, not war. Any stable government, however, had to be based on the will of the people.

He called for more industrialization. "Our capitalism is indeed too little." What was superfluous was foreign imperialism and native feudalism, but not native capitalism. China, however, would welcome foreign investments that obeyed the laws of the land. (This had long been the theme song of the Mexican revolution and soon was to become the attitude of many new independent backward lands in Africa and elsewhere.) He does not discuss the problems of neo-colonialism. He posed the issue squarely: Coalition or War.

By whatever means, China would become independent. The time was at hand. The great aspirations of China's martyrs for a hundred years had to be fulfilled in *this generation*. Any who opposed this achievement would fail. All through the twenty years of guerrilla fighting in China, Mao Tse-tung constantly hammered on the two slogans "land to the peasants" and "nationalism," now aroused by the struggle to drive out the Japanese.

Soon Chiang Kai-shek was backed by United States troops, money, and arms, and Chinese were being killed by American bombers, American tanks, and American machine guns. Mao's anti-imperialist talk became shriller. More and more people rallied to his support.

The people of the world had scarcely been informed of the Red Army's efforts in driving out the Japanese. Railroads, mines, factories behind the Japanese lines had been destroyed. Mao's armies had fought hard campaigns with increasing strength and confidence from the first important battle of Pinghsinkua to final victory. General Wei Lihung had fought against Mao in the early Chiang Kai-shek campaigns, but he and Mao stood together against the invaders at the battle of Chekuo. On the other hand, when the Red Army launched its "Hundred Regiment Campaign" in 1940, it had been forced to fight off a treacherous attack on one flank by Chiang Kai-shek troops. Even so, General Wei and Mao kept on fighting the Japanese in ever-bigger army actions and with greater experience—in forest tunnels, in city suburbs, on the plains. They sapped the Japanese of sleep, confidence, and resources. The Tokyo radio said the main army to be feared was the Chinese Red Army.

It was true, for by 1945 fewer than a hundred miles of railroad remained in Kuomintang hands and Chiang Kai-shek, despite all the outside aid, was powerless to launch a counter-offensive; the Red Army, however, was stronger than ever and continued to wrest territory from Japanese control. By then, Kuomintang troops were more obedient to Chu Teh than to Chiang.

In December 1944, Mao spoke to the People's Congress in the

border region about the tasks for the coming year. The Americans had reached Leyte again and might land on the Chinese coast at any moment. A simultaneous offensive by all the Chinese armies depended upon a coalition government, yet all efforts to set up a unified command had failed. Most needed was a mass anti-Japanese uprising; in lieu of that, a people's militia must be trained. Among the ninety million liberated, every man and woman citizen must be organized into defense units. The militia, already numbering more than two million, had to be doubled and must participate actively in guerrilla warfare.

The land-mine, he noted, had become the chief weapon. Easy to make, it might be merely a hollowed stone filled with gunpowder. At the same time organizing, training, and supplying a regular army on modern principles had to be carried on. The force must have the complete solidarity of officers and soldiers. All officer abuses had to be rooted out relentlessly. He launched "a support-officer love-soldier" movement in every unit. He also launched a "support-government love-people" movement.

Pending the reestablishment of agriculture and industries in the liberated areas, people must be supported and fed by the old areas. He called for a big reduction in farm rent in all freed territory. Every citizen should have on hand a surplus of food and clothing equivalent to one year's work. Finally he called for more art, more newspapers, schools, better public health. "Tyrants feed on the ignorance of the people; we rely on the intelligence of the people." He particularly stressed proper education of bureaucrats: no one should be punished for criticizing them, for many were corrupt, abusive, and arrogant, and people should be encouraged to speak out without reservations. Again he stressed the need for a coalition government, via continued negotiations with the Kuomintang.

On August 10, five days after the Hiroshima bomb, the Japanese government surrendered unconditionally. At once there began a race to the coast. Chu Teh ordered the besieging guerrilla forces to accept Japanese surrender everywhere. Chaing Kai-shek countermanded this order.

As early as August 15, Mao asked the United States to cease lend-lease to the Kuomintang. Additional weapons would merely be used against the Partisans. The plea was ignored, and Chiang Kai-shek at once planned to open hostilities against Mao's forces.

But the clamor everywhere was for peace. Reluctantly, apparently pressured by the United States, Chiang asked Mao for a conference. Mao's safety would be guaranteed by the Americans. He was filled with doubts for he did not trust Chiang Kai-shek or the Americans, but said he would be glad to go to Chunking "to discuss peace and national reconstruction" and signed this note, "Your younger brother." It was the first time Mao had ever flown in an airplane. He wrote a poem about it.

The two leaders drank toasts and praised each other in public appearances. *A modus operandi* was hammered out. All political parties would have equal rights, a people's consultative Council would be set up, popular suffrage would be established.

On October 11, Mao flew back to Yenan. He hoped for peace, but since no agreement had been reached regarding the armed forces or the Japanese surrender, the chasm had actually widened. "He treated me like a peasant," muttered Mao.

The Communists moved their capital into newly liberated territory —to industrialized Kalgan on the Yangtse River, where they established a good portion of the administrative offices, the University, Art Academy, and military and medical schools.

Already American forces had taken over Tsientsin and had established garrisons in Peking and other cities to guard the railways and to promote peace. But the only ones they fired on were Mao's troops. The aggression was protested by Chou En-lai.

The Americans had come, in short, to protect Chiang Kai-shek; which of course meant not peace but war. Despite Chou En-lai's protest, the United States announced the continuation of lend-lease (already totalling three-quarters of a billion dollars) to Chiang Kai-shek. The crisis had come, and Yenan was quickly evacuated.

High American officers were installed in Kuomintang headquarters —so-called operation MAGIC (Military Advisory Group). Soon Mao's forces were attacked massively by Chiang's troops armed with the latest American equipment. A million other troops were deployed against the Mao forces. The Shihpingchieh battle was said to have cost a hundred thousand lives. American war material flowed in through every port not controlled by Mao to aid Chiang Kai-shek. "The people abroad [i.e. the U.S.] are aiding the reactionaries. They are responsible for killing our soldiers, and if we are faced with mechanized war, we shall fight if necessary with our hands and our feet. Those fighting us do not want democracy at all."

Yet at no time were arms a serious problem for the guerrillas. In his famous work on guerrillas, Mao had said: "Our army's main source of manpower and material is at the front. Their arms, supplies and swarms of deserters, replenish rebel strength." He estimated that within eighteen months he would take over all China.

According to Lionel Max Chassin, Chinese Communist guerrilla forces increased from 10,000 men in 1923 to 300,000 in 1945, but only half were armed. Much equipment was obtained after V.J. Day "by disarming Japanese units in Manchuria, but . . . American material captured from the Nationalists . . . provided the great bulk of equipment . . . Russian material was almost never seen in the hands of Chinese Communists." (The Soviets had a pact with Chiang Kai-shek.)

In January 1949 the Chinese Communists reported that they had captured in all 1,709,000 carbines and pistols, 193,000 automatic weapons, 37,000 artillery pieces, 250 million rounds of small arms ammunition, 2,500,000 shells, 1,900,000 hand grenades, 857 locomotives, and 86 airplanes. Nearly all was American-made.

The United States did send the incredible General Patrick Hurley to attempt a reconciliation between Mao and Chiang Kai-shek. In spite of his propensity to burst out in Indian warwhoops at the strangest moments, for a time the Maoists thought him an honest negotiator. He failed, for he hated the Communists too strongly.

George Marshall personally made another attempt at reconciliation. But even while negotiations were going on, United States partisanship was apparent. It was then that American planes air-lifted the Generalísimo's forces to Manchuria to prevent the Japanese from delivering their arms to the Red Army, even though it had done nearly all the fighting in that area. In June General Marshall was able to organize truce teams made up of United States, Kuomintang, and Communist officers. But Chiang Kai-shek raided Yenan with six P-47 planes and a B-24 Liberator.

Thus Marshall's mission failed. The truce broke down, and the huge armies hurled themselves at each other. The United States blamed the Communists, but its emissaries were ignorant of China's history and the social forces. They held the Chinese in contempt, thus alienating not merely the Communists but large sectors of the Kuomintang they were supposed to assist. On his side, Chiang Kai-shek began jailing, torturing, and killing liberal and pro-Mao elements including students, professors, writers, and other intellectuals.

The war went bloodily on. By 1946 Mao's forces had wiped out one and a half million of Chiang Kai-shek's men and had come to control a fourth of China. More and more, Mao thundered against United States imperialism. In November 1948 he called for an alliance with the Soviet Union.

By then it had ceased to be a war of guerrillas. It was more than a war of mobility. Now, his forces stood at the gates of Peiping and other large cities. The Kuomintang generals began surrendering. The Kuomintang was dying, and Chiang Kai-shek could no longer organize effective defense. Even if he had had the forces necessary, his battle plans were too bizarre to halt the trend toward defeat. The provincial capitals fell one after another. In the middle of January, the victorious Mao army entered Peking, bearing pictures of Mao and Sandino, the

Nicaraguan guerrilla. On April 23, Nanking fell. Other cities capitulated. Shanghai, the one big industrial center, was entered with only token fighting.

Chiang Kai-shek reorganized his shattered forces, announced a new offensive, but steadily retreated. He said, using Mao's words, he was buying time at the price of space. He and his wife's family, the Soongs who had been looting the country, were squeezing it bloodless now, getting their wealth to safety abroad. Even United States Red Cross blood, with the connivance of a United States General, was being put up in $25 tins as a restorer of male virility. By October even Canton was in Mao's hands. Southern China was knifed apart. More Kuomintang generals surrendered. It took only a hundred men to seize Chungking.

Victory brought almost religious fervor. Mao's picture appeared on knapsacks and on walls as a youthful savior, though by this time "the Son of the Chinese Earth" was fifty-six years old. "Our victory," he said, "was not won by guns, but by the people, the support of all popular social groups. There is no other final power." Well before victory, though angry, he laughed at the vast armaments being supplied by the United States, which would fall into his hands. Reactionary rulers, he said, were "paper tigers—fierce to look at, but they melt in the rain."

On April 21, 1949, Mao spoke to the Red Army massed on the banks of the Yangtse, a million strong: "Advance boldly, resolutely, thoroughly, cleanly. Complete annihilation of all Kuomintang reactionaries who dare to resist. Liberate the people of the whole country."

A million troops crossed over that same day—a tremendous spectacle, with great banners, raised weapons, a mighty burst of song. Perhaps this was when Mao fulfilled a long-cherished ambition of swimming the Yangtse River. He wrote a poem about it:

> I swim across the great Golden Sands River
> And the sky of Chu unfolds before my eyes.
> I care not whether the wind blows or rain falls
> This is better than strolling idly in a patio;
> Today I am free!

By June 15, Mao reported that the Red Army had destroyed nearly six million Kuomintang troops, with small losses themselves, and he added, "We are in an era when the imperialist system is headed toward complete collapse . . . The Chinese people have the means to win complete victory."

October 1 he stood in Peking, flanked by Chu Teh and Chou En-lai on the balcony of the Tien An Men red-brass-studded Gateway of Heavenly Peace. Not long before, tribal gift-bearers had entered on their knees to prostrate themselves before the Emperor's yellow throne. Now everybody walked upright joyously. Mao, dressed in weather stained cap and worn clothes, watched the vast multitude moving into the square. A great roar burst from hundreds of thousands of throats. "Mao Tse-tung! Mao Tse-tung! May you live ten thousand years!" They burst into the battle song of the Red Army, "Arise, Arise, Arise, you who refuse to be slaves."

It died away as the Mao's voice spoke into loudspeakers: "The Central Governing Council of the People's Government today assumes power in Peking." Across the open space before the gate rumbled tanks now bearing the Red Star, followed by troops in armored trucks, followed by captured cannon. Sailors came with fixed bayonets. Red guards marched in with machine guns, and peasant guerrillas with red-tasseled spears—the only typical Chinese weapon. Bringing up the rear were white-costumed Yank-k'o dancers.

It was a quarter of a century since Mao had been a starving student at Peking University. It was twenty-two years after a thousand, ragged, hungry guerrillas had climbed the Mountain of Liberty into the forest of ice near Mao's birthplace in Honan. He had once led only a hundred armed peasants. Now he led ten million armed men.

Almost at once he took off for Moscow. At Potsdam, Stalin had disavowed Mao and the Chinese Communist Party just as he had disavowed Marshall Tito. Because of power politics, he had supported Chiang Kai-shek just as he had supported the Allied attempt to restore the Jugoslav monarchy.

Mao arrived in Moscow in a fur coat and fur cap, looking tired and aged. He was shown the usual sights—the Kremlin and a ballet at the Bolshoi Theater. Stalin granted him a loan of $300,000,000 to purchase urgently needed supplies and hire technical assistants, but the atmosphere was uneasy, not overly cordial. (In 1942 the United States had refused Chu Teh's request for only $20,000. So are the fateful moments of history decided—by big and little men.)

Mao's optimism revived as he took the train back across the Urals and Siberia, and he said that the alliance of China and the Soviet Union will influence the future of humanity all over the world.

He fell ill back in Peking. It was not until June that he announced a three-year program of agrarian reform, industrial development, and reduction of oversized bureaucracy, of governmental expenditures, demobilization, better education, and unemployed relief. He guaranteed freedom of speech. "If we are too proud, comrades, we will fail."

Only two years before, he had been hiding in the Shenshi caves reading history. His long hours of study during flight and battle and victory now stood him in good stead. He could still quote Confucius. But today his own poetic and philosophical utterances are quoted more than the aphorisms of Confucius. He was sensitive and subtle and knowledgeable, quick to acknowledge his own mistakes, flexible in his thinking and action, always patient. After coming to power, he was strong when he was close to the peasants of Honan and Central China; he seemed to waver only when he lost that intimate contact.

He knew the basis of power—the landlords were killed, stoned to death by the peasants or shot by Red Guards. The propertied classes were completely destroyed, thus ending all significant opposition to the new regime. Eight hundred thousand were killed, a small number compared to the number killed by Chiang Kai-shek—but a grisly business. Mao himself admitted in 1957 that nearly a million had been killed, mostly by local peasants.

From 1949 to 1968 China was successfully ruled by Mao and his entourage. At least one serious peasant-army uprising occurred.*

The image of impregnable Communist rule was strengthened by the Korean War in November 1950, when the flower of the Red Army was launched on MacArthur's forces and sent them reeling back in broken rout. That victory boosted Mao's prestige and the prestige of the state, and it raised nationalist sentiments to euphoria.

In September 1966, as a result of the new outside threat in Vietnam, Young Red Guard terrorism—a far-reaching power struggle promoted in Mao's name—stirred all China. Such purges are usually preludes to war. Stalin's purges and Hitler's killing of Jews were preludes to Russian and German participation in World War II. Under the fear and stress of United States invasion of Southeast Asia, a new militant revolutionary force has emerged, likely at any time to fight for Chinese security now seriously menaced.

Mao's monthly salary was and may still be $200, though he is wealthy from the sale of his books, of which about 600,000,000 have been sold. *Selected Works* alone has sold three and a half million. In 1966, while the Western press had him ill or dying, he repeated his

---

* Nearly a decade ago in Tibet, religious leaders staged a two-week insurrection against Chinese attempts at land, social and church reform. Tibet had been absorbed into the Chinese empire seven centuries before the United States existed—about the time of the Norman conquest of England—so both Chiang Kai-shek and Mao Tse-tung consider Tibet (like Taiwan) an integral part of China. So have all foreign countries. But after the 1910 revolution, the British promoted separatist tendencies, a task aided later by United States agents. However in 1940 the Chiang Kai-shek government, before it was driven to Taiwan, imposed the six-year-old son of a previous Dalai Lama to head the Tibetan government. In May, 1951, fearing the influence of the western powers, Mao Tse-tung sent in troops, a "pacific" occupation arranged by treaty. By 1959 a brief counter-revolution was ruthlessly put down, and the Dalai Lama fled to India. With the abolition of serfdom, the breaking of the power of the religious establishment, plus Chinese military occupation, it is unlikely that guerrilla fighting will reappear in the near future.

swim across the Yangtse River—during the great Purge. His head was again bobbing and grinning with pleasure in the river—he was seventy-three. He is still a young man compared to Chiang Kai-shek, but his rule is drawing to a close. It is not likely that it will result in a restoration of old-style imperialist controls.

10

ASIATIC GUERRILLAS AND HO CHI MINH

A serious guerrilla outbreak occurred in 1965 in Aden, at the tip of the Red Sea near the Indian Ocean. Aden has been a key British air and sea base ever since the relinquishment of Cypress. It has an enormous oil refinery to refuel shipping and planes.

Earlier step-by-step concessions had already been made. The British promoted several semi-independent federations of sheikdoms (one soon joined by a nearby revolting oil protectorate) and retained only the 72 square miles of Aden under full British rule. But even this could not be controlled.

Outbursts, aided by antagonistic federations and by Cairo and Saudi Arabia, soon made the situation intolerable. In February 1966, the British announced they would withdraw all their fourteen thousand troops by 1967. Some forces were transferred almost at once to Bahrein Island in the Persian Gulf, an oil protectorate claimed by Iraq. Even these outposts are to be abandoned after about 1970. Great Britain, though it has been joining with the United States in constructing various Indian Ocean island bases, is withdrawing all forces east of Suez, in truly a sunset of empire.

In spite of promised withdrawal from Aden, *The New York Times* reported in late 1966 that there had been thirty terrorist killings in fifteen months—that these were soon on the increase, mostly against British soldiers and officials or Arabs who work for the British. Egypt and Yemen made protests early in 1967 against the British for bombing areas north of Aden. Outbreaks grew more bloody up until the end. The British pulled out on schedule, leaving a shaky government in charge.

The guerrilla resistance of the Kurds in Iraq is endemic and has brought down various governments. In June 1966, Prime Minister El Bazzaz declared over the radio that the five-year war against them had used up the entire proceeds derived from oil export. He had made an harmonious agreement with Mustafa Barzani, head of the Kurd Democratic Party, to grant full autonomy, the use of their own language, and Parliamentary representation. A leading Kurd was put in charge of the Commission working on nationalization of the oil industry then owned by the Iraq Petroleum Company, an American, British, and French consortium. The Kurd question (promises were not kept) was involved in the 1968 and 1969 Army coups.

There are ever-increasing Arab guerrilla attacks in Israel since the late war, particularly in territories seized from Jordan and Syria and in the Gaza strip. These groups are operating mostly out of Jordan and Lebanon.

Elsewhere in Asia, guerrilla warfare by the Naga and Mezo peoples is widespread in India's Assam State north of East Pakistan. In 1968 it required massive army mobilization. Guerrilla fighting promoted in part by Pakistan in the Indian-held portion of Mohammedan Kashmir led to near war. Uneasy peace arrangements were made under Soviet auspices, but Kashmir remains an open sore on the flank of India. The Kashmir leaders remained in Indian jails until early 1968. More guerrilla outbreaks are all but inevitable, perhaps more war also. The Indian government keeps reconnaissance helicopters operating constantly. In late 1968, Pakistan (the eastern sector particularly) was harassed by antigovernment riots and some guerrilla activity. In March 1969 a new military dictatorship attempted to meet the growing crisis.

Malaysia is the artificial jigsaw state of mainland and scattered islands put together in 1963 by the British after twelve costly, bloody years of putting down a guerrilla movement. The country is still plagued by guerrillas, particularly in the islands. The secession of Chinese Singapore has curtailed the country's economic and political authority.

A guerrilla movement headed by Ahmed Zaldi Aldruce is fighting in the jungles of North Borneo—Kalimantan—rich in rubber and minerals. His delegate spoke at the Havana Tricontinental in January 1966. He was warmly greeted by Fidel Castro—"The people of North Kalimantan are a people who fight bravely for its liberation." The guerrillas were aided by Indonesia, but assistance was cut off because of the 1966 military regime's rapprochement with Malaysia. The struggle had grown acute again by early 1968. The Philippines also claim this area and the Filipino government has been training guerrillas to try to take over—who may have participated in recent attacks. Relations with Malaysia are very strained.

In Burma after World War II guerrillas came to control two-thirds of the country, but were gradually hammered back with British aid by General Ne Win, the present "neutralist" military dictator. But they are still active all along the Chinese frontiers and in Thailand.

In 1965 China warned that guerrilla warfare might break out in Thailand against "the feudal overlords of Thailand and the puppet ruler for American imperialism." Guerrilla refugees, expelled from both Burma and Malaysia, make constant raids from their new jungle settlements in Thai. The country was also plagued with outlaw fighting by the Laotians in the northwest and by Shan tribesmen in the northeast. On August 25, 1966, Stanley Karnow reported in the Paris edition of the *Herald Tribune* that the police "range through villages, squeezing the local population for food, lodging, and girls. Uncooperative peasants may have a bone broken, or worse, find themselves detained as communists." By 1968 guerrillas organized as the Patriotic Front had appeared in much of the country and close to the capital. An attack was launched on an American air base.

The United States has been feverishly building a half-billion-dollar complex of jet airstrips, ports, naval bases, depots, barracks, and roads aimed toward the guerrilla areas, toward Cambodia, Laos, and China: by 1968, it had more than fifty thousand troops in the country. Bombing flights over Vietnam and Laos are being made from five Thai bases that by 1967 were the takeoff for 80 percent of heavy bombings. Much of the air transport (as in Laos) is in CIA hands, including defoliation activities in South Thailand. Ruthless punitive actions, bombing, police brutality, and the burning of villages, have served as an excuse to step up American intervention—a steady escalation, with customary peace talk. When and if the Vietnam War ends, the American people will rub their eyes at discovering a full-fledged armed involvement in Thailand.

United States "advisers" are now training "Green Beret" Thai brigades for use at home and in Vietnam. The local authorities stated that in mid-September 1966, United States forces were participating actively in the fight against northern jungle rebels. To enlighten the American people, this was flatly denied by the State Department, but in November, it admitted that its military pilots were flying helicopters—and by November, bombers—against the guerrillas and stationing "advisers" in the area. However, on February 4, 1967, Foreign Minister Thanat Khoman said with a straight face, "Thai is not a colony, but a democracy."

In Cambodia guerrilla warfare (reportedly promoted by the CIA) plus the danger of invasion, led half a dozen provinces to be placed under martial law in February 1968.

Guerrilla fighting continues in Laos by the Kha Kha tribes people, the lower mountain Meo Meo, and the Cao Caos above the four thousand foot level. Food and weapons for resettled villagers are flown in daily by CIA airlines. In January 1968, the United States rescued some one thousand Laotian soldiers when North Vietnam and Lao guerrilla forces overran strong points near the jungle trail. Soon after, Leftist Pathet Lao forces were overrunning towns in the central highlands not far from the capital.

United States planes continually bomb in Laos along the Ho Chi Minh road, also near the capital and elsewhere. It was reported in

December, 1966 that American troops had crossed from Thai to occupy a southern strip of the country. Yulian Semijonov of *Pravda* reported after a visit made to Laos in February 1968—hardly an unbiased observer.

> The ground is lacerated by craters from one-ton bombs. The land in the mountains is not allowed to feed people . . . The intricate terrace system of irrigation of the rice fields is covered with bomb craters. One-ton bombs are also dropped on the cliffs, which accommodate hospitals, schools and inns. Not a person can live in his own house—everything in the liberated areas has been burned and demolished. The Laotian people live in cold caves. In them, they study mathematics . . . wash laundry, give baths to children . . . write books and have concerts.
>
> By day there is the roar of jet planes bringing death. At night there is the nerve wracking whine of AD-6 planes in the black sky . . .
>
> We fell to the ground and crawled to one side of the path toward the cliff . . . The ground shook . . . There have been cases of eyeballs breaking from their sockets and eardrums broken from the blast waves.

In the caves where a little boy had been blinded, heavy smoke hung like cotton wool over the floor. They could not move out of the cave for more bombs began falling. Yet "the rhythmic pulsating life of the country, fighting for unity, neutrality, peace, and prosperity" goes on. From one large cave came the "majestic liberation song 'Chan Pon.' " Clearly Laos is another site of a major United States escalation of the war that still threatens to engulf all southeast Asia.

The major stage for guerrilla fighting today is South Vietnam. After its liberation from the Japanese and its 1945 declaration of independence, the French tried to reconquer it with the aid of American planes, arms, and money—80 percent of all costs. But 800,000 French and Vietnamese soldiers were unable to put down the guerrillas. Since 1956 the entire job has been taken over by the United States, first with advisers, then with troops, ships, and planes. By 1968, 550,000 U. S. men had been sent in, plus more than 70,000 South Korean, Australian, New Zealand, and Thai soldiers, mostly of whom are outfitted and paid by the United States. After bitter debate, the Philippines finally sent in a tiny technical contingent.

Ever since the Paris talks began in May 1968, the war has been steadily escalated. There were more bombings in the Panhandle than previously in all North Vietnam, more bombings in South Vietnam and Laos, more United States troops, 10,000 more Thai troops, an added number of South Korean fighters, and stepped up shipments of material. More equipment, rifles, planes, tanks, and artillery, bombs, and rockets are supplied by the United States; more chemicals, poisons, gases, and defoliants. This in addition to augmented Saigon forces, nearly a million.

This manpower figure does not include 50,000 American troops in Thailand, 270,000 Pacific Navy personnel, or the vast army of civilians, private construction workers, specialists, aid and development people, and CIA and other secret service agents. It does not include 60,000 American troops in South Korea, which permit the United States to send in such a large force of Korean mercenaries. Nor does it include the increased military personnel in bases in Japan (36,000), Guam (25,000), Okinawa (25,000), the Philippines (25,000), and forces of unknown number in the Indian Gulf, Australia, and Hawaii—headquarters of the whole enterprise.

Besides conscripts, the United States has flung in a mighty air force, at least 4,000 planes and helicopters, also a flotilla of hundreds of naval vessels. The direct military costs in Vietnam itself by September, 1966 had reached $1,500,000,000 a month, and by 1967 the year's total was well over $30,000,000,000. The total direct outlay by the United States has been over $100,000,000,000. By the end of 1968 United States casualties totalled more than 250,000 but Vietnamese and Viet Cong losses have been higher.

It is the biggest guerrilla war in history, a mammoth invasion, a power drive that in many aspects surpasses that of World War II, despite the small size of the under-developed country. It is a great elephantine display of power, which tramples all the cabbage plants, but which thus far has failed to daunt the little men under the cabbages.

The Viet Cong heroes [or villains] who lead the guerrillas, the NLF in the south, are not much known. Most are educated men, devoted and competent, though scarcely mentioned in the American press, where their names sound strange and remote. NLF executives are Communists, Catholics, Buddhists, and representatives of other religions, as well as lawyers, architects, and businessmen who have fled from Saigon. They are not directly subordinate to China or the Soviet Union—countries from which arms keep coming in.

By February, 1968, after years of war hailed repeatedly by American generals and politicians as being near victory, the Viet Cong were able to stage attacks in 1968 and early 1969 on every town and city in the country including Saigon, Hué, and Da Nang. Eighty percent of Hué, much of Saigon, and many provincial capitals had to be wiped out by United States bombing raids, with great loss of civilian life and the creation of hundreds of thousands of additional refugees. President Johnson called it a victory. Yet by July, 1968 the Marines had to abandon—with much loss of life and equipment—Khe Sanh and surrounding outposts. Da Nang itself was under frequent bombardment and ground attacks. Bombs were still falling a few miles from Saigon and in Saigon. Terrorist attacks continued in the beseiged city. Eighty percent of the United States army was pinned down around Saigon and along the demilitarized zone. The rest were in outposts, under repeated attack. The rural areas are still largely in NLF hands. Time and again the guerrillas are cleared out of surrounding areas, but the news reports a few days or weeks or months later showed they were back at the old stand. In mid-December, 1968, they were again attacking shipping in the channels to Saigon. In January a strong offensive was staged in the Mekong Delta areas. By March, every town and city was under artillery and rocket, and often ground attack.

By the 1954 Geneva agreement, North and South Vietnam (much of which was voluntarily surrendered by the Ho Chi Minh guerrillas) were considered one country. The provisional partition at the seventeenth parallel was to be made permanent or be ended by a 1956 plebiscite. The United States and its imposed puppet President Ngo Dinh Diem refused to carry this out, thus making new guerrilla warfare in the South and presently intervention by the North inevitable.

Actually, Cuban liberator José Martí noted, Vietnam's independence struggle was resumed in strength back in 1898. The country had never been wholly pacified since Napoleon III—dreaming of imperial conquest—invaded it. The liberation struggle became very active more than twenty-five years ago, first against the French, then against the Japanese, then against the French again, and their United States backers. Catholic dictator Ngo Ding Diem, installed by and backed by the United States, began harassing non-Catholic religious sects with his army and police. The semiautonomous mountain people resisted, at first with bows and arrows, poisoned lances, and animal traps. Opposition spread. Protests were drowned in blood at Ngan-Son, Cho-Duoc, Mo-Day and elsewhere.

A Viet Cong leader later described the situation.

> Hundreds of patriotic students and intellectuals were jailed, thousands of union leaders, dozens of thousands of workers were cruelly tortured. Buddhist monks and laymen were assassinated. Thrown into bankruptcy, many bourgeois nationalists committed suicide. The cries of pain of the people from new born babies to old folk, moved all South Vietnam . . . Thousands of tons of paper, thousands of hours of work could not suffice to enumerate all those crimes.

Finally, the former guerrillas, aided by the Cao Dai religious rebels who started with fewer than a thousand guns, seized Tu Mai fifty-five miles northwest of Saigon, where they obtained a large supply of arms and ammunition.

The corrupt, bigoted Diem government, almost wholly dependent on American dollars, impressed "volunteers" and collected taxes at the point of the gun. Diem and his retinue became fabulously wealthy. Thrown out finally (with the assistance of the CIA unit of his own army), he and his brother were murdered.

The process was summarized by the *London Times* correspondent in 1957.

> Diem has divided the South. Instead of merely crushing his legitimate enemies, the Communists, he has crushed all opposition . . . He has been able to do this simply and solely because of . . . massive dollar aid, which kept in power a man who by all the laws of human and political affairs, would long ago have fallen. Diem's main supporters are to be found in North America, not in Free Vietnam.

His successors have had nothing better to offer. Diem—but not the Diem system—has gone. Nguyen Cao Ky, once a fighter for the French and who represents the local land monopoly, was a more successful Diem. Finally a constitution, O.K.'d by President Johnson, was drawn up. An election was held, and a new president was installed after he received about 30 percent of the actual vote—not more than 13 percent of the potential national vote. In mid-1968 the leading opposition candidate was jailed, and the leaders of one of the strongest opposition parties condemned to death in absentia. It is largely a military government, beholden chiefly to army generals and United States armed forces and money.

The present rulers, as before, are "Bourbons" who have learned nothing and forgotten nothing. As Walter Lipmann put it,

> They seek to retain those privileges they have and to regain those they have lost . . . [and] have depended on foreign bayonets for survival. For its own strategic and political ends, the U. S. is thus protecting a non-Communist . . . social structure that cannot defend itself and that perhaps does not deserve to be defended . . . I . . . worry . . . that in the process of waging this war, we are corrupting ourselves. I wonder when I look at the bombed peasant hamlets, the orphans begging and stealing in the streets of Saigon, and the women and children with napalm burns lying on the cots in hospitals, whether the United States or any nation has the right to inflict this suffering and degradation on any people for its own ends.

Where corruption is so great, where black marketeering is an outrageous scandal, there can be little control over money, men, or goods. Supplies are trucked directly from the boats to Cambodia. They melt into the jungle. Urgent calls come in for more. Some Vietnamese officers have been less interested in risking jungle death than lining their pockets or plotting a governmental takeover—anything for self-enrichment. The opium trade, centering in Thai and Laos has flourished fantastically, even on G.I. bases.

Wilfred G. Burchett, an Australian journalist who has covered Cambodia, the Viet Cong areas and North Vietnam (toward whom he is most sympathetic) tells how a whole printing plant was smuggled out of Saigon piecemeal, even its big rollers; how NLF propaganda was then smuggled in. Correspondent Malcolm W. Browne, in his *The New Face of War* (preface by Ambassador Lodge) tells how chemicals for explosives and even steel tubes for artillery are easily acquired by guerrillas in Saigon itself. All atrocities, including under-feeding the barbed wire "freedom" villages, are profitable. Chinese supplies such as steel sent in to Hong Kong actually go to the United States forces.

A few leaders in the North have become vaguely visible to American readers. Particularly Ho Chi Minh (the long-time guerrilla fighter and, since the 1945 Japanese surrender, President of the country) and his military commander Vo Nguyen Giap, who forced the French to surrender at Dien Bien Phu and has written important books about guerrilla warfare.

Ho Chi Minh * was born in 1890 as Nguyen Tat Tanh. He is a small slender man, with a tea-colored face and a stringy rice-colored goatee. His eyes are sharp behind spectacles. Highly educated, he speaks seven languages, some say eight—the eighth being enigmatic silence. His father Nguyen Sinh Hing was a peasant in the Nghe Tinh region on the Gulf of Tonkin, an area of green fields and gleaming beaches below the mountain foothills. In summer a hot wind from Laos cracks the earth and shrivels the crops. Typhoons bring torrential rains. In the eighth and fifteenth centuries it was the center of revolt against Chinese rule. It fought the French in 1880, and rose against them repeatedly. The French artillery wrecked much of Vinh, its capital, in 1947 and 1954. It has since been wiped out of existence by United States bombs.

Nguyen Siah Huy married his employer's daughter, receiving a straw hut and small rice paddy as a dowry. There Ho, the youngest of three children was born. His father studied, secured a degree, and became a teacher at Hué, later at Than Hoah. Then in 1905 he became a secretary in the imperial palace in Hué. He had become a mandarin; he served as deputy prefect in Binh Khe until kicked out by the

* During his long career as a revolutionary outlaw and leader, he has gone under at least eight names. [Ho's death was announced as this book was going on press.]

French. For twenty years he wandered from Saigon to Angkor and never rejoined his family, earning his living as a bone-setter, story teller, and as a scribe. He died in Cochin China in 1930.

Ho was brought up by an uncle who supported a nationalist guerrilla group. Ho's older sister, Tanh, practiced medicine and for a time managed a non-com officers' mess in Vinh where she stole arms for the guerrillas. "Other women bring forth children, you bring forth rifles," said the commissar who sent her to prison.*

Ho was ten when his mother died. He helped hide peasants from the French road levee. At fifteen he attended Quoc Hoc high school, where he became involved in the 1908 insurrections. At twenty-one he got a job teaching French and Quoc Ngu, but after eight months slipped off to Saigon where he shipped on a vessel as mess boy. He was at sea two years and saw North African ports from Cairo to Dakar; Marseilles, Boston, and New York. He went to London were he shoveled snow and washed dishes, read books, and hobnobbed with Fabians.

In 1917 he went to Paris, calling himself Nguyen Ai Quoc, where he mingled with one hundred thousand Vietnamese brought in to fight or labor. He endured poverty, became a photographer, dodged the police, engaged in Leftist demonstrations. He consorted with revolutionists, trade unionists, and pacifists at a back stall on the Quai Jemmapes and contributed *Reminiscences of an Exile* to *L'Humanité*, wrote a short play, the *Bamboo Dragon*, and articles for *Le Populaire* (published by Karl Marx's grandson).

He was described as a "wraith-like figure always armed with a book —Zola, Anatole France, Shakespeare, Dickens, Hugo, Romain Roland." His gaunt, gentle face was aglow with idealism. Once he attended a Saccho-Vanzetti protest meeting. Trying to deliver a Vietnam freedom proclamation based on Woodrow Wilson's Fourteen Points to the American leader at Versailles, he was booted out. (Had he been given a hearing, perhaps the history of the world would have been altered.) Presently he toured France, organizing Vietnamese workers. At the Socialist congress in Tours he made an impassioned talk about the brutalities and injustices of French rule in Vietnam, but made little dent, so he joined the Cachin-Froisard Communist group and wrote a violent pamphlet based on his North African experiences, attacking French imperialism—*The French Colonial Process*. He denounced the killing of Annamese and blacks by using them as conscripts "on the banks of the Marne and in the mud of the Champagne—to water the laurels of the French chiefs and provide their bones for the shaping of marshals' batons." He organized the Intercolonial Union, founded, edited, and distributed as its organ, *Le Paria*

---

* Quoted in the biography by Jean Lacouture. Ho's brother, Khiem, a teacher, died in 1950.

(The Outcast). *Le Paria* contained material about Vietnam, Syria, Algiers, and the Rif War in Morocco.

The Minister of Colonial Affairs set a spy on his trail.* Ho wrote the minister a sarcastic open letter, saying he would publish his daily schedule so that the workers' tax money would not have to be wasted on such nonsense, *viz*:

> 8–12 Workshop.
> Afternoon. Newspaper offices 'Leftist, of course,' or at the
>   library.
> Evening, At home or attending educational talks.
> Sundays and Holidays. Museums or other places of interest.
> There you are!

When Marshal Lyauty left Rabat, he wrote crudely, "The disreputable old fogey is leaving Morocco so he can nurse his syphilis in France."

His last article in *Le Paria*, sent in from Moscow, was "Hands off China," a warning to British and American Imperialists.

In 1960 Ho himself told in *L'Écho* how he had turned to Leninism. The great discussion in France was whether the Socialists should join the Second, the Second-and-a-half, or the Third International. All Ho wanted to know was which sided with the peoples of colonial countries. (It was Lenin's Third International, of course.) He shouted with joy when he read Lenin's words on the subject. He flung at his comrades, "If you don't condemn colonialism, what kind of a revolution are you waging?" He remarked, "At first it was patriotism, not communism, that gave me confidence in Lenin." His ideas "illuminated the path to final victory."

Ho spoke at the Ninth Communist Cell, the intellectual group where he met Boris Souvarine and went with him to the 1921 Party Congress. He also spoke at the Club du Fauberg on colonial exploitation, telling the French workers to get rid of their narrow prejudices against Africans and Asians.

He reached Moscow a few days after Lenin's death. On January 27, 1924 he wrote in *Pravda*: "Lenin dead? What are we going to do?" The people of colonial lands were "anxiously awaiting the answer."

He studied at the University of Peoples of the East, wrote articles and two pamphlets: *China and Chinese Youth* and *The Black Race*. Among others, he met Bukharin, Radik, Zinoviev, Stalin, Li Li-san, and M. N. Roy, the Hindu revolutionist whom he was to see again in China—where both went in 1927 as Comintern agents to work with Mikhail Borodin at the Kuomintang War college. Roy did not like him.

* Paul Arnoux, who dogged Ho across Europe and Asia for years and later was able to supply many details of his biography.

He participated in the Fifth Congress of the International in Moscow from June 7 to July 8, 1924, and criticized that organization for doing "nothing whatever" in behalf of colonial liberation. He exposed the systematic dispossession of Vietnamese peasants and the way Catholic missions worked in behalf of imperialist exploitation. "The revolt of colonial peasants is imminent. They have already risen in several colonies and been drowned in blood." His slogan was "national emancipation via international revolution." His main objective was always the destruction of the colonial system in Indo-China.

Early the following year, he went to Canton to aid Borodin. By midyear he had set up the organization Vietnamese Revolutionary Youth and published a newsletter with that name in which he stressed nationalism and a bourgeois-democratic regime to be followed by social transformation. "One becomes a revolutionary because one is oppressed . . . The bourgeoisie rose against the feudal system which was oppressing it. Today the same bourgeoisie is tyrannizing over the workers and peasants, which as a result are the driving forces behind the revolution." He sent agents and students to Moscow and to Indo-China. When Chiang Kai-shek seized and purged the Kuomintang, Ho left for Moscow as did Borodin and Roy. He traveled through Europe, then embarked for Siam (Thailand). He spent the next few years agitating and organizing in Indonesia, Shanghai, Malaysia, Thailand, and Vietnam.

In Hong Kong in 1930 he brought Left Splinter groups together in a federation—which he effected at a soccer match in the stadium. The Central Committee was stationed in Haiphong, later in Saigon. The February 18 manifesto called for the overthrow of French imperialism, feudalism, and the reactionary Vietnamese capitalist class; and for the establishment of full independence. Under a government of workers, peasants, and soldiers, he asked for confiscation of all foreign-owned property, land for the peasants, an eight-hour day, abolition of unjust taxation, all freedoms to the masses, universal education, and male and female equality.

That year the Tonkin native garrison revolted and killed its officers. French bombers strafed it and surrounding villages. Rebel leaders were guillotined. On September 12, six thousand peasants staged a hunger march on Vinh. They seized and distributed large estates and set up People's councils called Xo - Viets—a ready-made pun. Ho was in Hong Kong, but was condemned to death in absentia. His extradition was demanded. He was arrested on June 6, 1931.

At this time, according to a fellow worker, he was thin and agile, clean-shaven except for a few hairs on his upper lip, his face sharp and gray. He was insanely frugal, always energetic, taut, and vibrant. He had only one thought in his head: his country. He was no doctrinaire but a militant, tireless organizer.

In Hong Kong he was taken to the prison hospital with advanced tuberculosis, which he had had for years. Among those who fought against his extradition was Sir Stafford Cripps. In 1933, he was proclaimed dead, and funeral ceremonies were held in his honor! Actually his lawyer had smuggled him out and put him on a steamer bound for Amoy under an assumed name. He went on to Shanghai and finally got to Moscow, where he was a delegate to the Seventh Comintern Congress. He studied at Lenin Institute and taught Asian history there. He gave his lectures in verse, for it made studying "easier."

He combatted Party bigwigs by calling for a Popular Front and opposing a Far Eastern Congress of militants in Maçao in 1935. Extremism, he contended, would merely play into the hands of Japanese imperialists. He wanted a broad democratic national front of French and Vietnamese bourgeoisie, civil rights, amnesty, and legalization of the Party; but no compromise with Trotskyites, "henchmen of the Fascists." Communists should avoid leadership, merely make the greatest sacrifices, and set the example. He was sent to Sochi to be cured of tuberculosis and was not discharged from the hospital until 1938. He next traveled to Yenan, pushing a cart all the way. The Kuomintang was asking for instructors on guerrilla fighting, and he became a military strategist for Chiang Kai-shek (perhaps one reason why he is independent of Mao today). He met Van Dong and Vo Nguyen Giap, at that time a history teacher.

In 1941 he entered North Vietnam and in a cave at Pac Bo founded the Viet Minh. He trained cadres, translated a history of the Soviet Communist Party and Sun Tze's early treatise on war, and turned out several pamphlets on guerrilla warfare. Guerrilla bands were being led by Nguyen Giap and Chu Van Tran, a highlander. Special "propaganda units" were set up, and operations were pushed on into Tuyen Quang and Thai Nguyen provinces.

He returned to China under the name Ho Chi Minh ("The Enlightened One") to get support from Chiang Kai-shek for his Vietnam Independence League and against Japanese imperialism. He was arrested as soon as he crossed the frontier. Chiang Kai-shek wished to set up his own Vietnamese party subservient to the Kuomintang.

Word came back to Giap that Ho had died in prison. "We were almost paralyzed with grief. We organized a ceremony of commemoration for our revered leader." Van Dong prepared the funeral oration. A few months later a newspaper came through with a verse in the margin unmistakably in Ho's handwriting—he spent his time in prison writing poems. Later they were published in Hanoi as *Prison Notebook*. They are not so good as those of Mao:

> The clouds are setting the peaks aglow,
> The peaks are hugging the clouds—

> I wander alone, roused to feeling,
> Scanning the distant southern sky:
> I am thinking of my friends.

He was being marched hither and yon in irons with a yoke around his neck, but he found time to write: "I shall versify until I see freedom." "It is your body which is in prison, not your mind."

> The rice-grain suffers under the pestle—
> But admire its whiteness when the ordeal is over.
> It is the same with human beings in our time—
> To become a man you must endure the pestle of misfortune.

> "The rose blooms and the rose withers,
> Unaware of what it does.
> The scent of a rose merely has to drift into a prison
> And all the world's injustice
> Shrieks within the prisoner's heart."

> "Being chained is a luxury to vie for.
> The chained have a place to sleep,
> The unchained have none . . .
> The State treats me to its rice
> I lodge in its palaces
> The guards take turns escorting me.
> Really the honor is too great. . . ."

He finally learned why he was in jail. Roosevelt and Chiang Kai-shek were devising a joint plan for China to take over North Vietnam after Japan's defeat. What price victory!

Suddenly in 1943, Ho was released from prison and was made head of the Dong Minh Hoa, the Vietnam independence league set up by Chiang Kai-shek, which had been foundering, getting nowhere. The recent convict was subsidized with one hundred thousand dollars a month to fight the Japanese and win Vietnamese independence!

A fellow worker described him: his cheeks had hollowed, he was shaking with fever, his eyes were sunk deep in their sockets, but flashed with joy. His beard was dark with a few new gray threads.

The Viet Minh now entered the lists in force with banners and slogans. Giap soon linked up with the Tan Tho guerrillas and began infiltrating toward Cao Bang and Thai Nguyen. The French hit back hard.

Already in 1944 Ho saw anarchy looming from a five-way struggle to seize the country between the Japanese, the French, the Chinese, the United States, and the people. "The phase of peaceful revolution is behind us," he told Giap. "Stealth, stealth, continual stealth. Never attack except by surprise. Retire before the enemy is able to strike back." He devised a program for propaganda: concentration of forces plus local autonomy for training. Guerrilla tactics should be "rapid, active, now in the east, now in the west, arriving unexpectedly and leaving unnoticed."

By October 29 he had moved deep into Indo-Chinese territory, setting up a new headquarters on the limestone slopes of Thai Nguyen. Ten months later his forces entered Hanoi. Meanwhile Giap intensified indoctrination. He has told how Ho would drop in on his courses by fording the river with his trousers rolled up to his knees. One student said after class, "How odd to find that little old man here, so interested in politics in spite of his age."

The French decided to wipe out Ho and the guerrillas, but at dawn March 9, 1925, the Japanese suddenly arrested every Frenchman of the least importance throughout Vietnam. By overtly assuming power, the Japanese proclaimed that the Viet Minh had become the single enemy. Only French groups wishing to fight them would be aided.

The guerrilla bands were united into a single Army of Liberation, but Ho fell desperately ill. Whenever he was not in a coma, he talked to Giap over the telephone, giving instructions. "Independence at all costs," he reiterated, "even if the entire Truong Son mountain range has to be set on fire."

Presently he was visited by General Albert Wedemeyer and various O.S.S. agents. Statements differ on how much weaponry he was given. One agent said, "If I had to recall one quality of this old man sitting on his hill in the jungle it would be his sweetness. Ho was certainly a sweet guy." Via a Canadian and American officer, terms were sent to Jean Sainteny, head of the French military mission in south China.

These terms were: Universal suffrage for parliamentary elections, a French governor to act as president until final independence, a cabinet approved by parliament, independence to be granted after five years but no more than ten. Vietnamese resources were to be restored to Vietnam with proper compensation to French owners. United Nations freedoms were to be granted to all Vietnamese. The sale of opium was to be banned.

The French plan, issued March 24th, proposed to divide Viet Minh into three parts, to be federated with Cambodia and Laos. There was nothing left but to fight them tooth and nail.

The bombing of Hiroshima on August 5 shook Japan, Vietnam, and the French. Ten days later Japan asked for an armistice. Ho had waited patiently for the precise moment when the Japanese would be weakest and France had not had time to recover its positions. The day for starting the seizure of power was set for August 13. Giap struck out for Hanoi at once. Ho called for general insurrection: "Move forward courageously." For the moment the United States favored Indo-Chinese independence. General Wedemeyer blocked Sainteny's return to Indo-China until late August. On August 16, the Japanese handed over power in Hué to the weak wastrel Emperor Bao.

On August 17th occurred a strike of the civil servants' union of Hanoi. Tens of thousands poured into the streets and marched in the the monsoon deluge. By the 19th the imperial flags had almost disappeared. Only the red flag with its lone golden star waved over the vast crowd. From then on, French people were hunted down and ten were killed. It was worse in Saigon. A six-month nightmare began for the colonialists. On August 25 Bao's abdication was forced. The new "Democratic Republic" inherited the mandate from Heaven. The Viet Minh now controlled all Vietnam. When Sainteny arrived in Hanoi August 22, he was interned by the Japanese.

Ho had arrived the day before, but lay low, in contact only with Giap and other trusted friends. A caretaker government was set up, to be headed by him. He appeared at a larger gathering of the National Committee of Liberation on August 26. He was clad in a shirt and shorts and used a walking stick. On his head was a curious brown-painted colonial helmet—he looked like a peasant fresh from the paddies. But a packet of American cigarettes sticking out of his shirt pocket showed he was somebody.

It was a month before "Uncle Ho" issued a proclamation. The first was to the children. "Eighty years of slavery have debilitated our country's strength. Now . . . we must catch up with the other nations of the world." Its fame and glory would depend on their studious efforts. In his proclamation to the old people, he began, "It is as an old man that I address . . ."

Independence was proclaimed September 2. A hundred thousand people took part, including many Catholic priests. Ho's speech was almost word-for-word the one with which he had indicted French imperialism more than twenty years before at the Socialist Congress in Tours. But he added, "We hereby end colonial ties, end all French foreign obligations and abolish all French special privileges they have unlawfully acquired." It was a moment when a new cloud hung over the area. The Chinese, per previous negotiations with the Americans, were moving in to take over everything above the sixteenth parallel.

One enemy of Vietnamese freedom had been eliminated, but a Chinese horde was overrunning Tonkin and elsewhere. A French force was advancing from the south. Only the United States, for the moment, was inclined to support Vietnamese independence. As early as August 26, a United States mission arrived and was given an enthusiastic welcome. The Star Spangled Banner was played by the bands, and Vo Nguyen Giap lifted his fist in guerrilla-style salute to the American flag. The American emissaries were frequently in Ho's company during the negotiations with the French—who hoped to win back their colony by consultation rather than by a blood-letting conflict for which they lacked resources. Ho realized the need to placate them. He remarked, "It is better to sniff French dung for a while than eat China's all our lives."

Giap was less flexible. Nodding his round head and huge brow, his eyes blazed as he told Jean Lacouture that the new government would resort to a scorched-earth policy if necessary. But Ho told Lacouture how he had passionately read Victor Hugo and Michelet year after year. They had spoken the language of the ordinary Frenchman he loved. How different were the Frenchmen who come to Hanoi and so badly misrepresented France! "Ah, monsieur, colonialism must certainly be evil if it has the power to transform men in such a degree."

The French delegation in Hanoi headed by General Leclerc and Sainteny was more intelligent and liberal than the high commissioner in Saigon and less ignorant than the ministers in far-off France. Yet they found it difficult to abandon the superior attitude of colonial overlord and appreciate that they now had to deal with a sovereign state. Ho was willing to have Vietnam remain within the French Union and even in the Indo-Chinese Federation, but as "a free state." The ideas of what constituted an Indonesian Federation were obviously far apart. Also, France would not cede Cochin China or South Vietnam, saying that would require an act of Parliament. An agreement was reached March 9: a plebiscite would determine the status of the south.

Negotiations were continued in Paris. On May 30, 1946, Ho boarded a plane for Paris in company with French General Salan. Over Damascus he learned that High Commissioner Admiral Thierry d'Argenlieu had arbitrarily violated the agreement by setting up Saigon as a "free state" with its own parliament, army, and finances—as part of the Indonesian Federation and French Union. Ho was stunned. He was still more disconcerted when his plane was diverted to Biarritz and he was ordered to remain there until a new French government should be formed!

Sainteny met him at the airport. Ho said there was nothing left to negotiate; he was flying back at once. The Frenchman calmed him down, assuring him that the Saigon plebiscite would be celebrated. Ho had to loiter on in Biarritz until June 22. Georges Bidault became premier. Ho flew on to Paris. The La Bourget airport was black with people welcoming him, but many were hostile. He was hustled to a car guarded by sixteen motorcycle police. One open letter accused him of agreeing not to independence but only self-government. The signers said they would follow along the path he had not been able to follow to the end.

On September 4, French Minister Marius Moutet, worn out by the deadlocked negotiations, went home pessimistic. There, Ho showed up at midnight with a Vietnamese bodyguard and shoved the desired agreement under his nose. It reiterated the promise of a Cochin China plebiscite. Moutet sat up in bed in his pajamas and signed it. When Ho reached Haiphon—and indeed, all the way of the sixty-mile rail trip to Hanoi—he was received with almost hysterical acclaim.

Meanwhile Giap had been preparing for the worst and had feverishly worked to strengthen the armed forces. Ill-feeling between them and the French army grew tense. Trouble broke out in Haiphong over the landing of arms by a Chinese vessel, and the French tried to root out all Vietnamese from the European quarter. A ceasefire was finally arranged in Hanoi.

A cable came from Saigon to the French Commander to clear all Vietnamese armed forces out of Haiphong. The French officer in command opened fire—the guns of the *Suffren* opened up, wiping out refugees and villagers in a frightful carnage. Paul Mus put the body count at six thousand. Despite efforts to calm things down, French aggression spread to Hanoi on December 18. On the following night, Giap launched a full-scale attack. The French seized the Palace, and the next day Giap and Ho headed back for the rice paddies and their old strongholds in the north. The battle between the tiger and the elephant was resumed. As Ho put it, "If the tiger pauses, the elephant will impale him on his mighty tusks. But the tiger will not pause, and the elephant will die of exhaustion and loss of blood." As he had told a French minister in Paris, "You will kill ten of my men for every one I kill of yours. But even at that rate, you will be unable to hold out and victory will go to me."

Now he was back in the jungle in his shabby tunic and auto-tire sandals. Thirty years of struggle had left him almost where he had started.

At a rally of defenders, eight Commandments of the government of the Democratic Republic of Vietnam were given to the troops. The rivers were swollen from two days of torrential rains, and villagers were afraid to cross over. Ho forded them without faltering, the villagers after him, and reached the rally at the designated hour. Giap gave a vivid description of this odyssey.

His serenity, stoicism, and confidence were never shaken during this trying period. He lived among the peasants. He dwelt in crude huts or caves near the troops, typing out orders of the day, inspecting volunteer commando groups. Wearing a ragged lumber jacket, he climbed steep slopes, stick in hand, his beard and hair blowing about his head. He seemed always to be at the right place at the right time. At Quang Nap he lived in a hut built on piles . . .

> It stood exposed to the four winds and was bare except for his portable typewriter, some colored pencils, and writing paper. His only companion, a dog, was eaten by tigers. Later on he lived in a small house where he grew morning-

glories, mustard seeds, cabbages, pumpkins, and sweet potatoes. He was tremendously proud of his garden.

He still sought peace via the March–September agreements. But always Ho has preferred to win his popularity and the acceptance of his measures by argument and persuasion rather than by force, though always he has said, "Power comes out of the mouth of a gun." DeGaulle harshly closed the door to negotiations, and sent an emissary to demand capitulation. He told him, "There is no room for cowards in the French Union, and a coward I would be if I accepted your conditions."

He had abolished the Indonesian Communist Party two years before. With the more indigenous Lienviet Lao-Dong Party, he reorganized the Vietnam Republic in a session of two hundred delegates.

Mao had been victorious in China, and Ho welcomed his ambassador with champagne. Before long, Ho had been recognized by ten outside governments. It was all-out war now; French forces were pouring in by thousands, paid for, clothed, and armed by the United States, to the tune of billions.

But by 1953, France was tired of the fruitless, costly struggle. Ho willingly agreed to negotiate while Giap pushed the offense everywhere. Twenty thousand French troops were sealed up in Dien Bien Phu, and the French were unable to succor it. Vice-President Richard Nixon called for American soldiers to be rushed over, but the American public were sick of the similarly catastrophic Korean War. On May 7, under a rain of shells, the stronghold surrendered to Giap's guerrillas.

It was more than a victory for Vietnam; it was a notice to the world that the military role of the West was forever over in Asia, that a new era had begun. Nearly the whole world knew it—except for a few French die-hards and Washington bureaucrats. For Ho and Giap and their guerrillas, military success came after eight years of exhausting effort and bitter privation. They now believed that all Vietnam would fall into their hands. This alone can explain their generous willingness to retire above the seventeenth parallel, surrender 80 percent of the terrain they held, and once more to place their reliance on a promised plebiscite within two years, to decide the fate of South Vietnam. Furthermore, the Geneva accord of July 21, 1954 called for the withdrawal of all foreign troops from Vietnam. This was a guarantee against French reoccupation and Chinese intervention—but unfortunately not intervention by Americans, whose advisers promptly moved in on the heels of the departing French.

Among those active at Geneva was Chou En-lai. He consulted with Mendes France and flew back to Asia to consult with Ho, Nehru, Nu, and other Asian leaders. China's adherence to the final treaty was a necessary guarantee of Vietnamese independence and the proposed 1956 plebiscite for South Vietnam. Thus its later violation by the United States was an affront to China, to France, and to the fourteen nations who became signatories; a return to international anarchy and lawlessness.

Peace brought a period of feverish construction in the north. It was marred only by revolt in Nghen Province, brought about by a hasty, harsh land reform that hurt small peasants as badly as the great landholders. It was put down with implacable ferocity. A third of those condemned, Hanoi reluctantly admitted, had not been "feudalists" at all. Dissident extremist intellectuals, including the head of the official party, were purged in 1957.

Because of the United States bombing, in 1961 Independence Day was celebrated by small gatherings with music, flowers, and speeches. In a small hall, Ho sat on a platform with his Big Five—Pham Van Dong (Government), Giap (Army) Le Duan (Party), Truong Chinh (Parliament) and Nguyen Duy Trinh (Foreign Affairs). Behind them in four rows sat thirty more personages. Pioneers wearing red scarves presented flowers to the Big Five. Undulating arms symbolically warded off the imperialist demons. The battle hymn "We Shall Win," was sung. Giap, in his general's dark uniform, clapped in time with the music. Dong handed his flowers graciously to the orchestra leader. "Let's have an encore. The whole world knows we shall win." Ho Chi Minh spoke, stroking his small beard. "The front rows didn't sing very loud . . ." he began. Presently everybody slipped away in silence through the blacked-out city.

In 1924, Ho had written:

> Colonialism is a leech with two suckers, one of which attacks the metropoliton proletariat and the other that of the colonies. If we want to kill this monster, we must cut off both suckers at the same time . . . otherwise the animal will continue to live, and the cut-off sucker will grow again. . . .
>
> In our country the national issue is basically a peasant issue, and the agrarian problem is at the heart of the problem of democracy.

The government microfilms classic Vietnamese books for the soldiers. Recently Ho was asked if he did not think of publishing articles or books, as Mao had done. "If there is a subject Chairman Mao has not written about, let me know and I'll fill the gap."

During the next fifteen years, until the bombing by the United States, North Vietnam forged rapidly ahead of South Vietnam in industry, farm production, education, culture, health, and living standards.

Ever *since* the United States began bombing, North Vietnamese in-industrial and farm production has increased faster than ever. Education has been expanded to more than twice as many children and teachers. Scores of technical schools and half-a-dozen new universities have been started. Higher education and technical instruction have been increased four-fold. There are hundreds of new bridges and thousands of miles of roads—more than before the bombing started. Within three months of the bombing halt above the nineteenth parallel —according to a United States General—all damage to bridges, roads, and industry inflicted by more than two years' bombing (heavier than in World War II or Korea) had been repaired. However, the numerous cities and towns reduced to rubble with such great loss of civilian lives, have not been rebuilt. But hundreds of villages have been supplied with electric light and power, never enjoyed before. All industry, much of it now underground, is able to continue (should central power be knocked out by bombing) within a quarter of an hour by manual operation or by independent electrical generators now being installed everywhere. Numerous power plants have been hit, but the electrical output, according to official statements, is greater than before the bombing began. Food rations have been increased. Air shelters exist throughout the country. The streets of the cities are lined with concrete tubes, large enough to house a man or two, or a woman and child. These can be reached in seconds and will protect them from Lazy Dog darts and the thousands of pellets from antipersonnel bombs. (Apparently napalm and white phosphorus were little used in the North.)

More than ever, Ho Chi Minh is an almost God-like figure to the Vietnamese, North and South. If less prolific than Mao Tse-tung, he has published a considerable amount of polemics, philosophy, and addresses to his people and to the world. The memoirs of his year in prison in verse, *Prison Diary* (translated by Allen Palmer) appeared in English in Hanoi in 1966 and has been translated into French. His *Collected Works* (four volumes) were translated and published in English in Hanoi, from 1960 to 1962. Little exists in English about his life. A brief master's-degree biography can be read on film at a number of leading United States libraries. Several books by Bernard B. Fall, the French authority, including selected writings 1920–1960 on Ho's Revolutionary ideas, appeared just before Fall's death. A brilliant biography by Jean Lacouture, the noted French journalist, was published by Random House in July, 1968. Many aspects of Ho's life and personality are presented in Jean Sainteny's *Histoire d'Une Paix Manquée*.

Vo Nguyen Giap has also published notable works. He is quoted extensively in Nguyen Luong Bank's (fellow revolutionary) *Recollections of Ho Chi Minh*, which has appeared in a French publication. Giap's *People's War, People's Army* includes his incisive commentary on guerrilla warfare. It repeats many of the standard rules, but with Vietnamese experience and applications. (This was published in English in New York in 1962, with a Profile by Fall.) Giap also published his personal account of the capture of Dien Bien Phu; an English edition was issued in Hanoi in 1964. It is not as full-bodied as the 1967 account by Fall, who had access to French documents and interviewed French survivors. In 1968 Frederick H. Praeger published his *Big Victory, Great Task,* with a knowledgeable introduction by David Schoenbrunn. This is a hard-hitting account of American defeats, a critique of American strategy and tactics, which he claims have failed and can end only in defeat. He is aware of the deep sickness in American society and the confusion and differences in high government levels, the growing world antagonisms to the United States and its isolation. The war has warped and dislocated the global obligations of the United States, which impose a limit on the degree of involvement in Vietnam. He describes North Vietnamese military organization methods: how the guerrilla have been steadily reinforced by regional units and main force units, and by a powerful political and propaganda organization. In addition "our urban compatriots of South Vietnam will play an ever more important role and directly hit the enemy in their deepest dens." This was before the Tet and 1969 offensives or the ignominious surrender of Khe Sanh.

As for guerrillas, they "have fought with primitive weapons such as spikes, mines and traps as well as with . . . modern weapons . . . They have recognized the enemy's weak points." Methods of attacking cities have been developed. Enemy communications are nowhere secure.

During much of the period that the United States was backing the French against Ho Chi Minh and his government and then his guerrillas and his army, this country's government unsuccessfully backed Chiang Kai-shek against Mao Tse-tung. This policy was running contrary to the world-wide, post-war trend of national liberation of previous colonies. This made inevitable the degrading little war, eating up lives and resources, which by early 1969 had no sure end in sight, despite the Paris "peace" talks.

United States planes in Vietnam have been pierced—even downed —by powerful arrows; helicopters have been brought down with spears; war clubs have battered the brains of G.I.'s. One government outpost was captured by hurling in hornet nests. In November 1966, it was reported that hornets drove off defenders of a big United States convoy. The rebels have also made use of large, savage bees. In cleverly concealed animal traps or in streams or swamps, American soldiers have been impaled on sharp bamboo sticks that can pierce the stoutest army shoes. Whole villages—men, women, and children —make these deadly-sharp sticks by rubbing them on stones. The large Vietnamese cross-bows, using bamboo arrows often poison-tipped like the sharp sticks, are sometimes set up in batteries of ten or more.

The South Vietnamese independence fighters soon learned how to make guns, artillery, landmines, grenades, and explosives.

Some home-made weapons are curious. The "Sky Horse," a most effective shotgun that sprays death, is made of plumbing smuggled out of Saigon. A hole-center French ten-centime coin is soldered into a brass tube to hold a percussion cap. In one Viet Cong factory-shop, Malcolm W. Browne saw a home-made lathe turned by an ancient Japanese marine diesel engine. Bellows were operated by tricycle pedals to make grenade launchers and 60 mm. mortars. (Similar grenade launchers were manufactured by the Algerian guerrillas.) Presently, modern weapons—home-made, captured, bought, or imported —became plentiful, except for machines that fly in the air. These too are at hand in ever-greater numbers in North Vietnam.

Probably until mid-1965, 90 percent of Viet Cong weapons—Browne believes at least 98 percent—had been captured from American supplies or purchased from corrupt army men. Various United Nations on-the-spot reports bear out his estimate. Burchett (about the only newsman, except for French correspondent Jean Lacouture, to get behind the lines prior to 1965), quotes a regimental southern commander who claimed that as early as 1963, his force had captured nearly 600 carbines, plus machine guns and 57 mm. recoilless cannon. They had captured five modern weapons for every old one they had started with—from rifles and grenades to artillery, machine guns, and bazookas. Captured American-Vietnamese outposts and supply convoys provided large quantities of arms and ammunition. Practically none, at that time, had come from North Vietnam. After American air attacks and escalation, the NLF received ever-increasing aid from North Vietnam, China, the Soviet Union, and the central European countries, as well as token supplies from Cuba. It buys arms from Asia, France, England, and Sweden.

It seems absurd that a great nation, straining its resources with one of the most massive military expeditions in history, with more bombs dropped than on Germany in World War II, with the unstinted use of the most terrorizing weapons (many previously outlawed by the Geneva Convention), with scorched-earth tactics that wipe out thousands of villages, and with the set-up of concentration camps, has not been able in so many years to bring the foe to his knees nor appreciably blunt the fury of his attacks. In 1969 the Viet Cong still held the initiative, despite the revival of several (so-called) search-and-destroy operations.

One mortar attack in late 1967 inside Saigon came close to hitting General Westmoreland's headquarters. Many did hit his new headquarters at the Saigon's air base. Vietcong rocket and mortar attacks are expected anywhere, any day. Soviet tanks rumble far inside the war zone. In spite of our steady escalation, not merely in Vietnam, but also in Thailand and Laos in spite of our bases and manpower in Japan, Korea, the Philippines, Australia, Guam, and Hawaii, we are

increasingly isolated. Our domestic disorders, divisions, and disintegration grow worse.

Mao Tse-tung had much to say about the mess the United States
is now in. As we noted, he believed that victory does not depend
primarily on technical or industrial superiority, that the secret of
success is not so much a question of arms, logistics, and manpower,
but *political mobilization*. (This was the belief also held by T. E.
Lawrence.) The true guerrilla weapons, said Mao, are "time, space
and will." Of these the most essential is *will*. Territory or space can
always be surrendered and traded off for time, for time strengthens
the will. It permits penetration of the popular mind and creates the
belief that sacrifice is the highest moral value, stirring passionate
loyalties, love of independence, and hatred for the enemy. It makes
possible the winning of the good-will of the people of the rest of
the world—something against which attackers can never prevail.
"We shall create a great sea of people and drown the enemy in it,"
was Mao's much-quoted adage, albeit not an original one.

In Vietnam, the United States military retort has been that the
sea has to be drained, i.e., the people must be driven out or wiped out
entirely. Civilian deaths have been from two to five times that of
the enemy forces engaged, according to the *London Observer*, which
estimated losses of from 320,000 to 800,000 men, women and children.
By this date, the figures must number well over a million. After a
visit to the war zone, Representative Clement Zabloski of Wisconsin
estimated the ratio to be at least six to one. The Associated Press
(October 23, 1967) reported that more likely the ratio was ten to
one, a ratio also given in the *American Medical Association News*
in May 1966, by a member of a United States health mission. This
would put casualties at over two million. *Ramparts* for December
1964 put the total of civilian dead at not less than 415,000, of which
250,000 were children under sixteen—*plus* more than a million casualties since 1961.

The Vietnamese *Black Book* calculates that up to November 30,
1967, "imperialist aggression" had left 970,000 casualties, 400,000 jailed,
and 5,000,000 in barbed-wire concentration camps called "strategic
hamlets," later called "freedom villages"—as brutal an uprooting as
under Spanish General Valeriano Weyler in Cuba and modeled on
French methods in Algeria and British methods in Malaysia and
Kenya.

How many civilians have been killed by poisoning water and crops
is not known. Few of these victims have received medical attention; only a handful receive hospital care of a primitive sort. Probably
fewer than a hundred doctors are available for millions. Many Vietnam
hospitals do not even have running water. The victims are piled up

with napalm burns and other wounds, moaning and dying on cots and floors, eaten by flies, menaced by rats. Most die in the halls and the alleys.

In 1967 a limited number of controlled villages in a fifty-four-square-mile zone in Quangngai Province, midway north on the coast, were to be models for creating anti-Viet Cong sentiment—a task being carried on by specially-trained units under the supervision of Major Fred S. Korrer of Greensboro, North Carolina. This required more than ten thousand militia soldiery and marines. The first step was police and army interrogation of all villagers, a "census grievance" program to attempt to ferret out Viet Cong sympathizers. Can such interrogations arouse anything but the most bitter animosity? Naturally no guerrillas were discovered—but the rehabilitation unit was attacked at night in the school house in a bloody, prolonged fight. After that the cadre members have had to disperse to different houses to sleep. Despite the vast military protection, optimism for pacification programs seem exaggerated. The effort—the irrigation projects and the horrible tin-roof school additions to be done by the people—plus the implacable military regimentation scarcely seem likely to make most villagers happy. It was described as "modest and realistic." How can it fail with such vast manpower and money outlay? It was a camel straining to swallow a gnat. It would have been far cheaper to ship the whole village to some other land.

Collapse came in 1968. Most of these villages were overrun by the Viet Cong during and after the Tet offensive.

Another tactic was a combination of military pacification plus arming the people, a joint action by specially trained United States battalions and Vietnamese PUC's or provincial reconnaissance units wearing a skull-and-crossbones emblem. The PUC's were originally trained as a counter-guerrilla unit utilizing assassination, destruction, and terror. An Associated Press dispatch (January 18, 1967, by John Nance) from Rach Kien in the Mekong Delta described these continuing brutalities against civilians.

Are the guerrillas any better? Their own counter-terrorism grows worse as fighting grows more savage. But, though innocent villagers have suffered dreadfully, reprisals are supposed to be in theory at least, directed against officials and collaborators, as at Hué in February, 1968.

Instead of stopping communism—the only stated United States aim—the war has strengthened resistance and encouraged communism across the globe. To combat communism with the ever more fragile weapons of inflated money improperly and corruptly distributed and by armed force improperly applied, is a fatuous hope. Our official anticommunist slogans merely delude our own people and destroy the progressive, more democratic forces everywhere, thus blocking free political evolution. The guerrilla wars we hope to prevent become inevitable on all sides.

There are no more cheap Little Wars. Great Britain carried on a twelve-year war against the Malaysian guerrillas, mostly citizens of Chinese origin. It is now abandoning all of Asia. Great Britain carried on a futile war in Cypress for some years. Its long war against the Mau Mau in Kenya was even more costly. Each of these Little Wars cost more than did the bloody Boer War, which so debilitated the empire at the beginning of the century. Each was completely futile. South Africa and the three countries recently involved are now independent.

Our march into Asia began with United States meddling a century ago in China against the Taiping people's government in the Yangtse Valley (we were in favor of the decadent Manchu dynasty of the north) and our opening up of Japan by United States battleships under Commodore Perry. That march led later to the crushing of the independent Aguinaldo government in the Philippines. The latest chain links have been the bloody Korean war (a partial defeat) and the open-ended war in Vietnam. The Vietnam war has already cost the United States more than two hundred times as much as did the Spanish-American war, and has taken more American lives. It is now costing as much as World War I. Before long, it is likely to cost as many American lives as did that epic struggle.

The United States is now fighting against guerrilla warfare far and wide over the earth, or is preparing to do so. We wish to maintain the status quo everywhere, but in much of the world the status quo is not worth maintaining, and it grows less attractive in the United States itself. Abroad, it means keeping in power shaky regimes and dictatorships that rest on poverty, hunger, land monopoly, and military oppression—even as that in South Vietnam.

It is unlikely that either American money—so badly squandered everywhere with so little benefit for the people—or American arms now largely stalemated in Vietnam—can prevent the rising of the peoples against such regimes. There are alternatives, but the U.S. is not likely to follow them—at least not in the near future. Other "great guerrillas" are bound to arise in the decades that follow. There would seem to be more decent and more humane ways to settle the affairs of mankind.

11

CUBA LIBRE! FIDEL CASTRO

After the ill-fated landing from the *Granma* in December 1956, which had seen the major part of the little revolutionary forces wiped out, Fidel Castro was fleeing with a tiny group of guerrillas through the mangrove swamps and canefields on the south coast of Oriente province. Government planes flew over seeking them; he waved his hand, "They are frightened because they know we will destroy them."

Che Guevara wrote that in the early stages of guerrilla warfare, the airplane is useless to get at small bands in the forest. Open plains can be crossed at night.

In September 1966, Castro told a correspondent, "We won against Batista with only rifles and mines, although he had airplanes, artillery and tanks." Castro jumped out of the jeep and pointed to the Sierra de Escambray:

> What damage could the enemy's bombs do in a terrain like this? . . . I know a massive air attack has a psychological impact . . . but a fighter gets used to it and, if well dug-in, masters its effect. Have they achieved anything in Vietnam? The attack there . . . exceeds in destructive capacity and lack of scruples the Nazi offensive against Poland; yet in spite of poison gases and bacteriological warfare, and though hundreds of planes participate every day, the Vietnamese people go on resisting. The terror has not created more fear but less . . . not more respect for the U. S. army but more hatred.

When the refugees from the *Granma* finally reached the rugged Sierra Maestra that stretches for 5,000 square miles across western Oriente province below the guardian majesty of 7,000-foot Pico Turquino, only 12 men were left of the 82 who had crowded into the little, old yacht in Mexico to start revolt in Cuba. They had lost everything—their food, their ammunition, their supplies—all but their faith and determination. They had salvaged only a few rifles with telescopic sights and their olive-green uniforms with a red shoulder patch and the black insignia *M-26*—July 26 Movement—which referred to the unsuccessful attack on the Moncada fortress in Santiago in 1953, the birthday of the revolution.

For days their only food was sugarcane. At times their only water was the sap of lianas. Once they were hemmed in on three sides and the cane fields were on fire. But within two years the guerrilla band had become an army, and Dictator Fulgencio Batista and his police and army heads who had ruled by bloody terror, were fleeing the island.

Among the handful of survivors from the *Granma* with Castro in the Sierra were his young brother Raúl, the Argentinean Doctor "Che" Guevara, Doctor Faustino Pérez, the mulatto Juan Almeida (later to become head of the new people's army) and Camilo Cienfuegos —a handsome golden-haired giant, lost two years later in a plane flight near (ironically) Cienfuegos.

"The voice of principle out of a cave is stronger than an army," Castro told the court when he was on trial for leading the unsuccessful 1953 attack on Fort Moncada. He told the judges what he expected to do when the inevitable downfall of Dictator Batista occurred. He would make Camp Colombia in Havana into a school for orphans. (He did. There, he built a new education building and set up one of the greatest educational centers in the history of Cuba.*)

Fidel Castro was born August 13, 1926 on his father's plantation in Birán in the municipality of Mayarí, near Nipe Bay on the north coast of Oriente province. His father Angel Castro Argiz had been born in Galicia, Spain and had gotten hold of peasant lands, largely by banditry. He then got the titles confirmed by backing Conservative leader Carlos García Menocal in his struggle for power.

After the death of his first wife who had given him two children, Lidia and Pedro Emilio, he married his mistress Lina Ruz González. She bore him five children (most of them, it has been said, out of wedlock): Angela, Ramón, Fidel, Raúl, and Juana.

Fidel had a fierce hate-love relationship with his father. Except for the close tie between Fidel and Raúl, there was little love between the brothers and sisters. One sister was to become a CIA agent, working against Castro's government, but he has never spoken ill of her. The most favored of the children, Fidel, used to ride the tractor with his father, hauling timber from the hills. Lumbering added to the income from the sugar estate. The family fortune, confiscated by the revolutionary government, has been estimated at over half a million dollars.

Fidel was registered in the Colegio La Salle in Santiago, a Christian Brothers School. He learned to blow a bugle and wore a navy blue

---

* It was bombed by planes from the United States the day before the 1961 Bay of Pigs invasion.

uniform. After attending the Jesuit Colegio Dolores, he was sent to Jesuit Colegio Belém in Havana in 1942. He played basketball, ran track, and pitched on the baseball team—he is still a fanatic baseball enthusiast and in 1968 broke a finger in a game. The 1945 graduation yearbook said he had distinguished himself in his studies, was a good athlete who had defended "the flag of the school with bravery and pride," and had won "the admiration and affection of everybody." He would "fill the book of his life with brilliant pages."

After spending the summer at home in Oriente, he enrolled in the University of Havana Law School. He was then nineteen and over six feet tall. In 1947 he interrupted his studies to join a filibuster expedition at Cayo Confites to overthrow Dictator Trujillo of the Dominican Republic. President Grau San Martín had his navy intercept the vessel. Castro escaped arrest by jumping overboard with a machine gun and swimming ashore.

Returning to the university, he became president of the student body and was inevitably led into the maelstrom of Cuban politics. The students split into bitter factions, either pro-Catholic or pro-revolutionary. Castro was bitterly denounced as "a traitor" by the Communists, whom he opposed. He was almost gunned down by one rival faction and went into hiding. Two opposition leaders were killed. Castro's enemies claim he actually killed them himself, but the charge has never been authenticated.

The following year he headed a Cuban delegation to the anti-imperialist student conference scheduled to meet in Bogotá, Colombia, at the time of the Pan American (Inter-American) Conference attended by Generals George Marshall and Matthew B. Ridgeway—symbols of the new Yankee military diplomacy. En route, Castro visited Panama City and Caracas, Venezuela where he talked with President Rómulo Betancourt, at that time very anti-American.

In Bogotá, the students advocated the "independence" of Cuba and the internationalization of the Panama Canal. They denounced United States "atrocities." The police sought Castro, Rafael del Pino, and others for showering down anti-imperialist leaflets on the Pan American Conference. Castro ducked out.

He interviewed a number of leading Colombians including the president of the large "free" university. With other students, he had an appointment at the daily newspaper *El Tiempo* to talk with Jorge Elicer Gaitán, head of the leftist wing of the Colombian Liberal Party. Just before reaching there, Gaitán was gunned down. Later, smear-critics tried to implicate Castro in the slaying.

Bogotá erupted into a city of angry rioters joined by the police. The center of the great city was gutted; buildings went up in flames. The angry crowd, dragging the body of Gaitán's assassin, besieged the National Palace. They raced through the nearby Inter-American Conference hall, where the delegates cowered in fright under the tables.

What role Castro played during the next few flaming days has been tossed about by every writer. A turncoat Cuban fellow-student later accused him of having killed three priests—except that no priests were killed. Police headquarters and all its documents were destroyed. A falsified postdated document by secret service Agent 6 (never identified) was later published in a Dominican Trujillo newspaper to prove Castro had been collaborating with Communists. This document has never been accepted by any serious Colombian investigators, not even by the President's private Secretary Rafael Azúa Barrera, a firebrand anti-Communist who published a massively documented eyewitness study of the *Bogotazo*.

In any case, Fidel took refuge in the Cuban embassy and, with other students, was shipped home by special plane.

Soon after his return to Cuba, Fidel married Mirtha Díaz Balart, a philosophy student, in Banes, Oriente. They honeymooned in Miami, where he had to pawn his watch and other valuables until he could get money from home. A son was born September 1, 1949. Castro graduated in 1950, set up law offices with two friends and joined the radical nationalist Cuban People's Party (Orthodox). Its founder, Eduardo Chibas, later committed suicide after Batista seized power. His funeral is said to have been the largest ever held in Cuba.

In March 1952, the exiled ex-President Fulgencio Batista was allowed to return to campaign anew for the Presidency. He walked into Camp Colombia and took over the armed forces, ousted President Prío C. Socarras, and assumed dictatorial powers.

In 1933, Batista—then a thirty-two-year-old army sergeant and courtmartial stenographer—had been secret head of the army wing of the clandestine A.B.C. terrorist organization instrumental in overthrowing Dictator Gerardo Machado. Batista was of mixed Spanish, Negro, and probably Maya Indian blood; an orphan brought up by Protestant missionaries. From the age of fourteen he had worked on the cane fields and on the railroad. Finally he enlisted in the army.

After Machado fled from the island (practically ousted by F. D. Roosevelt) the provisional De Céspedes government was set up, handpicked by Ambassador Sumner Welles. De Céspedes had been a Machado tool, and in a few weeks Sergeant Batista staged "the shower-bath revolt." He had called a meeting of non-coms to ask for a proper clubhouse (they were excluded from the officers' club) and shower-baths. When he learned that he and others were to be arrested, he seized all the officers in the dead of night, discovering to his dismay that he had overthrown the De Céspedes government!

He sent messengers racing to round up the heads of the student and professor groups. It has been said that by mistake he got the leaders of the leftist rather than moderates he sought. One banker was routed out of his bed in his nightshirt and forced at gunpoint to become a member for a few days of the five-man civilian governing Junta. It was headed by the physician Dr. Grau San Martín, who was suffering from tuberculosis of the bones. On becoming President, he broke with the A.B.C. terrorists and tried to institute a few mild reforms, a reduction in electric light rates, a minimum wage, and civil liberties.

Sumner Welles was furious with Batista for the overthrow of the De Céspedes government and conducted clandestine negotiations with the A.B.C. heads in the Embassy garage.* Welles wanted to install Carlos Mendieta, a member of a wing of Machado's Liberal Party, as provisional president; to which the A.B.C. agreed. (I had lunch with Mendieta at the Yacht Club. He was a prosaic stuffy bureaucrat without a spark of imagination.)

One twilight, Batista (whom I had been seeing nearly every day), walked with me through the Camp Colombia athletic field. We sat on the bottom of the empty spectators' stands, and he told me he was going to kick Grau out and install Mendieta as acting president. "A Cuban government cannot survive without the approval of the United States," he told me, "and they want Mendieta." Maybe it would work, but he was not overly enthusiastic. Besides the A.B.C., much of Machado's discredited Liberal Party that had so long abused the Cuban people would back the proposed president. I told Batista that Grau was my friend. I said I was glad to be leaving Cuba, for I did not want to be a witness to his gross betrayal. (A few years later, I interviewed Batista. The meeting was not very cordial, and in 1957 he refused to see me at all.)

Batista seized the police stations. Planes flew over the National Palace, dropping a few bombs, and Grau handed over office to my friend Colonel Carlos Hevia, "The Flower of Three Days," who was to hand authority over to Mendieta. All very legal!

Mendieta's two years of office resulted in brutal terrorism as bad as that under Machado. As a reward for Mendieta's docility, the United States formally abolished the Platt Amendment that had made Cuba an involuntary protectorate subject to armed intervention any time Washington wished—and, as quid pro quo, received an enlargement of the Guantánamo Naval base.

For the six years after Mendieta, Batista ruled through puppet governments. Then in 1940 he ran for the presidency. He legalized the Communist Party, which supported him. Higher-ups such as poet

---

* I recall how Welles' neck muscles grew rigid and his face flushed when I asked if he did not think that lowering the light-rates, then the highest in the world, was a good thing. "They can't be changed," he shouted back. "They were set by the U.S. military occupation after the Spanish-American War, and the Cubans signed on the dotted line to enforce all the previous military acts."

Juan Marinello received government posts. Thanks to the war in Europe, Cuba was then fairly prosperous.

Batista tried to impose a handpicked successor, but Grau San Martín was swept in by a landslide. Batista, determined not to let him to take office, was obliged by United States Embassy pressure to leave the island. The Embassy was backing the man it had ousted ten years earlier as a dangerous radical!

Grau initiated a few reforms, but his chief claim to fame was corruption. He and his coterie stole the country blind. Not since the days of Zayas and the John R. Brooke's Marine government was Cuba looted more brazenly. Incoming President Prío Socarras of Grau's Cuban Revolutionary Party (*Autenticos*) was more circumspect, but blindly obedient to the United States Embassy. Ironically, a few years later he was marched in handcuffs through the streets of Miami for shipping arms to the revolution against Batista (after the latter's second armed seizure of power in 1952).

In the fall, Fidel ran for Congress on the Orthodox ticket. When Batista's coup aborted the elections, Castro daringly brought court charges against him for overthrowing the constitution. Boldly he reviewed Batista's "crimes" that made him "liable for more than 100 years in jail." If there were any bonafide courts left, said Castro, the dictator would be punished. Otherwise, "Hang up your robe, resign your post . . . let a corporal sit at once with his bayonet in the august courtroom of the Magistrates."

His brief was rejected. He gathered young friends in an apartment at Twenty-fifth and O Streets in the Vedado to devise a military stroke to rally the people.

Other plots were afoot. Dr. Rafael García Barcenas, head of the clandestine National Revolutionary Movement, tried to capture Camp Colombia in April 1953. He was sent to the Isle of Pines prison. In the prior trial he was defended by young lawyer Armando Hart, who was twice taken into custody and made spectacular escapes. (Later Hart became Castro's Minister of Education. He wiped out illiteracy in a year, doubled the classrooms and teaching force of the island, and revamped the methods and curricula of the educational system.)

The most ardent of Castro's group were Abel Santamaría and Abel's sister Haydée. They raised funds and bought guns, which were often smuggled in egg crates to a chicken farm in Oriente bought by the conspirator Renato Guitart, a member of the revolutionary unit. They planned to attack Fort Moncada near the heart of Santiago and seize its large supply of arms. One hundred and seventy do-or-die young men converged on the farm on the night of July 25 and slept on cots Haydée had provided. Thirty others were to make a simultaneous attack on the Bayamo Garrison to the west, so as to block the sending of more government troops to Santiago. Final plans, the designation of duties, and the selection of officers were all worked out that night.

The attack was scheduled for 5:15 A.M. It was carnival time, when people went to Mass at daybreak, so police were not likely to halt the conspirators. They entered the city in two cavalcades of ten and sixteen autos. Their uniforms were similar to those of the army, and soldiers in patrol jeeps saluted them as they went by.

The two lead cars peeled off at the Civic Hospital across the street from Moncada. Abel Santamaría led his men, Doctor Mario Muñoz and two "nurses" (his sister Haydée Santamaría and Melba Hernández) inside to be ready to care for any casualties. The third car, commanded by Raúl Castro, stopped at the Palace of Justice two blocks from Moncada. They seized a soldier and a sleeping guard and set up machine guns on the flat roof overlooking the Fort.

The fourth car, the "suicide" assault car, swerved to the Fort's side Gate 3. Three leaders—Renato Guitart, Jesús Montané and Ramiro Valdés—jumped out and seized the guards. One was killed. All rushed inside and held fifty sleeping soldiers under their guns.

The rest of the cavalcade was accidentally blocked by a military jeep. Fidel Castro, who was driving the fourth car, bucked it around on the sidewalk. Gustavo Arcos, a lad in the back seat, was cut down by machine-gun fire, and the other rebels had to take refuge in doorways. But about fifty, including Fidel, raced through the bullets to Gate 3. Dashing in through a fusillade of machine-gun fire, they took over several buildings. Raúl's roof sharpshooters picked off Batista machine gunners.

The battle lasted for two hours. Five rebels were killed, four wounded. Twenty-two government soldiers and officers were killed, and fifty-seven wounded. Fidel ordered his men to retire in groups of eight or ten. Those who escaped shed their uniforms and melted into the city. Castro and a few others got to their cars and raced back to the poultry farm.

About sixty were taken prisoner. They were horribly tortured, their eyes gouged out, their testicles crushed, their skin burned with hot irons. Many were taken out to country fields and killed "in battle."

Seeing the fight was lost, Raúl and his men discarded their uniforms. Raúl opened the outer door to face a patrol of fifteen men. He snatched the pistol from the hands of the sergeant, took them all prisoner, herded them inside and locked them up. He then casually strolled to the railroad tracks and walked the ties out of the city. He was captured about forty miles north.

At the hospital, Dr. Muñoz quickly put bandages on Abel Santamaría and twenty other rebels, who got into bed as patients. Still dressed as nurses, Haydée and her companion quieted the children in one of the wings. An informer gave the prisoners away. Their bandages were ripped off. They, the doctor and the two girls were seized. The doctor was pushed into the street and shot in the back. Later the soldiers presented Haydée with her brother's gouged-out eyes.

Archbishop Enrique Pérez Serantes persuaded General Alberto del Rio Chaviano, Oriente Commander, to halt the tortures and killings. He then went into the hills to get the escapees to surrender, under his guarantee they would be given a trial.

While asleep, Castro and two companions were captured by Lieutenant Pedro Sarría, who had been a university classmate. Sarría prevented his men from killing them and took Castro to the Vivac—the Santiago civilian jail—instead of to the barracks. For this he was cashiered several weeks later. Fidel was taken to the Puerto Boniato prison. The prison head, Lieutenant Yanes Pelletier, was given orders to kill him. He refused, was arrested, and dismissed.

By a ruse, Castro was separated from the trial of the others at the Palace of Justice and was brought into court ten days later on October 16, 1953. His trial was conducted in the ante-room of the provincial hospital—in secrecy, with no witnesses or spectators, only six court stenographers.

Castro pled his own case. He spoke to the three-man judge panel for five hours, delivering his famous "History Will Absolve Me" speech. He told the court of his adherence to the ideals of Martí, the great liberator of Cuba and gave them the story of Cuba's long struggle for independence and the abuses of United States interventions and economic subjugation. He told of the great American estates extending from sea to sea, of the four hundred thousand cane workers toiling for four months for a few cents a day, then thrown off the plantations to starve the rest of the year. In their whole lives they had never had shoes; most had never tasted meat. He described the condition of workers in foreign-owned factories. His judges tried to stop him. He told them he had no intention of sticking to narrow legalism "like a slave turning a millstone." He called on the judges to resign. They did not represent a legal government, only an illegitimate military tyranny. They condemned him, as they had Raúl, to fifteen years' incarceration in the Isle of Pines Penitentiary.

He managed to smuggle out much propaganda. Under great public pressure, a year and a half later, Batista granted amnesty to those who agreed to "respect" the régime. Though Castro had been incarcerated for sixteen months, he answered that he was still strong enough to reply with dignity. If his freedom depended on his making a shameful and cowardly agreement with the usurping government, his answer was an unequivocal "No!" Rafael Díaz Balart, Castro's brother-in-law and a high Batista official, was unable to alter his stand.

Batista had himself installed as a "legal" president following a one-candidate election in February 1955. On May 15th, all members of the Oriente uprising still alive and in prison were released. Fidel and Raúl were met by Haydée Santamaría and Melba Hernándes, who had been released ahead of them. In Havana they attended an all-night celebration by the national committees of the Orthodox Party and the National Student Federation.

Two months later, Castro flew into exile in Mexico and began preparing the armed invasion that took place the following year in December. An hacienda was leased outside Mexico City, and Spanish Civil War veteran General Alberto Bayo * began intensive training of volunteers. Some were from other Latin-American countries.

Castro established his M-26 organizations in a dozen cities on the two continents, a new independent revolutionary organization— "without sugar barons, without stock-market speculators, without industrial and commercial magnates, without lawyers for the big interest, without provincial *caciques* (bosses), without small-time politicians of any kind"—a movement of the "humble" for the "redemption of the Cuban working class . . . land for the peasants who lived like pariahs in the country their grandfathers liberated, bread for the hungry, justice for the forgotten."

Eighteen months later they started back to Cuba in the motheaten *Granma*. The vessel was delayed by stormy weather and shipped water which those on board had to bail out with pails, tin cans, hats, even cupped hands.

On the island, uprisings that were supposed to strike simultaneously with the landing from the *Granma* occurred two days ahead of time and were crushed. Underground M-26 coordinator Frank País García led the attack in Santiago from an old-fashioned apartment in the center of town. The attackers raided a sporting goods store for guns, then moved against the Maritime Police in their yellow brick headquarters on Intendente Hill above the docks. Thirteen lads in three automobiles stormed into the Customs building and took fifteen officers prisoner—two dead, two wounded—and made them lie on the sidewalk outside. The youths began hustling out rifles and ammunition to a supply car.

But at the Police headquarters, the guards directed a withering fire against the thirty assailants. Only one youth got inside, but he was killed. Though fires were started with Molotov cocktails, the attack had to be abandoned.

The revolters also failed in their attempt to seal off Moncada Fortress troops until other places were occupied. An 81-millimeter mortar with fifty-six shells had been set up in a school five blocks northeast

* In Bolivia he had published a notable two-volume treatise on guerrilla warfare

of the barracks. But the four men who knew how to operate the gun were picked up on their way there by a roving army patrol. Ambuscades set up on streets to stop troops coming out of the fort were also a fiasco. Leaders and men failed to show up. Truckloads of soldiers roared out unopposed.

They reinforced the National Police in their burning building. All rebel leaders were killed; the others fled. Government troops set up a mortar and two machine guns in front of the high school and blazed away. The defenders slipped out the rear through the athletic field and climbed an eight-foot wall.

In Holguín a rebel force tried unsuccessfully to seize dynamite from a warehouse. That same day, Colonel Fermín Cowley presented the people of that city with the spectacle of more than twenty bodies of badly-tortured young men hanging in the public plaza. More mutilated bodies were found in the cemetery and adjacent fields.

The *Granma* was discovered and bombed by planes. The survivors hid out in the mangrove swamps. Not until December 19th did the Almeida group find Castro and his brother, who had survived on sugarcane, edible cactus, prickly pears, and an occasional tortoise or broiled snake. They drank the sap of *bejucas*. On one occasion, Che Guevara's emergency breathing device for his acute asthma was used to suction water out of porous rock. Not until Christmas day were they able to slip through the Batista lines into the foothills—thanks to an expert *guajiro* (peasant) guide provided by prominent landowner Crescencio Peréz.

Batista announced that all the rebels had been dispersed or killed. He dismissed the idea that Castro had landed on the island. Then on January 17th, the doughty twelve fell at night on La Pata outpost just below the foothills, killing eleven and seizing weapons to arm more peasant volunteers. Three other raids were carried out that month. There was always a lightning retreat to higher ground where pursuers could be picked off by high-power rifles with telescopic sights.

Fidel Castro fought mostly with captured American weapons. Later in his July 26th speech in the José Martí plaza, he reminded his listeners that after the loss of the *Granma,* he began with seven men and seven rifles. "Who then believed that seven men could try to organize an army?" The seven became twelve, then nineteen, then a host. "In our first surprise attack, we took eleven guns from our enemies." Only after he succeeded did he begin buying Belgian, French, Soviet, and Czech rifles, sub-machine guns, tanks, and anti-aircraft weapons. But when he lay under a tree to read Montesquieu, the powerful telescopic rifle by his side was made in the U.S.A.

The area was sparsely settled, but the peasants provided whatever they could for the guerrillas. As the band became larger, the food supply problem forced them to split into smaller units. By then the guerrillas had many faithful peasants who went into Bayamo, Manzanillo, Santiago, and other towns and brought back loads of canned goods and other supplies along steep trails no mule could follow. They provided dried codfish, rice, beans, hammocks, blankets, boots, clothing, and plastic shower curtains for shelter against the heavy night rains—a protection Guevara stressed in his book as absolutely essential for the guerrilla. (Earlier, the Philippine Huks had stressed linoleum or oilcloth.) Women couriers brought out guns under their skirts.

However, the more prosperous peasants still aided the Batista military. A few such were tried and shot under the Castro revolutionary code. As the "free territory" widened, youths who were anxious to join the Castro revolt but who could not be properly armed were organized into bird-gun groups that ambushed Rural Guard sorties into the area. "We always knew where the soldiers were," Fidel said, "but they never knew where we were. We could move through their lines at will, but they could never find us except on our terms."

It was classic guerrilla fighting—shadowy, elusive, the flea hopping ahead of the heavy finger—so a Civil War Florida guerrilla once described his activities. "An elephant can trample a garden patch, but never hurts the grasshopper." The search became more difficult as the population grew more hostile to the soldiery.

Resistencia effort in the towns and cities was not easy because of Batista's control over the Confederation of Workers, whose dishonest leaders sided with the government and sometimes with American gangsters. Labor leaders stole the pension and benefit funds to promote private enterprises such as the magnificent Havana Riviera Hotel, radio stations, newspapers and other lucrative businesses. Even Communists were favored by secret *botellas,* i.e., government sinecures. Though most were secretly anti-Batista, many criticized the Castro effort as a stupid bourgeois effort.

Growth of guerrilla strength was hidden from the press. News filtered through Cuba mostly by word of mouth. The revolt in the mountains was belittled or ignored in every official pronouncement. It remained almost mythical. Determined to break through the silence, Castro sent René Rodríguez to Havana with instructions to bring a foreign correspondent to the Sierra. On February 15, Herbert Matthews of *The New York Times* and his wife were driven to Oriente by Xavier Pazos—son of Felipe Pazos, former head of the National Bank—and his wife. Lilian Mesa (a young woman leader) and Faustino Pérez came along. From Manzanillo, Matthews was taken by jeep to the foot of the Sierra and reached Castro's headquarters in the dripping forest just before daybreak on the 17th.

Castro strode into the grove, "a powerful six-footer, olive-skinned, full faced with a scraggly beard." His personality was "overpowering." He had "caught the imagination of the youth" of Cuba all over the island. He was "an educated, dedicated fanatic . . . of ideals, of courage and of remarkable qualities of leadership."

Matthews saw clearly that the old corrupt colonial order in Cuba was threatened for the first time since the establishment of the Republic. This was a real revolution, not a struggle of the outs to get in and enjoy the spoils. It could not fail. *The New York Times* man prophesied Batista was not likely to finish out his term of office (to expire in February 1959).

The truth and insight of Matthews' reportage were to bring down on his head an avalanche of envy by less enterprising or reactionary fellow journalists. He faced attacks from Washington officialdom, venom from two United States ex-Ambassadors who were to fall flat on their faces, and the hate of the ruling regime in Cuba and its many corporate beneficiaries in the United States. Few men have ever suffered more opprobrium for a job well done. General Martín Díaz Tamayo, chief of operations Oriente, called the *Times'* account, "a fantastic novel . . . a wholly imaginary interview." It had been "impossible" for anybody to get through the tight army lines about the area.

Matthews's disclosures were soon followed by the able firsthand reporting of Robert Taber, correspondent of CBS, who also made his way to the Sierra and witnessed actual engagements.

On March 7th General Francisco Tabernilla, head of the armed forces, said that the guerrillas had been "completely overcome." Three days later Batista called Castro "an agent of the Soviet Union" and claimed that there were scarcely a dozen rebels left. Nevertheless, the dictator began bombing villages and spewing napalm.

More and more armed volunteers streamed into the Sierra. Among them were three American youths from Guantánamo Naval Base. On March 13, a few days after Tabernilla's confident announcement, students of the University Federation congregated at a building on 21st Street in Havana and at 3:25 P.M., sallied forth to the Palace to attempt to assassinate Batista. Another group seized Radio Reloj station and announced that the dictator had been killed.

Racing through the Hall of Mirrors on the second floor of the Palace, the students tossed a hand grenade through the glass doors of the Presidential suite and ran in past two dead bodies.

Batista had already fled up a secret stairs to the heavily-guarded third floor. Thousands of troops began spraying the buildings of Plaza Presidente Zayas in front of the Palace with machine-gun fire and mowed down students emerging from the Palace. At least thirty-three died.*

That night students all over the city were rounded up and killed. The prominent scholar and ex-Senator of the Orthodox Party, Pelayo Cuervo Navarro (who a year earlier had blocked an attempt to raise the telephone rates) was taken from the home of a wealthy financier and killed by the head of the Narcotics Squad on President Batista's personal orders. His body was tossed beside a lake in a fashionable suburb. Dr. Vidal Morales, a prominent lawyer, was held for four days and made to drink water out of a toilet bowl. Four students were gunned down in an apartment at Humboldt 7. That killing outraged *The New York Times,* which commented that despite official denials Castro was stronger than ever. Fear and police terror combined to strew all Cuba with bodies.

When I reached the island in mid-1957, two or three police killings occurred daily in Havana, as well as others elsewhere. Day after day, I saw murdered victims on the main streets of Havana, posed on their knees, a noose around their necks, suspended from a miniature cross and sometimes sardonically provided with crepe and a bunch of flowers. Members of their families who came to recover the bodies were arrested. After Batista's downfall, other bodies, nearly all horribly mutilated, were disinterred in police headquarters and various barracks.

Everywhere on the island the police and soldiery seized suspected students and young men, tortured them, killed them, and threw them into empty lots—as, for instance, fourteen-year-old William Soler. His murder precipitated the first open protest in Santiago. Marching Catholic women from the Dolores church bore white banners: "Stop assassinating our sons." A year later under the eyes of the new United States Ambassador, Earl Smith, a similar group of Santiago women protestors was broken up with clubs and firehoses. Practically all Cuban civic and professional groups joined in protests against police murders: Lions, Rotary clubs, Sports associations, the Masons, benevolent associations, architects, lawyers, doctors, dentists, professors.

The morale of Batista's troops began sinking. They always came to grief whenever they tried to climb into the Sierra. Maintaining the troops on an active footing over a far-flung circumference increased demands for ammunition and supplies and began to hurt the public treasury.

More and more arms were getting through to the rebels. Arms were also bought from government forces. Castro had a regular scale of payment for Batista's cartridges, pistols, rifles, machine guns, and

* Their names are now inscribed on a bronze plaque in the Palace entrance— ". . . may injustice and oppression never again return to Cuba."

grenades. According to one report (never authenticated), Che Guevara bought for a million dollars Batista's great final troop and munitions train that was being rushed to central Cuba to try to save Santa Clara. This is probably a fantasy, though the Colonel in charge of the train did sail away in his private yacht to live at ease on the Florida Gold Coast.

Castro agents were buying arms in the United States. Exiled President Prío, said to have spent five million dollars in the effort to drive out Batista, was also sending in arms, though only to his own followers.

In spite of the stepped-up rebel activity, Batista announced he was withdrawing all forces from the Sierra because of the *decline* of guerrilla forces. By then Castro was in firm control of about five thousand square miles. In April he got a heavy shipment of arms in oil drums via Bayamo and Manzanillo on the coast: machine guns, bazookas, rockets, semi-automatic weapons, and thousands of rounds of ammunition. On May 28, the rebels struck into the lowlands for the first time, seizing Ubero on the southern coast. The attackers claimed that thirty of the seventy soldiers were killed, only eight guerrillas.

On that same day, certain striking electric workers (having no connection with Castro) blew up the main light conduits in retaliation for drumhead court trials of union members.

The conspirators rented a house near the power station and burrowed a tunnel under the street to set off a tremendous dynamite charge that wrecked one building and damaged others on both sides of the street. All Havana was plunged into terrifying darkness for fifty-seven hours. No elevators worked, no newspapers were published, meat rotted in the warehouses, butter melted and turned rancid. The streets were dark, and no radio stations were on the air. There were no movies, no night clubs, no restaurant service, no telephones.

I reached Havana the day after power service had been restored. Workers were still feverishly trying to clean up the debris and fill in the great canyon in Calle Suárez; two thousand feet of cable had had to be replaced. Three men were shot for the crime and their bodies placarded in the streets, but the actual perpetrators escaped.

Batista began sending out planes loaded with napalm and bombs in dawn-to-dark saturation sorties. Villages and civilians were burned, but no guerrilla casualties were reported. It did not add to good American relations that the napalm came from the United States and that the American military mission was actively aiding Batista. Special church services were held for peace. Women's organizations clamored for an end to Batista's new scorched-earth policy; women in peace parades were clubbed and dispersed.

A new scorched-earth "Zone of Death" demanded the dislocation of fifty thousand people. Peasants were driven out of the foothills. (This, again, is the desperate tactic always attempted at a certain advanced stage of antiguerrilla drives, as by "Butcher Weyler" in 1898 in Cuba, by Chiang Kai-shek in China, by the British against the Mau Mau. Starving, sick peasants carrying live chickens, pots and pans, bundles, and pictures of the saints piled up in Holguín, Manzanillo, Santiago, and elsewhere. I talked with many of these bewildered victims. Anyone who remained in the desolated area was to be shot on sight as a guerrilla sympathizer. The government, however, simply did not have the resources to carry out such a brutal enterprise. Moreover, it gave the lie to Batista's repeated claim that Cuba was at peace and that the Castro revolt was not really serious.

Except for the nightly killings, Havana did give an impression of busy prosperity. Its streets were jammed with automobiles and diesel buses stretched bumper to bumper as far as the eye could see. But there and in the provinces, particularly in Santiago, house-to-house searches were being made. The home of the dean of Cuban scholars, Fernando Ortiz, was invaded in the dead of night.

Presently long-sought Frank País, the underground leader in Oriente, was shot down by secret police. His funeral prompted the greatest gathering of people in the history of Santiago. They chanted, "To die for one's country is to live." All shops were closed for five days and spontaneous strikes paralyzed much of the country. The Nicaro nickel mines shut down, the banks of Havana closed, and public buses quit running. In Holguín all power was shut off, and Fermín Cowley shot people recklessly. When the light came back on at 2 A.M., nine corpses lay on the street. One was a father who had gone out to buy candles for his daughter's sick room.

The next disaster for the regime was the naval revolt at the Cienfuegos base on September 5, planned by Prío's *Organización Auténtico* and Faustino Pérez of the M-26. The naval base of Cayo Loco ("Crazy Key") was easily taken over, and the sailors and rebels advanced across the causeway to the city and seized police headquarters. Only the Rural Guard post on the edge of the city refused to surrender.

Heavy army reinforcements were sent in by air and by land. Planes commanded by Colonel Carlos Tabernilla began bombing and strafing. Most of the rebels fled back to Cayo Loco. Cienfuegos became literally the "city of a hundred fires." But forty rebels still held out in the San Lorenzo school. They surrendered at one o'clock in the morning and were shot at once; their bodies were then run over by tanks. Two hours later the rebels holding the police station surrendered and were machine-gunned. Four M-26 men who refused to surrender held off the attackers until all four were killed at 8 A.M. The planes are said to have killed at least five hundred noncombatants. Six hundred bodies were dumped into a mass grave. The slaughter—two hundred were

allegedly buried alive—was denounced by a leading Cuban doctor
at the Eleventh World Medical Congress. The *Washington Post* called
on Batista to resign. But the Pentagon sent the Canal Zone Air Force
Commander, Major General Truman Landon, to Cuba to decorate
Tabernilla.

Adam Clayton Powell read accounts of the Cuban atrocities into
the Congressional record, and he as much as any one person obliged
the State Department to place an embargo on arms to Batista. "Get
that nigger Powell," became a byword in certain Pentagon and State
Department quarters. From then on, he was put on the hot griddle,
secretly persecuted by business interests, harrassed by income-tax
agents, and assessed outrageously high court damages for his "bag-
woman" speech. In 1966 he was dislodged from the House of Representatives.

Cuban urban guerrillas gathered momentum everywhere. Oil tanks
were burned near Havana. The Havana aqueduct was dynamited,
pouring five million gallons of drinking water into the sand. Buses were
burned in their terminal in Santiago. Power lines, water mains, bridges,
and public buildings were blown up. Schools were wrecked, sugar and
tobacco warehouses were destroyed.

Castro launched eight attacks during the first week in December.
In Verguitas, 200 rebels attacked 300 soldiers, inflicting 170 casualties.
Castro did his Christmas shopping in that town, taking out four truckloads of supplies. On Christmas Eve the Castroites captured the big
Manzanillo airport and obtained medicines from a nearby hospital. In
spite of the bombs rocking Havana, Batista lauded "continued rising
prosperity and happiness in all Cuban homes."

The rebels again raided Verguitas and destroyed the telegraph office.
A motorized column speeding to relieve the garrison was blocked by
a mine that blew up the lead armored car. Buses were being halted
everywhere, the passengers ejected, and the vehicles burned. The
destruction of trains was reported near Bayamo and elsewhere. Much
of the Havana-Santiago road and railroad became impassable.

The army, pressured to produce "victories," took prisoners out of
Santiago prison, trucked them to a likely spot, then shot them, reporting a battle and victory.

A guerrilla group headed by student leader Eloy Gutiérrez Menoyo,
survivor of the 1957 attack on the Palace, opened a new front in Las
Villas province in the heart of the island—the Second National Front
of Escambray—and attacked army posts around Sancti Spíritus and
Port Trinidad. On February 1, 1958 Fauré Chaunont and other leaders
of the student Palace attack landed on the north coast and holed up
in the Sierra de Trinidad.

Two new fronts were set up in Oriente. Juan Almeida moved closer
to Santiago, and Raúl Castro moved to the north coast not far from
the American-owned nickel mines. More arms came in to Castro via the

Playa de los Colorados, near the site of the original *Granma* landing. Other arms steadily trickled through—a few pistols in a sack of flour, a machine gun in a lard tin, ammunition in oil drums. An attack on Piña del Agua, a Batista strong point west of Bayamo, yielded enough machine guns and rifles to arm a new battalion. By this time the M-26 forces openly rode armored jeeps and cars along the foothills of the Sierra.

The records of the Urgency Court of Camagüey were burned. In Havana the National City Bank was raided, and thousands of cancelled checks and drafts went into a bonfire. Radio programs were taken over repeatedly by armed youths. A sixth of Cuba's warehoused sugar was destroyed. A famous Argentine auto-racing champion was kidnapped, later released to his Ambassador. He told the press he had been admirably treated and had enjoyed the race—on television. Good-naturedly, he considered the episode "another adventure in my life."

An intrepid judge in Havana signed an order for the arrest of the top police killer, Estebán Ventura and the chief Naval intelligence officer, Lieutenant Julio Laurent. Batista suspended constitutional guarantees, and Ventura came for the judge, pistol in hand. But the judge had already fled by plane to Miami.

Cardinal Manuel Artega and all other members of the Catholic hierarchy called on Batista to resign in favor of a government of "national union." Forty leading civic groups demanded that the present regime "cease to hold power." The President of the Havana Bar Association, Dr. José Miró Cárdenas, disguised himself as a priest and hid in a church.

Batista ordered the enlistment of seven thousand more soldiers.

On March 12, 1958, the M-26 called for a general strike. It was an error of judgment, for labor was strictly controlled by Batista through the colossal grafter Eusebio Mujal, who enjoyed the active support of the American Federation of Labor.

Simultaneously Castro issued a twenty-one point "Declaration of War," his first real pronouncement since his Moncada Court plea. It was an ultimatum: he attacked the Batista regime for moral cowardice and military ineptitude and gave statistics of the number of *campesinos* murdered. Why had Batista refused to let newsmen visit the battle area? Because he could not permit the truth to be told. Cuban students, Castro ordered, were not to return to classrooms until Batista was ousted. All highway and rail traffic through Oriente province was forbidden; passengers would be fired upon. All tax payments and collections were prohibited. All judges, magistrates, and district attorneys were ordered to resign by April 5th or be forever disqualified. Members of the armed services were called upon to mutiny, desert, or join the revolutionary army. Those who brought their arms with them would be promoted in rank. New Batista enlistees would be court-martialed as criminals. Anyone who continued in the executive branch of the government would be tried for treason and have his home burned. Castro proclaimed "total war."

On March 26th, the State Department found itself under growing pressure and halted all arms shipments to Batista. It is doubtful, however, that the embargo was one hundred percent perfect. A Nicaraguan official stated that on at least one occasion, United States government arms sent to Somoza were transferred in the harbor to another vessel headed for Cuba. It has never been disclosed just how much of the arms and ammunition supplied by Dictator Rafael Trujillo were actually from the United States. With a straight face, the State Department declared that Trujillo had assured them that none of the arms sent had originated in the United States. But the napalm sent to Cuba was certainly not of local manufacture. Nor did the United States pressure England not to supply arms and airplanes to Batista, although some years earlier, it had managed to stop all European shipments to Jacobo Arbenz, President of Guatemala. Rather than transport arms for bombing Oriente, thirty-nine Batista pilots took refuge in the United States or elsewhere abroad.

Castro set up a strong short-wave radio transmitter, and urban terrorist groups were supplied with walkie-talkies smuggled in from the United States for them *by a Batista official.* "Big Lips," i.e., *Bemba,* word of mouth, replaced newspaper censorship. Mimeograph rebel instruction sheets were distributed simultaneously to all main centers. They provided information on how to make Molotov cocktails; how to cripple transport; how to sabotage machinery, police cars, and buses. Attacks mounted. In Santiago, the Castillo rum distillery was burned down. Fighting was going on in small towns close to the Oriente capital and near Guantánamo. Trains no longer went farther east than Camaguey; their crews were afraid to violate Castro's orders. By then most bridges in the east had been blown up. Only strong military convoys could get through on the highway.

Raúl attacked Mayarí Arriba. Seventy rebels entered in trucks, and the garrison ran away by jumping into the river behind the barracks. One soldier broke his leg.

As the strike deadline neared Batista began arming government employees, who were absolved of all legal responsibility for whatever use they made of the weapons. Judges were forbidden, under pain of instant dismissal, to issue legal rulings against any government official. Employers were forbidden to close their premises during normal working hours, and workers were forbidden to strike on pain of permanent dismissal.

Baracóa, a large place, was captured by the rebels. Manzanillo was isolated and could be supplied only by air. Government planes were now bombing villages just outside Bayamo and Manzanillo. The army killed seventeen boys and strewed their bodies along the Bayamo road as "proof" of a battle. Havana papers duly reported the "victory."

In Santiago, nobody ventured on the streets after dark, not even in automobiles. The custom of Saturday and Sunday strolls along the garden Paseo beside the harbor had been abandoned for more than a year. The only person I saw there the previous April was one little girl bouncing a ball.

But the general strike was sabotaged by the labor bosses and the Communists and was doomed before it started. Its greatest success came in Santiago. The bank clerks were the first to leave at 11 A.M. Fifteen hundred Bacardi workers left their plant at noon. By then the city was empty except for patrolling cars.

A running gun-duel began against the counter-guerrilla, strong-arm gangs of Senator Roberto Masferrer, an ex-Communist who had long been murdering students, youths, and workers in Oriente and elsewhere with *carte blanche* from the government. He also owned a daily paper in Havana, heavily subsidized by government.*

Three large Santiago warehouses were blown up. Gas stations were wiped out by Molotov cocktails. Four youths were gunned down near the cathedral by a police *micro-onda* car, and a boy ordering shops to close was shot. By nightfall the death toll had reached thirty. Masferrer's gangsters careened through the city firing at random. They took over the open cocktail gallery of the big Casa Grande Hotel and shot at everything that moved. In the morning the police and soldiers forced open shops "illegally" closed, but few owners or employers could be located, and there were no customers. The big oil refinery shut down that day.

In Havana the M-26 seized Radio CMQ, and issued the strike call. The banks and some stores closed. On the Prado a bomb blew up a gas main that sent flames skyward all day. Dynamite again cut off electric power to the city.

But two thousand underground resisters failed to materialize. Those who did were shot down in the streets. Probably a hundred people were killed that first day while several thousand patrol cars policed the city. CBS correspondent Robert Taber overheard a police-car radio. "We have a doctor who has a pistol."

"Kill him." A detonation was heard.

"We have ten prisoners."

"No prisoners. Kill them."

Though he had been reluctant to authorize the strike, once it broke out, Castro danced around, shouting joyously. He embraced Argentine correspondent, Jorge Masetti.** "The hour of liberation is here. You are going to Havana with us."

The April strike failure was a serious setback. Many people believed

* It was burned down when the revolution succeeded.
** Later Masetti headed up *Prensa Latina*, later organized a guerrilla operation in northern Argentina, and was reportedly killed, but this has not been wholly verified. I knew him well.

the Castro guerrillas would collapse. Though controlling a large area, his forces still numbered fewer than five hundred men. Raúl had gone north and west with sixty-five men, not all armed, and with only one Browning machine gun among them. Juan Almeida had advanced toward Santiago with seventy men, of whom only twenty-eight had rifles or machine guns. Another small force operated near Holguín under Camilo Cienfuegos. Half-a-dozen smaller units harassed highway and rail traffic. Castro's tiny forces faced a well-outfitted army of thirty thousand with air power, tanks, jeeps, artillery, and United States advisers.

In the rebel attack at El Cobre, thirty tons of dynamite blew up, razing the church containing Cuba's most revered image. Catholics were shocked, but miraculously of all the images in the church, the Copper Virgin came through unscathed.

Castro had opened an airplane field and plenty of ammunition came in. A big shipment arrived by plane via Costa Rica; other arms were flown in by Rómulo Betancourt, President of Venezuela. Attacks were stepped up below the mountain periphery. The port of Baire on the eastern end of the island was seized.

The rebels now had a crude local telephone system. A machine shop was working around the clock repairing arms and making grenades. Batista's unexploded aerial bombs provided explosives. The rebels maintained herds of cattle and built numbers of hospitals that were well-stocked with medicines.

Raúl began taking the initiative. He was established in a much more populated sector with good-sized towns (almost a necessity for successful guerrilla operations), rich coffee fincas, hundreds of farms, and big sugar plantations on the plain. Here the Sierra broke into half a dozen ranges with farming valleys between them. There were many country roads. On the north coast were the big United States nickel and manganese mines and refineries. There was considerable lumbering. Soon Raúl had six hundred men, all armed. The garrisons of small military outposts surrendered or fled. By the end of April, nearly all the region had been captured.

Batista sent in strong columns by truck, but often they were under sniper attack. One big convoy had to fight its way to San Benito through a hail of steel. They burned the coffee terminal, then were beaten back, beset with road mines, ambushes, and constant rifle and machine-gun fire. Other troops from Mayarí were able to reach the big manganese mines at Ocujal, but all attempts to supply the force were ambushed.

On a moonlit night in July, rebel trucks spaced half a mile apart, moved between Mayarí and the big nickel refinery at Nicaro on Nipe Bay. The men descended from the hills, single file. Detouring around a night-operated nickel mine, they disarmed a night watchman and set up ambushes for troops bound to come out from Yori. At four in the morning the rebels made a frontal attack on the local barracks. Five soldiers threw down their arms. Seven lay dead; the rest were wounded. The guerrillas set off with their prisoners and the wounded in jeeps.

Elsewhere, rebel road ambushes killed thirty-seven of one hundred soldiers. One jeep was blown up by a land mine. Planes flew over the next day, but by May 10th, all government forces had been driven out of the area. Raúl commanded a small airfield where planes began landing guns and munitions. The rebels fully controlled the rich coffee and food crops and great herds of cattle.

Two Batista air-force planes being used as bombers over the Sierra Maestra made emergency landings at the Guantánamo naval base and were refueled. There, too, the United States made delivery of rocket warheads. In retaliation, Raúl invaded the Moa Bay Mining properties. After a fierce battle his *barbudos* took over. They seized hospital supplies, captured nineteen jeeps and trucks, and carried off eight American and two Canadian engineers. Two days later, thirty United States sailors who customarily went to Guantánamo City for their high-jinks were kidnapped. Other raids were made on the Nicaro nickel mine and the United Sugar Fruit experimental station at Guaro, bringing up to fifty the total number of American hostages.

The prisoners were shown fragments of bombs and napalm casings stamped United States of America, but they were well-treated. Raúl's account book shows the sum of $1,400 for beer, soft drinks, cigarettes, and other small luxuries for the prisoners.

Grant Wollman, American counsul in Santiago, arranged an armistice and went into the Sierra by jeep to negotiate for surrender. His car was strafed and rocketed by a government plane. (His hosts told him he had probably been hit by warheads from Guantánamo Naval base.) After negotiations, the prisoners were released and taken back from a rebel air strip by United States helicopter. The United States Guantánamo base was taken out of the Civil War.

The government launched a big new offensive into the Sierra Madre. Two Batista battalions fell into a trap at Santo Domingo and were cut to ribbons. In July an entire battalion led by Major José Quevedo was cut off after ten days fighting. He held out for eight days, hungry and weary in a depression at El Jiguí. The heat was terrific. He tried to break out of the trap but only lost more men, most of the company's arms, all its transport, and thirty-nine mules.

Aircraft appeared and attacked Castro's positions from 6 A.M. until 1 P.M. and again the next day. Government reinforcements were massed at the river mouth, and a relief column climbed up from the beach. Castro sprayed them with automatic rifle fire and 50-caliber machine guns. The first two platoons were shot to pieces; the rest retreated. After twenty-four hours of fighting, another battalion had to retreat to the beach leaving thirty-eight casualties behind. Parachuted air supplies fell into rebel hands.

During a four-hour truce, Batista soldiers came to the rebel fox-holes to beg for food and water and embraced the rebels with tears of gratitude. After a long talk with Castro, Quevedo, a former class-mate, returned to camp and told his men he was joining the rebel cause. His idea was received with enthusiasm. After the wounded had been cared for Castro delivered 163 prisoners to representatives of the International Red Cross, which had forced Batista to accept an armistice. Quevedo became a valiant and loyal Castro guerrilla.

In the North, other army defeats occurred. The rebels celebrated July 26 with big banquets of barbecued pig and speech-making. By mid-August, after another serious government defeat, all fighting was over in the Sierra. Castro controlled nearly all Oriente province—fifteen thousand square miles.

Every day there appeared more rebel groups who had not acknowledged Fidel's leadership. In the rich Santa Clara sugarcane area, there was only a tiny group of Fidelista guerrillas led by Victor Bordón. Castro had to take charge of the area or the guerrilla drive would get out of hand.

Che Guevara led a small force from Oriente across the plains of Camagüey. He wrote Fidel that they had been hit by a "cyclone" just as they started out. They marched; they struggled through swamps; they were bombarded and shot down a plane. They were attacked repeatedly. Once they walked two days without food through a swamp, their arms high above their heads. Two miles away, the rail line was heavily guarded by soldiers stationed every few yards. On September 30th they reached the borders of Las Villas province. Scarcely able to walk, their water-soaked feet raw from fungus, they were met by friends near Ciego de Avila and supplied with food and horses. On October 15th, they evaded a thousand pursuers. The rain was pouring down and a hurricane struck. But they reached the "sheltering" hills of Sierra de Sancti Spíritus, below the Escambray mountain area.

Che wrote Fidel:

> Since we left the Cauco Zone . . . we have traveled without resting a single night, for forty days, many times without guides, but with the coastline as a compass for direction. For fifteen days we marched with mud and water up to our knees . . . evading ambushes and troops. In the thirty-one days . . . through Camagüey . . . we ate only eleven times . . . After four days without . . . food, we had to eat a mare—the best one of our poor cavalry—raw without salt.

The new offensive into Las Villas and stepped-up raids everywhere made a farce of the one-party elections Batista had called for November 3rd, even though they were backed and praised by the United States Ambassador who hoped to set up a new, acceptable President. The elections were boycotted. In Havana 75 percent of the voters stayed away from the polls; in Santiago, 98 percent. Andrés Rivera Agüero, one of the worst Batista grafters and a member of a reactionary Creole family, won by a landslide of more votes than there were voters—a ridiculous last-minute shadow play.

People were wondering what Batista could ever do against an enemy that could not be destroyed or even contained. Batista had lost nearly all support except for his small political clique of officeholders, army officers, and United States advisers—and even these, he later claimed in his *Respuesta,* were plotting behind his back. Ambassador Earl Smith, he wrote, was in contact with treacherous generals, secretly striving to bring about a coup.

Fidel had to move fast to head off any last-minute military seizure in Havana, which would prolong the struggle indefinitely. He personally led his guerrillas to seize mines and towns around Bayamo. When Guise was attacked on November 18th, a truckload of troops coming to help the garrison was blown up. The *barbudos* captured their first tank, fourteen trucks, and much ammunition. Bayamo, the third largest army post in the country, was isolated, all communications severed. Santiago was also cut off.

A few roving Batista counter-guerrillas still operated outside the big city garrisons. Major Jesús Sosa Blanco burned at least 130 homes. He would tie up peasants along with their wives and children, then burn them alive. *Time* magazine disclosed none of his crimes, and later shed tears for him when he was tried in a public courtmartial and executed.

By mid-December, more than half of the island's sugar crop was in guerrilla hands. The industries of eastern Cuba had all shut down, including the big nickel, cobalt, and manganese mines and refineries. Holguín and its eighty-five thousand people were without electric power. In Bayamo and Guantánamo, both surrounded by guerrillas, there was no gasoline, hence no cars, trucks, or jeeps. The water supply outside the Guantánamo Naval Base was taken over.

On December 12th, Senator Allen J. Ellender of Louisiana was visiting Havana, where rebels and prisoners were being murdered every night, where clandestine radio stations were broadcasting Fidelista successes in every province. He uttered the prize comment of the year: "Is there a revolution here? I hadn't noticed any trouble." In less than three weeks Batista fled the island.

Che Guevara's forces seized Santa Lucía on the road from Sancti Spíritus to the north-south highway, capturing machine guns and other arms. One hundred and thirty-six soldiers were captured in Escambray sugar central and the town of Fomento. Towns east of the highway were captured by Bordón. Guevara next hit Planceta. On

Christmas Eve the M-26 underground militia took Sancti Spíritus with the aid of the townspeople.

Further east, Fidel took Palma Soriano close to Santiago after two days of house-to-house fighting. Other towns were falling all over the island. The Escambray Front guerrillas joined with Bordón and moved on to encircle Santa Clara. Its capture would cut Cuba in two.

Chavaría, the Government Commander at Santa Clara, had been detected redhanded in conspiring to bring about a coup: Tabernilla and Batista were to be caught and killed. And Tabernilla had his own plot! The scandals were too serious to be made public, so Batista called long-disgraced retired José Eleuterio Pedraza back as head of the general staff. (He had been Batista's chief killer after Machado was ousted in 1933.) Chavaría was quietly replaced by Colonel Joaquín Casillas, to whom Pedraza sent off the famous million-dollar train with the last of Batista's arms to try to save Santa Clara. It was a crack train with electric kitchens and British armored cars, a million rounds of ammunition and two month's provisions. Che Guevara tore the tracks up and derailed it with dynamite. Molotov cocktails turned the armored cars into ovens.

Hundreds of volunteers were armed with this added supply of weapons. Street fighting began in Santa Clara. Civilians blocked streets with their automobiles; women made Molotov cocktails and threw them from windows at government armored cars. The railroad station was taken, then the fortified Gran Hotel. Planes came over destroying houses and buildings. In a flaming barracks, the Chief of Police and Batista's commander bickered over who had charge of the city. Each gave separate orders, but by New Year's Eve Santa Clara was in Guevara's hands.

Batista had been watching the lights on a great electric panel, a new gadget given him by the United States military mission. Each light represented a town, and he saw light after light on the big board go out one by one. When that of Santa Clara went dark, he knew it was time to move on.

Before departing, Batista put the armed forces in the hands of General Eulogio Cantillo and named Carlos Manuel Piedra, the head of the Supreme Court and one of his most shameless sycophants, as his "constitutional substitute." Batista and his close retainers—including president-elect Rivera Agüero and killer General Pedraza—took off for the Dominican Republic. Senator Masferrer escaped on his private yacht. Some fifty officers not included in the escape plans commandeered a plane at gunpoint and flew deep into the United States. A news picture taken of General Tabernilla boarding the escape plane revealed a countenance of utter terror.

Crowds surged through the streets, but their destruction was mostly selective. They smashed up the new pay telephones and the parking meters, from which a Batista relative had received graft. They burned the Masferrer printing presses and newspaper. They smashed the glittering gambling casinos owned by Batista, Eusebio Mujal, and American gangsters.

In the streets, I saw the ruined, smoking remains. From the Palace Hotel, the bar, the gaming tables, the upholstered chairs, and the frescoes of nude women had been torn out and burned. A foreign travel agency, known to be Batista-controlled, was gutted but a big American travel agency alongside was not touched. The mob attacked the home of labor-leader Eusebio Mujal, Batista's henchman. His furniture was tossed into the street for a bonfire, but this was stopped by hurriedly-organized M-26 militia that were racing through the city to control the angry mobs. Mujal abandoned his four million-dollar estate near Havana and fled to the United States, where he acted briefly as advisor to the American Federation of Labor as it issued false pronouncements against the revolutionary regime.

General Cantillo had been in charge of the flower of Batista's army in Santiago and had visited Fidel shortly before the downfall. He made a deal for the surrender of the city. But Cantillo was playing all sides against the middle, trying to ingratiate himself with Castro; plotting to depose Batista, yet pretending to be Batista's last faithful military support, while still making himself welcome at the United States Embassy. When Castro marched into Santiago and learned that the general had been named head of the army, he paced and circled furiously. As one officer described it: he wore a deep rut like a billy goat on a tether. At all costs he had to prevent a new military Junta and a new government set up by the old crowd. He ordered a general strike in Havana and hastened to swear in Dr. Manuel Urrutia Lléo, (who had refused to go along with his fellow judges in punishing captured guerrillas) as provisional President. The Santiago Archbishop attended the ceremony and administered the oath. Urrutia was sent posthaste by air to take over the National Palace in Havana.

Another non-Castro presidential swearing-in ceremony had been scheduled a few days earlier in the National Palace. In hurried Ambassador Smith, the Papal Nuncio, and the Spanish Ambassador—the only diplomats to attend. But the great Palace was silent, the drapes drawn in the glittering salon. No one showed up, for the Supreme Court had refused to give the head of their own body the oath to take over. And so another scheme to shortcut the revolution had fallen on its face. Still, General Cantillo had charge of Camp Colombia.

With Mujal gone and Communist labor leaders now jumping on the Castro bandwagon, the general strike was effective. Mountains of garbage were piling up on every street, and the semitropical city was beginning to stink.

Meanwhile, Castro had sent every available guerrilla unit—particularly the forces of Che Guevara and Camilo Cienfuegos—racing across country to take over Havana. But Colonel Ramón Barquín—leader of the 1953 anti-Batista military plot—had just been released from Pino del Rio prison. He flew to Havana, boldly arrested Cantillo, and took over Camp Colombia. Fauré Chaunont (a leader of the 1957 student assault on the Palace and head of an independent guerrilla force close to the capital) reached Havana before the Fidelistas and took over the University, the big arsenal, and the National Palace. Arriving soon after, Che took over Morro Castle. Cienfuegos finally took over Camp Colombia, throwing out Barquín.

Meanwhile, President Urrutia was pacing the airport, unable to go to the Palace. For hours, negotiations were carried on with Chaunont. Promises were made; Chaunont finally agreed to let Urrutia come to the Palace, provided *his* men were the ones to deliver it to him. They were then to retire peacefully.

The new President was duly installed, a ceremony not graced by the presence of Ambassador Smith. He had left for Washington, never to return.

Not until Castro finally reached the city nearly a week later was he able to pry Chaunont out of his other positions. Chaunont was demanding a new government by a "democratic" process, with representatives from all rebel factions. It looked as if an armed fracas, even though one had been narrowly averted at the Palace, would occur, but Castro's prestige was too great; Chaunont finally gave in. He was promptly shipped off with a big slush fund as ambassador to China, later to the Soviet Union. (Today he is high in the inner councils of the government.)

Castro led a leisurely victory parade the entire length of the island, displaying scores of captured tanks including the United States Sherman tanks sent to help Batista. But one was a homemade contraption, made by rebel blacksmiths who welded steel slabs to a truck. The parade was received by delirious throngs everywhere.

From ten in the morning until well into the afternoon, a million people waited in the frying Havana sun for Castro to appear. All restaurants and stores were closed; even shoe-shiners were not shining shoes. A few peddlers were soon stripped of wares. Some people had been wise enough to bring lunches. My own lunch consisted of two bottles of Coca-Cola, barely cooled. As Castro entered the city, I could hear the long deep rumble of the cheering crowds; the rumble grew louder as he neared. A few blocks away it became a mighty roar. He made his entry, standing in the turret of a tank with his arm about his young son, who had been loaned by his mother (divorced in 1957) for the occasion.

Reaching the Prado, Castro whirled off to pay his respects to Urrutia in the palace, then went on to Camp Colombia, arriving there at sundown to give his famous speech of peace. The people had been bombed with napalm and missiles, he said, but the planes were now in the hands of the Revolution and would be used to drop food and clothing and toys not available that Christmas.* The great land reform would soon be under way, he promised. A dramatic publicity stunt was staged and later repeated at other Castro appearances: peace doves fluttered around his head and perched on his broad shoulders. It was a stunt as old as Mahomet, who had kept corn in his ears. Castro denounced war and violence. He heaped scorn on the United States military mission: They had proved their uselessness. A handful of guerrillas had defeated their mighty army. There was nothing they could teach the Cubans, they should go home. Shortly he packed them off unceremoniously; they went on to Haiti, seventy of them, to advise Dictator Duvalier.

Castro's guerrillas were supreme in a rich little land of seven million people, ninety miles from the United States. The rebels had no reason to love Americans, nor did the people. Nor did Castro. His regime has lasted eleven years in the face of armed invasion, CIA plots, bombings, and a United States-Latin American trade boycott. A million people still pour out wherever he speaks.

* Forthwith a nation-wide collection was made. Militia trucks with banners carried bands. Scantily-dressed dancing B-girls and cabaret comedians went through their acts. Girls standing on street corners took donations.

12

THE LATIN AMERICAN EXPLOSION

In 1931, Oliver La Farge published a fine novel, *The Sparks Fly Upward*, about the guerrilla exploits of a Quiché Indian youth who leads a successful revolution for "Land and Liberty" against the landowners, the Army, and the ecclesiastics. In the end, the upstart leader is torn between his loyalty to the cause and his desire for status as part of the ruling clique.

After gaining power, most such South American liberators have become the hangmen of the people. Peasants are often shoved back into their hovels—until the volcano erupts again and new bands gallop across the land. Thomas Carlyle described the process as "vulturous quack and tyrant against Quack and Tyrant." Latin America's guerrilla calendar goes back nearly two centuries to the stirrings of Independence. It is marked throughout by repeated outbreaks of political, class, peasant, labor, racial, religious, nationalist, and/or anti-imperialist motivation.

The feudal-military systems no longer meet the needs of the people or the demands of the modern industrial and electronic age. The most recent military dictatorships, often promoted directly or indirectly by the United States to maintain an intolerable status quo, govern steadily deteriorating lands. Few army rulers know anything of justice or honesty: they make revolt inevitable. Guerrilla activities everywhere are coalescing into a continent-wide revolution, bound to grow more terrible as more injustices accumulate. No imaginable free government can easily fit into the "acceptable" pattern of fostering American goodwill, preserving law and order, and encouraging foreign investment.

The costly Alliance for Progress, a patchwork wall against Castroism, has scarcely matched-up to its promises. Except for a few brighter spots, the Latin American picture continues to darken: more illiterate, more unemployed, more homeless, less education, less public health, lower per-capita food production, mounting debt, wider trade gaps—and more dictatorships, more militarism. United States aid is insufficient to replace the money, resources, and talents being drained away. Science and technology cannot function in a military system of backward landholding and feudal bungling. Outside business invest-

220

ments only take out natural resources and absorb more capital than they put in. Guerrillas are part of the inevitable reaction.

Already there are guerrillas in at least ten southern countries: Paraguay (since 1960), Bolivia (1965), Peru (1959), Colombia (1948), Venezuela (1961), Honduras (1965), Guatemala (1963), Brazil (1967), Ecuador (1967), Panama (1969). In Argentina, guerrillas were quickly crushed, 1965–1966, as was a later effort by Jorge Masetti. But they continue. Petty local guerrilla flare-ups have occurred in Mexico. One occurred in the north in 1966, but was quickly snuffed out by federal paratroopers. Off and on from 1959 to 1966, reports have come out of Nicaragua (plagued by several conservative invasions, falsely labeled "Cuban-inspired") about guerrillas operating in the Segovias, Sandino's old stamping grounds.

In his recent *Death in the Brazilian Northeast,* Josué de Castro believes that this long-suffering area is headed for guerrilla war and may become another Vietnam. The largely Catholic underground in Brazil is called Popular Action (PA). In midsummer of 1966, somewhere in Amazonas, it was host to a meeting of guerrilla leaders who had come from five or six other countries to discuss tactics. The PA has spread to ten "regions," subdivided into zones, sections, and cells. It works in the *favelas* or slums, in trade unions, among the peasants and students. A parallel military organization of expelled army officers acts as instructor to ultra-secret guerrilla groups. Members hand over from 5 to 10 percent of their earnings. In December, 1968, the army suppressed Parliament, and made wholesale arrests.

Some Latin guerrillas may be romantic imitations of Castro and Guevara. Guevara's own efforts in Bolivia were somewhat romantic, but despite Guevara's failure, all such movements have classic reasons for growing more effective. A year after Guevara's death, President René Barrentos of Bolivia stated that guerrillas were still operating. He was faced by riots and the collapse of his pseudo-civilian cabinet.

Under the present Latin American system, the worst "imperialists" are not Americans but the home-grown rulers, landholders, army men and others who control the governments. The sad thing is that both native and foreign "imperialism" tend to join hands. Inevitably, the greatest breeder of revolutions abroad today is foreign capital—not Communism, Castroism, or home-grown despotism.

The rise of great Latin American cities comes about as a result of some industrialization, foreign investment, and continued land monopoly. But such urban centers have produced a new proletariat—often Indian; not mestizo or creole—that festers in slums where people live worse than animals. A Latin American writer calls the cities, "the beachhead of imperialism." By 1900 greater Buenos Aires led the world in slum clearance and city planning. Today it is a vast slum-ridden aggregation of more than seven million people—a fourth of the country's total population. Some three million of that once-proud city live without water, sewers, electric lights, fuel, paved streets, proper transportation, hospitals, or schools—only more police-stations and barracks. It would take *all* of the Alliance for Progress' budget for the the next decade to set merely that *one* city to rights—and this would be no assurance of permanent remedy. Caracas is nearly as bad. Beautiful Lima is becoming a cesspool. Handsome Mexico City now has more than four million people, and its slums have grown faster than the new apartment houses. Panama City tells a similar story. Indeed, the picture everywhere is the same: *over-developed* cities, glittering with neon lights, vice and gambling, rise in an ever-declining *under-developed* hinterlands. Obscene wealth was next to even more obscene poverty; spangled majesty is pitted against misery.

Josué de Castro gives a horrifying picture of the swamp slum of Recife among the mangroves; whole families live in mud, excrement, and garbage. They crawl after crabs and crayfish, their only food. "What their bodies throw off is returned to the mud to be made into crabmeat again." As I can testify personally, a similar or even worse poverty evists in nearly every Brazilian city including the handsome new Brazilia. What is more terrible than the enormous floating riverslum of Manaos on the inner Amazon? The filth-laden *favelas* of Rio de Janeiro crown the mud hills, and with each heavy rain, they avalanche into the avenues with death and disease.

Such horrors are not confined to Latin America. Big cities breed big slums: witness the incredible ghettos of Washington, D. C. Look at Madrid, Leopoldville, Brazzaville, Lagos, Teheran, Bangkok, the frightful cities of India, or Saigon, now bombed and burned, with 200,000 refugees living among the garbage heaps.

To sum it up, the economic balance has been shattered everywhere; the old cultures have been fractured. The ancient poor have grown poorer; they have been cast into limbo between worlds. The old productive life that created some amenities and graciousness in the last century has become insufficient. The press, radio, movies, and television advertise imported luxuries and throw miseries into sharper relief. Local production fails to match the soaring new hopes or the population growth. Low wage scales, limited demand, and sheer hunger block new enterprises.

Each automobile (mostly imported at excessive cost, though Mexico and Brazil now turn out some hundreds of thousands each year) that rolls over a few new roads into the hinterland, penetrates areas where there is no electricity, no doctors, no schools, little food. It transports well-to-do people, more soldiers, more police, more tax-collectors, but few teachers, doctors, or engineers. The tires that almost run over unshod feet are coveted for sandals, wherever they are discarded, be it in Peru or Vietnam. Five-gallon oil cans, fitted with wooden handles, replace the beautiful home-made terracotta jars, to tote contaminated water from the rivers.

Some years ago, mountain villagers in Oaxaca, Mexico, crowded around me excitedly to say that the Angel Gabriel—some said Jesus Christ himself—had just ridden overhead in the sky; they had seen him with their own eyes. It was their first glimpse of an airplane, one that had strayed from its usual flight route. When I told them that the pilot was my friend Tom Jones, with whom I had had drinks in the St. Regis bar, the villagers were so angered by my sacrilegious talk that they threatened to lynch me.

Presently little Mexican towns acquired short runways. Presently some women, who had never seen an automobile or a train, learned to stow their hampers of produce, their chickens and turkeys, into planes and fly off to the Mexico City or Guadalajara markets. They brought back shoddy mass-produced goods to sell; more local handicrafts are discouraged. They brought back not doctors or nurses or teachers, but new diseases and outlandish ideas.

A few years ago I visited the Colquiri tin mines in Bolivia—a day-long trip from La Paz. Wages there were less than a dollar a day. The miners chew the cocoa-leaf to numb their hunger pangs and to provide a temporary sensation of great energy. I was asked to talk to about five hundred miners. They were illiterate Aimara, who did not speak good Spanish, but their questions showed that they were more intensely interested in international affairs than most New York audiences. They were quite aware that what happens in Cairo or Bagdad, Cuba or Mississippi, has meaning for themselves and their families. They knew about Vietnam and Algeria, Mexico and Cuba, the Congo, South Africa; about United States race riots and freedom marches. For them darkness has been pierced by dazzling light, by the clangor of far-off wars. Everywhere on earth, the peoples stir restlessly; in the coming years, they are going to be on the march. (Within three years it came to pass in that same Bolivia.)

The workers were not Communists. At Colquiri, an outside Communist organizer ruefully told me he had been able to line up only five miners. A few miners were Trotskyites, but the majority were behind the official party of President Paz Estenssoro. He soon betrayed them, and now he is gone. The military upstarts now in power have exiled the leaders, murdered miners, and shot Che Guevara. A new guerrilla leader has now arisen to lead the people, guns in hand. Military rule nearly always worsens the disease it cannot and does not know how to cure.

Critics argue that being illiterate, such poor people cannot read the great free press. But some villager can always read to his neighbors. Critics argue that such poor people do not have radios, but today in all the world there are few villages, however remote, where there is not at least one radio set or television, if not in the homes, in the town hall where the villagers gather every night. In his *Children of Sanchez*, Oscar Lewis found that in the *Casa Grande*—a Mexico City tenement of 157 windowless one-room apartments—79 percent had radios, though their average income was well under $200 a year. Actually Brazil has long been *exporting* radios; they are manufactured in large numbers in Argentina, Chile, and Mexico, often by United States subsidiaries. Cuba turned out 40,000 sets in 1964; 100,000 in 1965.

Self-powered movie projectors travel to distant little places where people have never known electric light. With bated breath, the audience watches Hollywood gangsters and politicians and elegantly gowned gunmolls lurking behind potted palms in marble halls, or a near-nude starlet fighting off rape. That sumptuous fairy world is remote, but the onlookers ask why they should remain dirty, sick and hungry.

The new gadgets of so-called progress intrude into their lives—perhaps a communal motor to grind maize for their tortillas—to do in a few minutes what took hours of back-breaking labor. But change does not easily end four centuries of habit, and it brings uneasiness, dissent, and presently armed disorders—guerrillas in the hills. Technology itself is the greatest revolutionary conspirator of all.

Josué de Castro feels that the economic domination of Latin America —by American capital, American loans, and official intervention at all levels, the control of major production, the near monopoly of exports and imports—is overwhelming. Except in the cruel majesty of the new cities, this outside control stands against nearly all social progress and modernization. The new nationalism is inevitably antiforeign in an angry way.

Politicians fan smouldering animosity into hot flames. The foreigner, the foreign power, and foreign corporation become convenient whipping boys for all local evils and miseries. Slogans such as "Yankee, go home" gain potency. There is scarcely a place on earth where these words or even more insulting anti-American graffiti are not seen daubed on walls. They arouse a huge emotional response.

The Castro revolt in Cuba depended on the Cuba *guajiros* or peasants. "The city," said Castro, "is the cemetery of revolutionaries and revolutionary resources." "Those great Yankee branch offices [cities] are living purgatories compared to the great urban conglomeration of Europe and Asia," said French analyst, Regis Debray, now jailed in Bolivia for thirty years.

A first-page editorial in the Cuban weekly *Bohemia* (July 2, 1965) summarized the *raison d'être* (according to Cubans and many Latin Americans), that United States "imperialists" are hated and feared the world over.

To say guerrilla is to say peoples in revolt against the invading blond beast and his servitors—in Guatemala, Colombia, Venezuela, Peru, Vietnam. So worried are the Pentagon schemers . . . that they have invented an undefinable monstrosity, the "Antiguerrilla," a *reducto ad absurdum* of the authentic guerrilla. In Latin America particularly, the Antiguerrilla is an aspect of rural counter-revolution to suppress guerrillas. The result is that every day there are more guerrillas in the mountains—from the ancient homestead of the Mayas to the stage-setting of the Incas . . . one after another, the peoples are joining up with the great insurgency so prophetically announced in the Second Declaration of Havana.*

Bohemia continues:

The first aim of every guerrilla is to maintain himself—the second, to keep the enemy under constant check. These goals have been achieved on this continent. Only the third is still uncompleted; to sweep the Anti-People from every corner of the hemisphere. It is an inexorable process, which will be carried through to the last phase when the new liberators clasp hands across frontiers.

Mexico's leading novelist, Carlos Fuentes, wrote in the *Monthly Review* (January 1963):

No, my American friends, an agrarian revolution is only made through revolution, with weapons in hand. This is what the share-croppers of Peru, the peasants of northeast Brazil, the pariahs of Chile, Ecuador and Colombia are beginning to do. They are not allowing themselves to be cheated by false agrarian reforms: the distribution of sterile lands, without credit, without machinery, without schools or hospitals.

---

* This was a pronouncement made by Fidel Castro, September 2, 1960, to the Second General Assembly of the People. In it, among other things, he denounced the United States antiguerrilla schools in Panama and the United States military missions in Latin America as constituting "a permanent espionage machine in each country closely linked with the C.I.A., teaching officers the most reactionary sentiments and trying to convert the armies into instruments of their own political and economic interests." Millions of copies of this declaration have been openly distributed over the earth in many languages, and the declaration has already appeared in English translations. A diluted, mutilated version was subsequently printed by the Senate Internal Security Sub-Committee as a hush-hush document of Secret Cuban propaganda in the *Hearing Eighty-eighth Congress, Washington 1965*, pp. 184–197. The Mexican writer Jorge Carrión in *Política* (August 15, 1966) called the Declaration "the first real act in the independence of Latin America."

The "revolutionary impetus" cannot be stifled. "We want to live with with you as loyal friends, not as sick, poorly fed ignorant slaves."

Unfortunately, much of official Washington long ago came to the conclusion that every nationalist—who automatically becomes an anti-imperialist critic of United States policies—must be treated as a Communist. "The thinking of Guatemala's intellectuals . . ." said the 1954 United States White Paper, "became covered with a glaze of nationalism and Marxism . . ." This provided "a ready means to blame Guatemala's backwardness on foreign imperialist exploitation." Marxism "provided a dialectical explanation of 'imperialism' and a concrete cause dedicated to overcoming it." Maybe so, said a Guatemalan friend, "but the United Fruit and other gringo corporations own the country and run the government. They run the army, the newspapers, the ports, the vessels, the telegraph lines, the airplanes."

For Washington, nationalism has "gone out of style," remarks Juan José Arévalo, borrowing a phrase from a speech by John Foster Dulles (November 1, 1957) and "whoever makes claims for defunct sovereignty . . . does not live in this world or is a Communist."

The alarm has been sounded by the United States and by native spokesmen. "Sovereignty is a medieval concept," said Brazilian cabinet head Juracy Magalhaes, speaking in Buenos Aires when attending an inter-American conference in November 1966.

Foreign Minister Vasco Leotao da Cunha of the Brazilian Castelo Branco military dictatorship, asserted "The Brazilian frontier can be expanded just as the North American frontier has been expanded in . . . respect to Berlin."

"Nationalism," says Peruvian ex-Communist Eudocio Ravines, who has long made his living by professional anti-Communism, "has been converted into the best auxiliary of the Kremlin." This antinationalist, no-sovereignty thesis for weaker nations is advocated by former United States diplomat John C. Dreiser, participant in the Guatemalan Army coup, in his 1965 *The Organization of American States and the Hemisphere Crisis*. It has been repeatedly stressed by "hard-line" Lincoln Gordon of the State Department. It is also advocated by C. F. Black in his *The Dynamics of Modernization*.

Its crudest, yet haziest expression, is to be found in General Maxwell D. Taylor's book *Responsibility and Response*. He envisions the United States rushing in everywhere to suppress "wars of national liberation," which he sees as "inimical to our national purposes." The Taylor plan for subjugation of the South Vietnamese helped get us into the present impasse. He feels that even if American bombers destroy everything in North Vietnam, war may still be going on twenty years from now.

Ignoring treaties, President Johnson, once declared that the United States will intervene anywhere in the hemisphere wherever there is danger of a "Communist" take-over—even if the revolt is wholly in-digenous and non-Communist, as in the Dominican Republic in April, 1965. This is merely the revival of a long-standing policy temporarily abandoned by Franklin Delano Roosevelt. Today, however, armed in-tervention is being supplemented by covert control of local internal affairs—by money, diplomacy, technical, financial, and military mis-sions, propaganda, cultural and labor attaches, customs collectors, and secret police agents.

Johnson's universal interventionist position was backed by an even cruder Congressional resolution in September 1965. Any New World nation, Congress declared, has the right to invade any other country menaced by Communist take-over. For world-power planners, Wood-row Wilson's "self-determination of peoples" and his basic thesis of the War to End all Wars have passed into strategic limbo.

Unfortunately, the identification of "Communism" is even more blurred by Latin American politicians and dictators than by American officialdom. President Vargas once called one of the biggest São Paulo bankers a "Communist." In Nicaragua, all political opponents, labor leaders, Masons, Conservatives, and Protestants are lumped together as "Communists." That charge was openly levelled by "Liberal Party" candidate Nacho Somoza against the Conservative Party in his 1967 campaign. Dictators everywhere customarily brand all opponents as Communists, though on occasion they themselves have been allied, openly or secretly, with the Communists (as was Medina in Venezuela, Benavides in Peru, Vargas in Brazil and Batista in Cuba). Student rioters are always "Communist inspired."

This handy epithet, of course, frightens Washington into assisting dictators with more financial aid. Numerous dictators have found it advantageous to pull a few Communists, imaginary or otherwise, out from under the bed. Several years ago a usurping dictator in the Dominican Republic promoted a fake "Communist" guerrilla move-ment to hasten recognition.

The Congressional Resolution mentioned above that trampled on all existing treaty rights, incensed nearly all Latin Americans. Public figures and congressional leaders from Mexico to Patagonia and in Europe denounced it as "a bid for international anarchy." It stimulated more guerrilla fighting.

Castro has been accused of sending arms to Venezuela guerrillas. The evidence is not conclusive, but the FLN-FALN—the Venezuela guerrilla front—maintains a permanent mission in Cuba. Its head, Pérez Silva (known at the front as Leonardo Quintana) died there in October of 1966, and his funeral was attended by Raúl Castro, head of Cuba's armed forces. Fidel was displeased by the Communist abandonment of guerrilla efforts there, which temporarily disrupted the armed movement. Therefore Fidel supports by words and perhaps with arms Commander Douglas Bravo, who in 1967 refused to follow Communist Party orders any longer.

Apparently Castro has a finger in Guatemalan revolt, having backed Luis Augusto Turicos against Sosa, whom he accused of favoring Trotskyites. Also, according to *Spartacus*, an American Trotsky publication, Castro managed to disrupt the Trotskyite Peruvian MIR (Revolutionary Movement of the Left) and pretty well ruined the guerrilla movement in that country. Castro has sent military advisers to Ghana and Tanzania, and provided the Presidential Guard in the former French Congo. He has repeatedly offered aid to the Viet Cong, has an unused military mission in North Vietnam, and has sent sugar ships to Haiphong. In any case, guerrilla leaders from Peru, Colombia, Bolivia, Paraguay, Venezuela, Guatemala, and Honduras have visited Cuba before or after hostilities.

Castro has also been accused of training guerrillas in Cuba for many lands. He has likely done so, though the December 1964 *Reader's Digest* article, "Inside the Castro Terror School," by secret agent Juan de Dios Marín, is mostly fantasy. An American woman correspondent of a Chicago paper told Castro in August 1966, that she wanted to visit his camps for training Latin American guerrillas. He laughed. "Visit our sports fields," he said dryly, "We have gone in for international sports in a great way."

Sympathetic Latin American exiles or visitors customarily volunteer for Cuban militia duty. When in Havana I first tried to contact Juan Cooke of Argentina and ex-President Jacobo Arbenz of Guatemala, their wives told me they were out drilling.

What Cuba does is a drop in the bucket compared to American anti-guerrilla training schools in Panama, Guatemala, and Puerto Rico. There are seventy United States military missions in the southland countries. CIA and other money is lavishly spent to buy or influence individuals, organizations, and governments.

Nevertheless, the numerous international conferences held the year round in Havana, are themselves *ideological* training camps. Thus in September 1966 a number of national and international trade union congresses with delegates from fourteen countries were celebrated, besides the Latin American Students' Congress. In December, the permanent Havana office of the great 1966 Tricontinental Congress set up political training schools for the revolutionists of all countries. The great 1967 convention of the new Organization of Latin American Solidarity (OLAS) brought all anti-imperialist and revolutionary elements of the Western Hemisphere together under the slogan "Revolution Now." It called for guerrilla warfare everywhere: "A revolutionist is one who makes a revolution."

A lot of false fears have resulted. On July 6, 1966, the Nicaraguan police announced the arrival of thirty Castro and Moscow agents—a figment of heated election propaganda. The Brazilian government—also in July—reported that an abortive attempt on the life of the official presidental candidate Arturo da Costa y Silva was "on orders from Castro." Dictator Onganía of Argentina denounced a wave of pornographic literature as having come from Havana—"a subtle method" said the press, to soften the brains of "our splendid army officers." One Cuban said wittily, "Every time a banana is thrown at a cop, the cry goes up 'under orders from the Cuban government.' Pretty soon," said the Cuban, "they'll blame us for all the starvation and sickness in Latin America."

In Paraguay, Peru, Bolivia, Colombia, Venezuela and Guatemala, the United States has aided efforts to suppress outlaw fighters with money, supplies, airplanes, helicopters, gas, and chemical supplies, napalm, and sometimes by specially trained Green Beret rangers and military and police advisers. Joint antiguerrilla operations have been carried out in numerous countries. With great fanfare in September 1966 the Peruvian Army launched an all-out antiguerrilla operation in the Ayacucho region with helicopters, planes, paratroops, and commandos—similar to operations in Vietnam, said El Tiempo. "Just a show," said a labor paper "put on by the reactionaries to cover up the panic and desperation of the Balaunde government over the persistence of guerrilla nuclei." In 1968 the Belaunde government ceased to exist —not from guerrillas but "gorillas." A military Junta took over, a changeover—due to an oil-concession. By then guerrilla efforts had largely collapsed, though they persist in the eastern Marañón jungles.

During the 1966 Guatemalan elections, according to the Cuban Granma [Communist] and other papers, three thousand United States troops were surreptitiously introduced into the country, at least temporarily. In late 1966, Robert W. Porter, Jr., chief of the United States Southern command in Panama, suavely told the House Foreign Affairs Committee that American Army engineers were engaged in a "civic action" program on the Honduras-Guatemala border. That is where the soldiers of both countries have been conducting joint antiguerrilla probes. United States military "advisers" have accompanied Guatemalan antiguerrilla forces there and elsewhere. A thousand Green Berets, it is claimed, were sent to various mountainous areas toward the end of 1966, where two thousand people have been killed. American correspondents claim to have seen Green Beret soldiers in the mountains and on the streets. FAR, the official rebel news bulletin, claimed in late August 1966 that a state of United States military intervention "actually exists now and, since the Guatemalan army had proved incompetent, has been attempting to promote armed intervention by the rest of Central America." Occasional news of rebel fights occur, but the headlines are now held by urban terrorists. Wealthy Guatemalans, even high members of the government, have been kidnapped and held for ransom used to finance the guerrillas in the hills. Nearly a million dollars has been collected in this way. In 1968, two United States military mission officers were gunned down in the streets. In August, the American Ambassador was similarly assassinated. (There were parallels in the 1923 to 1925 Moroccan Rif revolt, when the Spanish government paid four million pesetas to ransom officers and soldiers. But of course, the United States paid the highest ransom price in history—$60,000,000—to get back survivors of the 1961 Bay of Pigs invasion.)

President Peralta called the guerrillas "cowardly bandits," because they refused to fight the army except when they chose. He put a price of $25,000 on the head of leader Marco Antonio Yon Sosa. But in October, 1965, Yon Sosa issued his manifesto. "Close ranks about the armed movement which fights for the downfall of the present military regime and for the taking over of power by the progressive and revolutionary sectors . . . making an open fight against oppression, hunger and ignorance." He told Argentine correspondent Adolfo Gilly about successful efforts to win over the peasants.

Among the Guatemalan guerrillas in early 1967, slender, intense, and angry, 24-year-old Luis Augusto Turcios Lima accused Yon Sosa (head of the MR-13 movement) of having permitted so-called Trotskyites to infiltrate into FAR (Armed Rebel Forces). He was backed by Fidel Castro's firebrand attack on Yon Sosa. Turcios, head of the Guatemalan Labor Party (Communist) assumed control of part of the guerrilla elements in the Sierra de las Minas. He followed Castro's line at the Tricontinental Congress, though presently he said his inspiration was not from Moscow or Havana but from Sandino in Nicaragua. In April, Yon Sosa expelled the Trotskyite Juan Posadas' splinter group from the MR-13 ranks and held conferences with Turcios to heal the breach. This revival of a stale Stalin feud with its outworn phrases, deep in American tropical forests, reveals a curiously sterile mentality —perhaps a peculiar power lust. Behind this Commad-Trotsky bickering some say, is involved a policy split between Maoism and Stalinism. However, on October 2, 1966, Turcios was killed in a flaming automobile accident, and his place was taken by twenty-three-year-old César Montes, a captain in the Edgar Ibarra front who has thrown off all ties with the Guatemalan Labor Party.

Guerrilla war on an increasing scale is almost inevitable in Peru, Venezuela, Colombia, Ecuador, and Bolivia. Late in 1966, however, ex-Assistant Secretary of State Lincoln Gordon told the United States House Committee on Foreign Affairs that the guerrilla problems which he considered "a communist phenomenon," had been reduced. Whatever the guerrillas' political complexion, their cause is not communism, but political and economic miseries, inevitably aggravated by wealth, power, and lack of comprehension. The population explosion and military rule compound the disaster. Latin American remains a powder keg.

13

GUERRILLAS U.S.A.

Only urban pseudo-guerrillas thrive in the United States. None inhabit the Rockies, the Ozarks, the Dakota Badlands, or the Appalachians. A considerable force of guerrillas cannot operate in near uninhabited places; they require food and supplies. This was one of Che Guevara's miscalculations in Bolivia, where he was unable to penetrate into productive rural areas. Still, a few young people these days seriously—and romantically—discuss the possibility of Che Guevara-type warfare in the United States. Mary Jane, a wispy, dainty blond girl whose rich boyfriend has been questioned by the F. B. I. regarding secret arms transactions, remarks, "I chose that Vermont College because the hills there are ideal for guerrilla operations and arms can be easily run in from Canada."

Considerable urban terrorism featured the Castro revolt in Cuba. The newsworthy accomplishments of guerrillas in Guatemala, where wealthy men have been kidnapped for ransom, have been urban attacks.

The most heroic example of urban guerrilla warfare was that in the Warsaw ghetto under Nazi occupation. Before and during that warfare, nearly half a million Jews were fed to the local glue factory. The final resistance is told in heart-rending style by John Hersey in *The Wall*. It is a picture of semistarvation and death: underground bunkers, secret attic retreats, the maze of basements, perforated walls, and roof thoroughfares. In those dark cellars babies were born, while grandfathers, the sick, and the wounded died. Ammunition and arms were smuggled through the wall. Grenades, bullets, and Molotov cocktails were fabricated, traps and ambushes prepared, tanks, armored cars, and trucks blown up, storm troopers burned alive or bombed to smithereens—naturally with great loss of life among the guerrillas. To end the resistance, the Nazis finally had to raze every building in the ghetto, leaving only a wasteland of rubble. It was a battle of desperation to the death; few Jews escaped alive.

According to Guevara, the genuine guerrilla is a revolutionist, one who seeks power and control of the state to establish the rights and freedom of the people. The journalist Regis Debray, now imprisoned in Bolivia for thirty years, wrote that the guerrilla could not long persist in a single region in the hope that his pressure would bring reforms. He must move on to full victory.

At the moment, only piece-meal victory can be won in the United States—in the cities. There have been rural protest marches, usually attended by violence and death, but the only night riders there have been Ku Klux Klanners, White Crusaders, and similar white terrorists. Most protests have been urban and have occurred either as spontaneous mass demonstrations in the ghettos or as sit-ins in Universities. Both are well corralled before they begin; mostly they are examples of what Debray has declared doomed to failure. They are small "corner" revolts. But they have their purposes and the word "failure" is too absolute. Even if by their very nature they are not "bonafide" (if such a word may be used) guerrilla drives, it is true that such demonstrators have learned and on occasion do utilize a few classical guerrilla tactics. But being a guerrilla requires continuous full-time dedication and resistance. A rural guerrilla may rejoin the community as a peasant and wait for the opportune moment to strike again. This technique plagued American commanders in the Philippines, as it has later in Vietnam.

So-called urban guerrillas in the United States have increasingly used Philippine Sandatahen tactics of seventy years ago: raining down missiles from rooftops and windows, sharp-shooting as in the initial riots in Chicago. Molotov cocktails have been widely used. Arson is a tactic of modern guerrilla warfare, both during riots and at other times. So is sabotage to cripple and disorganize everyday social life—sugar in gas tanks, sand in electric motors and gears, power failures, destruction of transformers, opening hydrants, damaging pipes and wires, breaking windows, false fire and police alarms, disconnecting public phones and police call boxes, stink bombs in public places and theaters, smashing traffic lights, terrorizing subway riders. These acts, though criminal in the conventional and legal sense, are not to be categorized as vandalism per se, however vandalistic they may be. They represent a pattern of organized or individualistic disruption. Persons already outside society's guide lines, wholly alienated from society by the abuses of society, see the breakdown of that society as guerrilla warfare's only possible means of success. Every such breakdown sows confusion and fear and leads more people to turn to violence. The greater the social disorganization, the more guerrilla ranks swell.

Demonstrators resort to hit-and-run tactics, dissolving before police confrontation to reassemble elsewhere—from the United Nations Plaza to Times Square or Washington Square. Using buses, the police learn to match their mobility. But the one truly guerrilla tactic, which has occurred on a few occasions, has been ambushing police answering false alarm calls. As noted, the university students occupying buildings violate all known guerrilla rules.

The right of people to demonstrate is an integral part of our democratic process. Even sit-ins have become more tolerated, especially in New York. Nearly all mass demonstrations have allegedly been pacific —the sinners are *always* the police. Both Martin Luther King, Jr., and his successor Reverend Abernathy, have been or are disciples of Gandhi. David Dellinger—editor of *Liberation,* chief organizer of the Chicago convention demonstrations so savagely smashed by Mayor Daley's police, and the anti-Nixon inauguration flare, is—or was—a devout nonviolent pacifist. The Voluntown community in Connecticut and elsewhere whose members trampled on Johnson's tulips at the Pentagon and who picket all atomic submarine launchings, are completely nonviolent and nonresistant—so much so they have refused to bring charges against the night-raiding Minute Men and Marines who attacked them several times, wounding some of them and burning their cars and buildings.

But few demonstrations are without a handful of violent types such as those in Chicago who threw sacks of urine and razor blades in potatoes. The result was what the investigating commission called "a police riot." Policemen are rarely inclined to be either rational or gentle, and protestors usually blame them for any violence. The fact is, many demonstrators are often intent on violent confrontation. No demonstration is considered a success unless a certain number of participants are bloodied or dragged off in paddy wagons.

But the spirit, the dedication, the self-sacrifice, the persistence that feature guerrilla activities elsewhere have not yet appeared in the United States. Demonstrations, however inadequate, serve to keep up courage and reinforce a continuing spirit of protest and alienation from the establishment. Saner tactics are being sought, especially by some students, as at State College in San Francisco. On November 13th, minority students at the college met to formulate demands on the President. At first, the police really had to hunt for students to club (and of course found them). The Negroes of the college—the BSO—and the Chinese, Mexicans, and Filipinos—the TWLF—passed the word to white supporters: "no mass confrontation."

As one said, "There are going to be a lot of disappointed people when they find out there will be no buildings taken over or any traditional crap like that." Mass confrontation was the wrong game—a good way to get killed; though it was "romantic" to throw rocks from behind the crowd and shout "Oink, oink." But in spite of this—and due to a small number of militants—police brutality was ruthless. A strike was called, and the protest then swelled to thousands; they were joined by six hundred faculty members and by labor-union pickets. Most demands have since been met.

Certain new mores have developed. Most demonstrators (the Blacks led the way in this) have learned to endure police clubbings and have lost their fear of going to jail. That—besides pushing toward a breakdown of court-processes—is a rupture of middle-class sobriety and respectability. For some younger people, it has become almost a stamp of dishonor *not* to have been dragged to jail—an indication that a whole generation has lost its respect for what is defined as law and order. It calls the police "pigs," it spits in their faces, it denounces them as Nazis and Storm Troopers, perhaps not wholly without reason. The more the police club and jail, the more converts are made for "revolution."

If neither the spirit or circumstances exist at present for successful wide-spread guerrilla operations, reasons for them do exist: poverty in a wealthy nation, ghetto unemployment and ghettos themselves, a society cracking apart with the spread of nonhumanistic computerism often directed against supposedly humane purposes. Indeed, cybernetics may be a greater breeder of guerrillas than either police-brutality or propaganda.

Furthermore, avenues of protest other than riots and demonstrations have been progressively closed. Single newspaper monopolies depend upon the existing power-structure, boss-selected candidates avoid all rational discussion of pressing problems. The election choice of Nixon versus Humphrey was scarcely any choice for the intelligent voter. "Tricky Dick" saved us from Humphrey's saliva just as Humphrey would have saved us from the pompous munching of mouldy crusts. For some millions it was no choice at all. The blatant evasion of such issues as the Vietnam War, conscription, racism, integration and desegregation, poverty, crime, and urban renewal was an insult to everybody. Guerrilla war will be the inevitable result of discredited elections. It is either that or marching Black Shirts, Brown Shirts, and sansculottes who bring about government terrorism rather than the millennium.

Such remedies as "ghetto capitalism" and "Negro free enterprise" are as absurd as similar proposals made in England and France more than a century ago. They attempt to divide the black from the poor in an effort to take the edge off Black Power militancy, not to solve problems. A million good jobs are needed *now*. The fact is that the ghetto is too costly to be sustained by the American taxpayer. The ghetto is at the root of much of the crime problem and hence the stronger police action, be it against crime or guerrillas. To shoot arsonists on sight sounds commendable to some, but it does not end arson or explain why arson exists. Each year J. Edgar Hoover has asked for more and more money; strangely, the more money he has received, the more crime has increased. The tougher and more varied the measures of repression, the tougher becomes the resistance. This is a vicious circle, and it erodes power at great cost. The real problem is not crime and disorder. It is a social sickness—the decay of our big cities, the Vietnam war, and ever-expanding militarism, the steady erosion of efficient public services, an unfair conscription law that destroys immediate opportunities for youth. All this can bring about more youthful revolt. The belief is enforced that injustice is institutionalized and that there is no escape from the nightmare tangle of corruption, procrastination, and red-tape.

Some goals, even if achieved, merely emphasize the contradictions. All over the country, universities hit by black revolt have scampered about seeking more black students and black professors. This, however, means a brain-drain from black institutions: the more affluent white university pulls away the best black students and the superior black professors.

In general, reformist piece-mealism promises to make no adequate amends within the reasonably foreseeable future. After all, the evils are deep. Some such as racism continue in the making. The breaking point has almost come, and no slow-paced, insignificant reforms are going to save the country from serious trouble.

The outcome is foreseeable. As Howard Zimn states it in his *Disobedience and Democracy*: "If the social function of protest is to change the unjust conditions of society, then the protest cannot stop with a court decision or a jail sentence." A morally justified protest is bound to continue beyond all penalties and all police clubs. It will not stop dead in its tracks "as soon as the very government it is criticizing decides against it."

Yet the cries for Che Guevara may also be thrown back by bloody repression. With violence, frustration is just as possible as success. At least Guevara represented action and purpose, not complacent conformity and acquiescence. In any event, there is fascination in "Revolution for the Hell of it"; students are more sensitive to this than most. Trustees and old-style professors (not the newer ones) find it difficult to understand why students prefer to jump off the corporate conveyer belt—which is what most present day institutions represent—than rush to repair it when it breaks down. Students are beginning to doubt if society can ever be repaired satisfactorily—and in any case, they do not like where it is taking them. Demonstrations, riots, and violence can become a way of life, a habit just as can pot-smoking or masturbation.

But most guerrillas of the cities are earnest people filled with an undying spirit of resistance. "We won't turn around. We ain't going to be turned around," the Negro leaders chant. Behind their chant is the upsurge of Africans and nonwhite Asians who will no longer be denied their rights to freedom and glory. Why should African blacks be free and American blacks continue to be sub-standard citizens—except in the mouthings of equality by politicians who seek to trick them with sleek programs or brush them off? The meager privileges the blacks have won have been gained not by peaceful petitions but by bold confrontations with existing authority. And they know that perfectly well.

Black Power has become the one credible militant slogan—a sort of reverse apartheid system, an accepted segregation. The cry is no longer for equality with the whites (which becomes demeaning for blacks). Equality of travel and public facilities yes, but not acceptance of the white life-style, not equality of black and white *individuals*. Even the poorest blacks in the South are often superior to poor-whites. The black has pushed up stronger in environment of poverty, whereas the poor-white has degenerated, morally and physically. For any black to seek equality with George Wallace would be an insult to his dignity, pride, and intelligence. The fact is, some whites are too low to make equality desirable.

Black Power goes beyond mere equality of political and economic rights. It means restructuring Negro society and the Negro community, a realization of cultural and social reintegration for dignified participation in a pluralistic society. It pretty well parts company with other previous immigrant minorities—the Jews, Italians, Irish, Poles—and projects a new concept of human society: a new Austro-Hungary or Swiss federation. There are some parallels in other lands.

Black Power is not without immediate goals and does seek some immediate economic and political penetration: wider job participation on all levels, control of local schools, local police, and official administration. In fact, as Black Power achieves immediate local goals, the likelihood and danger of guerrilla revolt will likely lessen. More traditional methods, though directed at nontraditional objectives, may blunt the edges of bitterness and violence, unless social disintegration proceeds faster. But that hope will require far more tolerance than the conforming middle-class or police-mentalities have yet displayed. They seem even less likely to display intelligence in the present confused atmosphere of deepening terror and fear. The black faculty member whose arbitrary dismissal from New York University produced such disastrous trouble, stated "White Americans have deluded themselves with believing they were invincible." Cuba, Vietnam, China, the black liberation, have broken in "on this comforting dream with frightening reality." Today the cadence of "Freedom by any manner necessary" has become sure and steady in their ears. But as Communist Henry Winston admits, "the overwhelming majority of the American people, including black people, are not yet convinced that the system must be changed, much less that it is necessary to do it by armed force."

A hope and possibility still exists for America that unfortunately no longer exists for most of the so-called Free World, or Third World. Where population growth proceeds apace, where hunger is growing into a national catastrophe, and where social change blocked by military dictatorships that offer law and order by terror, guerrilla warfare becomes the only method to redress the shames of inhuman oppressions. Two days before he was supposed to return to jail, Black Panther Eldridge Cleaver said:

> Any social science book will tell you that if you subject people to an unpleasant environment, you can predict they will rebel against it. That gives rise to a contradiction. When you have a social unit organized in such way that people are moved to rebel against it in large numbers, how do you come behind them and tell them they owe a debt to society? I say that society owes a debt to them. And society does not look as though it wants to pay.

INDEX

Abbas, Ferhat, 132
Abernathy, Ralph, 234
Abdel Krim, Mahammed, 100, 102, 108, 112
Abdel Krim, Mohammed (Mohand), 15, 99–112
  forces opposed by, 107–10
  government formed by, 102
  surrender of, 112
Abdel Krim el-Khatabi, 100–2
Abs, Hermann, 143
Adamic, Louis, 114
Addams, Jane, 24
Adekunle, Col. Benjamin A., 134
Aden, resistance to British in, 168
African Independent Party of Guinea and Cape Verde, 137
African National Congress, 140
Aguilar, Gen., 46
Aguinaldo y Famy, Emilio, 4, 8, 13, 15, 16–30, 34, 37
  capture of, 33–34
  Dewey and, 16, 20–21
  Otis and, 25, 27
  revolt led by, 18–19
Aguiyi-Ironsi, Gen. Johnson, 134
Alamazán, Gen. Juan Andrew, 62
Alemán Bolaños, Gustavo, 78, 95
Alexander, King of Jugoslavia, 118–22, 124
Alfonso XIII (ship), 110
Algeria, revolt in, 132–33, 138
Algoncillo, Felip, 23
Alliance for Progress, 220
Almeida, Juan, 194, 208, 212
Altamirano, Capt. Pedro, 87
Alvarado, Gen. Salvador, 50, 64
Alves, José da Felicidade, 136
American Federation of Labor, 84, 209, 217
American Medical Association News (periodical), 190
Anderson, Brig. Gen. Thomas W., 16, 17, 22
Angeles, Gen. Felipe, 53, 70
Angola, guerrillas in, 136–39

Angolan Revolutionary Government in Exile (GRAE), 138–39
Anti-Fascist Council of National Liberation, 126
Arauz, Blanca, 82, 87
Arbenz, Jacobo, 210, 228
Arcos, Gustavo, 199
Arévalo, Juan José, 226
Arévalo Martínez, Rafael, 85
Argenlieu, Adm. Thierry d', 183
Arias, María, 52
Ariel (publication), 76, 85
Arnold, Matthew, 3
Arnoux, Paul, 177n
Artega, Manuel, 209
Atl, Dr., 52
Azúa, Barrera, Rafael, 196

Bacon, Nathaniel, 75–76
Bakunin, Michael, 154
Balewa, Sir Abubakar Tafawa, 134
Balge, Mariano, 35
Bamboo Dragon (Ho), 176
Bank, Nguyen Luong, 187
Bao Dai, Emperor of Vietnam, 181–82
Barcenas, Rafael García, 198
Barcenas, Gen. Victoriano, 70
Barquin, Col. Ramón, 218
Barra, Francisco de la, 46
Barret, John, 21, 22
Barrientos, Réné, 1, 9, 221
Barzani, Mustafa, 168
Bass, John F., 18
Batista, Fulgencio, 1, 193, 194
  Castro pardoned by, 200
  coup led by, 196–98
  installed as president, 201
  revolt led by Castro against, 202–17
    Guevara in, 202, 206, 214–16, 218
Bay of Pigs invasion, 194n, 230
Bayo, Gen. Alberto, 201
Bell Trade Act, 35
Bemis, Samuel Flagg, 7
Ben Barka, Mehdi, 133
Benedetto, Commander, 138